EUGENIA

A TRUE STORY OF ADVERSITY, TRAGEDY, CRIME AND COURAGE

To Monty with regards,

EUGENIA

A TRUE STORY OF ADVERSITY, TRAGEDY, CRIME AND COURAGE

Mark Tedeschi

MARK TEDESCHI QC

SIMON & SCHUSTER
AUSTRALIA
A CBS COMPANY

EUGENIA: A TRUE STORY OF ADVERSITY, TRAGEDY, CRIME AND COURAGE

First published in Australia in 2012 by
Simon & Schuster (Australia) Pty Limited
Suite 19A, Level 1, 450 Miller Street, Cammeray, NSW 2062

A CBS Company
Sydney New York London Toronto New Delhi
Visit our website at www.simonandschuster.com.au

National Library of Australia Cataloguing-in-Publication entry
Tedeschi, Mark, 1952-
Title: Eugenia / Mark Tedeschi.
Subjects: Falleni, Eugenia, 1875-1938.
                Male impersonators--New South Wales--Sydney--Biography.
                Trials (Murder)--New South Wales--Sydney.
Dewey Number: 364.1523092

ISBN: 9781922052292 (pbk.)

Cover design: Christabella Designs
Internal design and typesetting: Midland Typesetters, Australia

Printed and bound in Australia by Griffin Press

The paper used to produce this book is a natural, recyclable product made from wood
grown in sustainable plantation forests. The manufacturing processes conform to the
environmental regulations in the country of origin.

I dedicate this book to the memory of my oldest friend, the late Dorothy Porter (1954–2008), one of Australia's finest writers, whose premature death cheated Australia of so much literature that she still had within her; and to the other members of the Porter family: Chester, Jean, Mary and Josephine.

CONTENTS

Acknowledgements   viii
Introduction   xi

Part I The Search For Love

Chapter 1: Discovery on the high seas   3
Chapter 2: Early years   12
Chapter 3: Parenthood   19
Chapter 4: Love   25
Chapter 5: Marriage   33
Chapter 6: Exposure   41
Chapter 7: Picnic   49
Chapter 8: Tragedy in the Park   55
Chapter 9: Discovery in the Park   62
Chapter 10: Anguish   66
Chapter 11: Lizzie   76
Chapter 12: Investigation and arrest   81
Chapter 13: Lizzie's discovery   91
Chapter 14: Exhumation and second autopsy   97

Part II Legal Proceedings

Chapter 15: The Press   105
Chapter 16: Judge, Crown Prosecutor and defence counsel   113
Chapter 17: The trial begins   124
Chapter 18: Family witnesses   135
Chapter 19: Sighting witnesses   145
Chapter 20: Expert witnesses   155
Chapter 21: Lies   166
Chapter 22: Police witnesses   170
Chapter 23: Defence case and case in reply   176
Chapter 24: Closing addresses   181
Chapter 25: The law speaks   188

Part III Incarceration and Release

Chapter 26: Prisoner   199
Chapter 27: Release   210
Chapter 28: Jean Ford   218
Chapter 29: To the bank   223
Chapter 30: Retrospective   227

Epilogue   237
Bibliography   248
Endnotes   251

Yet each man kills the thing he loves
By each let this be heard,
Some do it with a bitter look,
Some with a flattering word,
The coward does it with a kiss,
The brave man with a sword!

Some kill their love when they are young,
And some when they are old;
Some strangle with the hands of Lust,
Some with the hands of Gold:
The kindest use a knife, because
The dead so soon grow cold.

Some love too little, some too long,
Some sell, and others buy;
Some do the deed with many tears,
And some without a sigh:
For each man kills the thing he loves,
Yet each man does not die.

'THE BALLAD OF READING GAOL'
by OSCAR WILDE

ACKNOWLEDGEMENTS

I would like to single out for my appreciation and gratitude the following persons who have contributed to this book:

Alan Gold (writer, literary critic, educator and human-rights worker), my literary mentor and guru, for his unprecedented generosity of time and patience, for his excellent suggestions that greatly improved the manuscript, and for his wise counsel and unfailing encouragement.

My editors at Simon & Schuster: Larissa Edwards, Claire de Medici and Kate O'Donnell.

Louise Coleman (law student extraordinaire), who assisted me in researching some of the historical, social and institutional details of life in Eugenia's time.

My son, Benjamin Tedeschi, who edited Part I and made some excellent suggestions to improve several chapters.

Dr Rebecca Irvine (forensic pathologist, Department of Forensic Medicine, Glebe Coroner's Court, Sydney), for her expert assistance with the pathological evidence.

Dr Judith Perl (clinical forensic pharmacologist with the New South Wales Police), for information on blood alcohol testing methods.

Suzanne Falkiner, author, for discussing the project with me and for her permission to reproduce parts of her 1987 interview with Eugenia's sister-in-law, Olga Falleni (referred to in Falkiner's book as Anna). I have received permission to disclose Olga's real name from the Falleni family in New Zealand.

Phillipa Fioretti (author, Adelaide), for throwing the spark into the tinderbox.

Carol Baxter, author, for her advice on writing styles.

Dr Paolo Totaro AM, for correcting my Italian and suggesting some Neapolitan.

Kim Falleni (New Zealand), Eugenia's great nephew, for the photo of the Falleni family in New Zealand in about 1910.

Lisa Falleni (New Zealand), granddaughter of Olga and Louis Falleni and hence Eugenia's great-niece, for information about the Falleni family in New Zealand.

Tom Elvy (Sydney), great-grandson of Eugenia, and his wife Michelle, for information on Rita Elvy (née Whitby) and Arthur Whitby.

Nerida Campbell and Rebecca Edmonds (Justice & Police Museum, Sydney), for access to the museum's holdings on Eugenia Falleni and general assistance with the project.

Philip Selth OAM (Executive Director of the New South Wales Bar Association), for help in searching for material on Archibald McDonell.

Robert Parkinson and George Zabeth (Land and Property Information Division, Registrar General's Office), for their help in locating the exact site of the Cumberland Paper Mills.

Bruce Carter (Research Librarian, Family History Section, State Library of NSW), for help in searching old records relating to Eugenia Falleni, Annie Birkett and the De Angelis family.

Amie Zar, Local History Librarian, Leichhardt Library, for research help.

Staff of the ODPP Library, Sydney.

Ashleigh Smith, Police Prosecutor, Central Local Court, Sydney, for help with the history of the Central police station.

Sergeant David Shazaleh, Sheriff's Officer, for photographs of the Central police station before the recent renovations.

Assistant Superintendent Tony Dixon, Corrective Services Department, for access to his photographs of the Central police station before the recent renovations.

Robert Merchant and Duncan MacAuslan, for information about tram services in Sydney in the 1910s.

Bill Allen, who has been collating information about Sydney Ferries for over 60 years, for sharing his knowledge about ferry routes and the location of wharves.

Anne Bishop (Scone), granddaughter of William Coyle KC, for her assistance with materials about and photographs of her grandfather.

Anne Carolan (Middle Cove), for a host of material on Archibald McDonell and Zulu.

Frances Kenney (Cundletown), McDonell family historian, for information about the McDonell family.

Ian McDonell (Gisborne), for assistance and introductions to other members of the McDonell family.

Maureen McDonell (Mt Wagga Wagga), for help with the extended McDonell family.

Rod Corrie (Cowra), for information about and a photograph of EG Maddocks Cohen.

Marise Brass (Sydney), a niece of Maddocks Cohen, for information on her uncle.

Dr Jerome Stern, for bringing to my attention the legend of St Eugenia.

My remarkable wife, Sharon, for her ready acceptance of my eccentric enthusiasm for the project, her patience during the months of my literary monasticism, and her many words of masterful advice.

This book has emanated from my career as a barrister and Crown Prosecutor. I would like to take this opportunity to thank and pay tribute to some people who have played a major role in supporting that career: Chester Porter QC, Franca Arena AM, Nicholas Cowdery AM QC, Justice Reg Blanch AM, my parents Ruth and Robert Tedeschi and, yet again, my wife, Sharon.

INTRODUCTION

From a completely misunderstood childhood and adolescence, Eugenia Falleni boldly strode out in adulthood in an attempt to establish what she saw as her true self as a man. Within that identity, constantly fearful of exposure, shame and punishment by an unforgiving community and the law of her time, she sought what almost all of us seek: love, acceptance, security, respect and connection with other human beings. Part I 'Looking for Love' is largely an account of that search.

When, in middle age, she finally established an intimate connection, she was forced by her social circumstances and the strict moral confines of her day to maintain her deep secret from almost everyone, including her beloved. Threatened with the loss of her first real love and the opprobrium of society, in a state of complete panic she acted foolishly and unwisely. Part I is an unravelling of these events, interpreted with the benefit of nearly one hundred years of hindsight.

The reaction of society only eventuated nearly three years later. In the meantime, she had established another love relationship, with Lizzie, to sustain her, again based on a necessary deception. When everything fell apart and her history of sexual deception became public property, the full weight of the law and public opinion came crashing down upon Eugenia, branding her an outcast, a social misfit and a serious menace to the moral fabric and health of society. In the context of the hatred and fear that was whipped up about her by a voracious press, the result of her clash with the law and the Press was almost inevitable. Part II 'Legal Proceedings' is an account of the reaction of the law and the newspapers to her crime and her unique circumstances, and an analysis of her trial by the author, with the insight of more than thirty-five years' practice in the criminal courts for both the prosecution and the defence

The last section of Eugenia's story, covered here in Part III 'Incarceration and Release', takes place after the law has had its say about her alleged crime. It includes an account of the period of her incarceration and her later life when society has finally released its ferocious grip on her – at a terrible price. The ending of that part is so tragically poignant that one can only view fate in the guise of a cat playing with a mouse it has caught, setting it slowly down and letting it go, only to swipe at it with a fearful, final blow just after it has regained its footing. Part III also includes a retrospective analysis of Eugenia's trial and the medico-scientific issues that it threw up, as well as a discussion of the possible reasons why she chose to live the life she led.

Eugenia's story can be a valuable lesson for us today: as an account of how the law can be misguided and unsympathetic; as an illustration of the dangerous agitation that can be whipped up in the public by the media with a salacious story to sell; and as a lesson in the persuasive power of fallacious science. Part III also contains an analysis by the author of these lessons and how we can benefit from them today.

The historical facts of Eugenia Falleni's story that I have related in this book, including quotations from newspaper reports and evidence from her trial, are based upon contemporary public records, press reports, court transcripts and other written accounts, as well as subsequent recollections of people who had direct contact with the main personalities. I could have provided footnotes or endnotes for the historical facts, but I believe that including numbered notes in a text creates a visual and psychological hurdle for the reader to overcome. For this reason, I have instead included a bibliography at the end of the book and I have only inserted numbered endnotes in the text where they are essential for an explanation. Where I have referred to personal thoughts and emotions, these are generally inferred by me from the background factual circumstances in which they occurred. Most conversations are taken from police statements or evidence given in the committal proceedings and the trial. In those two instances (in chapters 1 and 8) where, in the absence of established facts, I have engaged in conjecture about significant events, I have clearly indicated that this is the case and stated the basis for my supposition.

Inevitably there were difficulties in deciding what name to ascribe to Eugenia at different stages of her life, and whether to refer to her as 'he' or 'she'. The decision I came to, and have adopted throughout this account, is to use the name and pronoun appropriate to the identity Eugenia assumed at any particular time of her life. For that reason, I have used four names for her in different parts of this book: Eugene, Eugenia, Harry and Jean.

Mark Tedeschi QC
June 2012

PART I

THE SEARCH FOR LOVE

CHAPTER 1

DISCOVERY ON THE HIGH SEAS

The year 1897 was a momentous one for the whole world. In May of that year, Italian inventor Guglielmo Marconi sent the first ever wireless communication over open seas for a distance of more than three miles. The message traversed the Bristol Channel from Lavernock Point to Flat Holm Island in South Wales and read '*Are you ready?*', thereby initiating a new age of wireless electronic communications. In that same year, the world's attention was also focused on Irish writer, poet and playwright Oscar Wilde, who was released from Reading Gaol in Britain after serving a sentence of two years' hard labour for 'gross indecency' with another man.[1] In mid-1897, Wilde wrote '*The Ballad of Reading Gaol*', a poem that narrated the execution of a man who murdered his wife for her infidelity, highlighting the brutal punishment that prisoners endured. On the other side of the world, in the middle of the South Pacific Ocean, another event took place on a four-masted, iron-hulled Norwegian barque carrying freight between the South Pacific Islands, New Zealand and Australia. Although this event had no international importance at the time, it led many years later to one of the most extraordinary legal, ethical and moral controversies ever known in that part of the world.

Eugene Falleni, a twenty-two-year-old seaman on the Norwegian barque, would not have known much about Marconi or any of the other scientific luminaries of the late Victorian age, and it was unlikely that he would have known anything of Oscar Wilde. He certainly would not have read 'The Ballad of Reading Gaol' because, like many of his fellow seamen, he could neither read nor write. Eugene came from an Italian family that had migrated to Wellington, New Zealand when he was two. He had left his hometown and family about eighteen months earlier to take up a life at sea. Since leaving New Zealand, he had worked on a number of sailing ships as they plied their trade in the South Pacific Ocean. The present one was a Norwegian barque with four masts – three square-rigged and the fourth rigged both fore-and-aft. This sail plan resulted in a slower vessel, but with greater manoeuvrability than some others, requiring fewer sailors to man it. This barque had a crew of between fifteen and twenty sailors. The goods they transported from the Pacific Islands included sugar from Fiji, sandalwood from Hawaii, mother-of-pearl, bêche-de-mer (sea cucumber), sealskins, tortoiseshells, whale oil, whalebone, pineapples, banana, coffee and copra. On the way back, they would bring coal, wool, shale oil and kerosene to the islands.

Eugene loved the freedom of life at sea and the camaraderie of his fellow sailors. Working ships attracted a wide variety of characters from many parts of the world, so that the crew comprised men of vastly different ages, backgrounds and circumstances. Many of them had little education and most had learned about sailing solely by experience. Signing up as a seaman enabled people to put their pasts behind them, so there were a fair few men at sea who had unresolved problems with the law, unpaid debts, families they had deserted or social conflicts they had avoided by removing themselves from their previous lives. It was a little like joining the French Foreign Legion, but without the risk of having to fight in a war. Not that life at sea was without its difficulties and risks. Many a sailor had been lost during a storm and some captains were ruthless in dealing with troublemakers. Eugene, however, never tired of the many smells on the ship and the constant movement. He loved to climb up the masts, with the wind whistling past him and the upper sections of the ship furiously rocking as he toiled next to several other sailors to furl or unfurl the sails. He never grew weary of the uncompromising, hard work that was required of seamen. When the day's work was done, he would join the other sailors in consuming their daily allocation of alcohol and revel in the raw banter and crude allusions to what they would do to the women they came across when the ship was next in port. His favourite ports were Suva, Papeete and Honolulu.

Eugene was a good worker and was well liked by the other seamen. He was a fine-boned, good-looking young man, with penetrating eyes and wavy, dark hair always precisely parted on the left. His small, wiry body belied his strength, and what he lacked in size, he made up for in determination. He could drink and swear like the best of them, and seemed to relish the harder aspects of work at sea. He had an engaging charm that made him good company, especially when he had had some drink. His most strange quality was his extreme modesty, which the other sailors found bizarre. In the close confines of the crew's shared quarters below deck, he would always wait until it was completely dark before washing at the single tub of water in their cabin or changing his clothes. While he would always join them in a drinking session, he would never engage afterwards in their 'pissing game' at the back of the ship. Behind his bonhomie was an underlying reserve that could not be penetrated, although among crews on sailing ships that was not an unusual characteristic. He was a man whom the other men could rely on in a storm. When anyone asked him about his family in Wellington, he would quickly dismiss their enquiry. Everyone knew that you did not press a fellow sailor for personal details if he showed any reluctance to talk. To do otherwise was a recipe for a fight and then for the much more terrible wrath of the captain.

The captain of this ship, which Eugene had joined in New Zealand several months earlier, was an Italian, originally from Naples, named Martello. Nobody knew his first name and everyone merely called him 'Capitano'. After working on other ships, Eugene was pleased to find someone with whom he could converse in his native language. It brought back memories of his life as a young child in Wellington when his beloved grandmother was around and everything seemed much less complicated.

That late afternoon, as Eugene stood on the deck of the barque absorbing the salt air and the gentle rocking, as he had done numerous times before, he had no forewarning that on this unremarkable day his life would irretrievably change. The exact details of what happened are not known, but it must have been something like this.[2]

While the other sailors continued their drinking on the middle deck of the barque, Eugene made his way towards the captain's cabin at the back of the ship. Since he had joined the crew, the captain had on several occasions invited him to come to his cabin to open a bottle of Italian wine that he had carefully put aside to share with someone who would appreciate it. Today, the captain had invited him again. They had all been working hard, and now it was time to relax.

He knocked on the captain's door, and a loud baritone voice bellowed, '*Entra.*' Eugene opened the door and cautiously ventured into the dark cabin. Captain Martello, a large, handsome, forty-six-year-old man with silver streaks laced through his otherwise dark hair, was sitting at the table in the middle of the room, clearly drunk. He beckoned for Eugene to sit down on the only other chair at the table. Eugene followed his instructions. The captain poured him a glass of wine from a bottle that was already half-empty, and Eugene noticed a part-empty bottle of whisky on top of the cabinet under the sole porthole, which looked out to sea from the stern. After offering a few pleasantries and pouring Eugene a glass of wine, the captain launched into tales about his time as a sailor in the Italian navy, serving on an iron- and steel-clad battleship that had been built at La Spezia. Eugene had heard most of it before, but politeness and respect compelled him to listen attentively once again.

The captain's language was an odd mixture of standard Italian laced with Neapolitan dialect. Some of the time, Eugene had difficulty understanding him, because Eugene's family had come from Livorno, where the dialect was quite different. Occasionally, the captain would roar with laughter and, at other times, when he was telling a story of tragedy or loss, tears would well in his eyes. They soon finished the bottle of wine, and the captain pulled out another identical one from the cabinet. Eugene listened to his stories and occasionally interjected with a question or a short comment, but the captain seemed almost oblivious to his presence.

Towards the end of the second bottle, when Eugene was feeling the pleasant effects of the wine, the captain suddenly shifted his focus to him and said, '*Dimmi qualcosa di te* (Tell me something about yourself).' Eugene paused and thought quickly about what he could possibly tell the captain that would match his war stories, and decided to speak about his beloved grandmother, Eugenia, after whom he had been named, and who was the only person he had missed during the long months at sea. Eugene spoke in the manner one would expect of a young person, because his Italian had been restricted to family life during his childhood and he had never received any education in his native language. His mind went back to the time when he spoke only Italian to his parents, his siblings and his grandmother and to the numerous occasions when he would escape from the home of his parents – where he was so misunderstood and frequently criticised – to the home of his grandmother, who accepted his eccentricities and strange ways. Lost in his thoughts and memories, he began to tell Martello about his grandmother: '*Mia nonna …*' he began.

Eugene was surprised that the captain was listening to him intently. He moved on to describe his childhood in Wellington, truanting from school most of the time and working with the horses at the stables that belonged to his grandmother's second husband. He told the captain about his love of horses and how well they responded to him. He bragged that even at a young age he was better able to control the wilder ones than the adults were. The captain intervened: '*Pur essendo piccolo, sei molto forte* (For someone small, you are very strong).' Eugene had always been small, even as a child, and as his mind drifted back to that time in his life, he said to the captain, '*Anche durante la mia adolescenza, mia nonna mi chiamava "mia forte piccolina"* (Even as an adolescent, my grandmother used to call me "my strong little one").' As soon as he said it, he knew that he had made a terrible mistake. In English there are no word endings that delineate gender, but in Italian almost every word has a masculine or feminine word ending. By using the feminine '*piccolina*' instead of the masculine '*piccolino*', he had inadvertently said something that no native-born Italian would ever say in error.

The captain repeated the last word he had just heard, but this time in a puzzled and questioning way, cocking his head and looking at Eugene with a quizzical expression. Eugene pretended that nothing of importance had happened and continued his story. The captain kept listening, but with a renewed emphasis, and he was now staring at Eugene with great intensity, as if trying to assess his inner soul. Eugene was aware of his stare but pretended that he was oblivious to it. Within minutes he had completed his story and the captain made it obvious that the session had come to an end. Eugene thanked him for his hospitality, paid his respects and quickly backed out of the cabin.

Once outside, he found a place on the ship where he could stand by himself and mull over the mistake he had made. What would the captain make of it? Would he dismiss it as a language error by someone who had been raised in an English-speaking country and who had not spoken much Italian during his time at sea? That night, as he came into the large cabin where all the crew slept on straw mattresses laid out on wooden bunks three levels high, he noticed that a few of the older men who would ordinarily be quite chatty to him were uncharacteristically silent and avoided looking at him. He was hardly able to sleep as he contemplated the various ways in which events could unfold.

The next day, work began as usual. Most of the men were their usual selves towards him, but those who had been silent the night before were still taciturn. Eugene was on guard and hyper-attentive towards everyone and everything. He noticed whenever two or three of the men stood together chatting at the far end of the ship, and he was easily startled by their sudden laughter. He paid particular attention to anyone who talked to the captain. If the captain spoke for more than a minute or two to a sailor, he would watch to see with whom the man next conversed.

As the day wore on and nothing untoward happened, Eugene began to relax his vigilance a little. However, towards the end of the afternoon, the captain roared at him to come to his cabin and his level of fear and tension rose to a crescendo. This was not the way that past invitations had been extended. Eugene looked around and had a terrible sense of foreboding as he noticed that several of the men, including those who had not spoken to him for the last twenty-four hours, looked away as though they had not heard the captain call out. In trepidation, he made his way to the captain's cabin, and for the second time in as many days he knocked on his door.

'*Entra*,' he heard the captain call out. Eugene carefully opened the door and entered the dark cabin. He was relieved to see Captain Martello with a bottle in hand and two glasses in front of him. Eugene relaxed as he thought that his concerns had all been for nothing. He sat down opposite the captain, who pushed a glass of whisky towards him. This was an unusual act of generosity, as the captain rarely shared his whisky with anyone, not even those men who had been at sea with him for many years. Eugene appreciated a good whisky as much as any man, and he downed this one with relish and relief. It was followed by two more in quick succession, as the captain uncharacteristically moved about his cabin, seemingly rearranging some objects from one side to the other. Eugene had a passing thought that it was strange that the captain was still on his first glass while he was already on his third. Usually the captain was ahead of him and ready to start the next glass while he was still halfway through the previous one. He put it down to whatever task it was that the captain was engaged in.

As the captain moved across the cabin behind him, without the slightest warning he grabbed Eugene's hair at the back of his head, yanked his head back hard and wrapped his right hand around the front of Eugene's throat, gripping the windpipe so tightly between his thumb and forefinger that he could barely breathe. Eugene reached up to try to prise the captain's large fingers away from his throat. Then just as suddenly, the captain let go of his throat and, still holding Eugene's head back, reached down between his legs on the outside of his pants. The look of horror on the captain's face when he felt nothing in the groin was something that Eugene had never seen in all the years he had been at sea. Reverting to his native Neapolitan, the captain exclaimed, '*Mannaggia 'a marosca, ma tu sì 'na femmena!* (Bloody hell, but you're a woman)'.

The captain let go of Eugene as suddenly as if he had picked up a stick and discovered that it was a snake. His face showed a combination of anger and disgust. A swift kick of the chair from behind sent Eugene flying to land flat on the floor. Before he had a chance to pick himself up, the captain had his boot pressed firmly down on his neck, hard enough to make him choke, but not enough to break his hyoid bone. He looked up pleadingly at the captain and saw a face flushed with lascivious desire after weeks at sea without female company. '*Qual' é il tuo vero nome?* (What is your real name?)' he barked. Despite his struggle to breathe, he managed to get out one word: 'Eugenia'.

Martello released the pressure on her throat, but instantly there was a kick to her temple, causing flashes of lightning inside her brain, and for some moments she lapsed into unconsciousness. As her senses returned, he was roughly ripping her clothes from her body, and then suddenly he was upon her, penetrating deep inside her body. The pain and sense of invasion was something she had never experienced before, and she desperately wished for unconsciousness to intervene. She felt as though her internal organs were being ripped out of her body and replaced with the entrails of an animal. She tried to cry out, but no sound emanated from her throat. It was as if an alien presence had taken possession of her body, leaving her only with raw nerve endings to feel pain but depriving her of any control over her actions. Inside her head, she went somewhere else, back to the times when she would play alone in her grandmother's yard in Wellington. It was the only time in her entire childhood that she had felt totally secure and untroubled. The passage of time had no meaning. Then suddenly, almost without warning, it was over. The captain slowly got up and adjusted his clothing. As she lay there, near-naked like a deeply wounded animal just before death, he looked down at her body with a mixture of pity and revulsion. '*Cosí impari a far finta d'essere uomo* (That will teach you to pretend you're a man),' she heard him say.

He darted across the cabin, and she heard him whip open the door and call out, 'Come and look at what we have here!' Many of her fellow sailors crowded into the cabin and in what seemed like an endless silence they gazed down upon her femaleness. Their faces showed a combination of bewilderment and fury. One of the oldest superstitions among sailors was that a woman on board brought a ship bad luck. How dare a female be amongst them in the guise of a male, challenging their pride in their strength, agility and prowess as seamen? Men at sea had their own unspoken code of conduct, which applied almost uniformly from ship to ship. It was unlike the rules or laws on land because the conditions at sea were so different. The code was the invisible cohesive glue that bound the crew together during the long weeks at sea. The divide between male and female was so basic, so critical to their identity, so universally accepted and honoured, that a transgressor could not be allowed to breach it without a fearful penalty. To have not only crossed over into their domain as men, but to have deceived them for so long was a violation so heinous that the months of friendship and camaraderie at sea counted for nothing.

She heard the captain say to them, 'Take her away. Put her down in the store'. Struggling for breath and cowering with fear and humiliation, she was roughly manhandled by four of them out of the captain's cabin to the stairway and down into the bowels of the ship. They placed her down on the bare wooden floor in the 'store' of the ship's hold, which was a small cell-like area up against the side of the ship, lined on the other three sides with vertical metal bars, exposed to the air but secure from any prying hands. Usually it was the place where the captain would stockpile the barrels of beer and rum and other valuable commodities that he wanted to keep secure. He had also occasionally used it as a punishment cell if one of the men had gone too far in fighting or committed some other infraction of his discipline. As the men who had carried her there turned and began walking away, she heard the captain say, '*Questo è per tua protezione* (This is for your own protection).'

This cell was to be her home for what was the haze of the next two months as they slowly progressed from island to island. Every few nights the captain would descend into the hold on his own. As he came down the stairs, he would taunt her with '*Ecco la mia piccolina* (Here is my little one).' She was so weakened, physically and emotionally, that she could not resist him. Occasionally, she was taken upstairs onto the top deck and into the open for a little exercise and air, but she was kept in the brig whenever the ship was in port. Apart from the captain, not one of the men would look at her or say a single word to her. Most of the time, she was locked up in her cell. Over the weeks of her incarceration, she became more and more pale and, unusually for someone with her experience at sea, she became seasick.

The next major port of call was Newcastle, a thriving coal and timber port on the east coast of Australia about one hundred miles north of Sydney. With twelve hydraulic and five steam-driven cranes, the Newcastle docks were some of the busiest and dirtiest in the south Pacific, with coal dust constantly hanging in the air. The area surrounding the docks was a bazaar of pubs, inns, brothels and seafarers' establishments. The captain told her a few days before that she would be put off the ship there. Her protestations that she knew nobody in that locality had no effect. The captain saw her off the ship. This time, he had an apologetic tone. He went to say 'I'm sorry', but the words wouldn't come out. He handed her an envelope with a few notes in it, turned around and left her on the dock. Perhaps he suspected what she already knew – that she was with child.

When Eugenia Falleni was forced to disembark at Newcastle, she was alone, traumatised, destitute and pregnant. Her defilement by the captain had left her feeling contaminated by his evil seed, and now there was a foreign body growing inside her – a part of her, but also separate from her. She felt resentful that she would have to wait many months before she could expel the product of the trauma from her body. All she could see was the coal dust permeating every inch of the docks and even the air she breathed. She was desperate to escape from this alien environment, but where would she go? What was she to do? How would she cope? How could she live life as a man, as she was driven to do, if she had a child to look after? What had led her to such a dreadful predicament?

CHAPTER 2

EARLY YEARS

The year 1875 saw some momentous instances of worldwide cooperation: the establishment of the Universal Postal Union and the Universal Bureau of Weights and Measures. That year also witnessed the creation of the International Committee for the Red Cross, which was to have global ramifications in the twentieth century for defining the rules of war. In 1875, Italy was still a brand new nation. Although the 'Risorgimento' or reunification of Italy had commenced many decades earlier,[1] it was only in 1870 that Rome had joined the other Italian States, and the following year it had been designated as the capital city of the new nation.

Eugenia Falleni was born on 25 January 1875 in Ardenza, which was then a very small seaside village just outside Livorno in northern Italy.[2] She was the firstborn child of Luigi and Isola Falleni. Luigi worked as a coachman while Isola was a tailor. Since the 1580s Livorno had been an important port-city of the kind known as 'Porto Franco', which meant that goods traded through that city were duty-free. As a result it became one of the most important and cosmopolitan ports of the entire Mediterranean region. In 1868, when Livorno became part of the new Kingdom of Italy during the Risorgimento, it lost that status and the city declined in commercial and civic importance. The 1870s witnessed the beginning of what was called the 'Italian Diaspora', as many Italians emigrated, fleeing widespread poverty and overcrowding within the newly unified nation.

With the end of the gold rush in New Zealand in the late 1860s, the government instituted an assisted-migration scheme to lure prospective migrants from southern Europe into the country. The scheme offered free passage in exchange for working on the construction of New Zealand's railways, roads and other public infrastructure projects. A majority of the Italians who emigrated under this scheme came from Livorno during 1875 and 1876. This was partially due to the efforts of a New Zealand government agent, John Glynn, who was situated in Livorno. He was able to entice several hundred Italian men and their families to emigrate to New Zealand with the promise of well-paying labouring jobs. These men were initially set to work on the Featherston railway. Within a short period, however, they were declared by the New Zealand government to be utterly unfit for the manual labour for which they had been employed. Most of these men subsequently found more suitable work within the main urban areas of New Zealand, but the failure of the original employment scheme resulted in the government viewing these Italians as 'undesirables'. This was one of many reasons why these immigrants were the subject of considerable prejudice and hostility from the local Anglo community.

In 1877, when Eugenia was two, her parents migrated to New Zealand with her on the ship *Waikato*. By then, she already had a sister, Lisa, who was too young for the ordeal of the long sea journey to the other side of the world, and so was left behind with relatives and not reunited with her family for several years.

When the three members of the Falleni family arrived in New Zealand, there were already a substantial number of Italians from Livorno living in Wellington who had arrived under the assisted-migration scheme in 1875 and 1876. The prospect of employment was not the only reason Eugenia's parents chose New Zealand. They came because Eugenia's maternal grandmother, also Eugenia, was already in Wellington, having migrated two years earlier with her second husband, Vincenzio Buti.

When Eugenia and her parents first arrived, they lived in Wanganui, and Luigi Falleni worked as a fisherman. Not long after, they moved to the Wellington suburb of Newtown, where her grandmother lived, and Luigi became an 'express man', which was the term used for carriers who were involved in the recently introduced express mail service using a horse and cart. His business also involved the carriage of goods, such as furniture, as well as fruit and vegetables. Isola worked as a tailor, but her main activity over the next twenty-five years was giving birth to and raising a multitude of children: ten boys and seven girls. The family remained engrossed in their traditional Italian ways, and they spoke only Italian in the home. Eugenia was known to her parents and siblings by various nicknames, including Eugenie, Nina and Lina.

As foreigners in a predominantly Anglo-Saxon society, the Falleni family faced a considerable amount of prejudice and social discrimination from their neighbours. New Zealand society in the 1880s and 1890s was characterised by widespread intolerance and antagonism towards immigrants from non-Anglo countries, particularly those from Southern

Europe, who were treated with suspicion and often outright antagonism, as New Zealand sought to promote a racially homogeneous and civilised image as the 'Britain of the South'. Italian immigrants were viewed by both the government and the broader public as lazy, immoral and exploitative of the country's assisted-migration scheme. Many Italians found solidarity with their compatriots in clubs and societies which were founded at this time. Even after years of residence, these immigrants were still regarded as aliens whose speech, appearance and behaviour rendered them entirely distinct from the British race ideal. Even though she had come to New Zealand at the age of two, Eugenia was still viewed as a foreigner and was often taunted at school about her Italian origins.

As a child, Eugenia developed into a tomboy. She loved to dress in boys' clothing and to play rough games with the boys. With so many brothers and their friends, she had no shortage of boys to play with. Unlike most other girls in her neighbourhood, she had no interest in frilly dresses or dolls. As the first-born daughter in a traditional, patriarchal, Italian family, she was expected to play a major role in helping her mother look after her younger siblings, but she continually resisted fulfilling this expectation of her. In her early teenage years, she was considered quite beautiful, but wilful, restless and uncontrollable. She clashed continually with her conservative Italian father, who was unable to accept that his eldest daughter was not interested in leading a conventional female existence, while her mother readily went along with her husband's hostility towards the strange ways of their first-born child. Only her grandmother accepted her as she was, loved her unreservedly and refrained from constantly trying to change her ways. Eugenia frequently truanted from school, and was more often than not to be found working around the horses in the stables owned by her grandmother's husband, Mr Buti. As a young adolescent, she had a natural facility for working with horses and she was immensely proud of the fact that she was better at riding them than most of the men. Her parents blamed Mr Buti for leading Eugenia astray by allowing her to remain at the stables instead of going to school. As a result of her poor attendance at school, Eugenia was unable to read or write – a handicap that was to remain with her for all her life.

At fifteen, in the early throws of adolescent rebellion, Eugenia caused her parents terrible trauma by running away from home. In desperation, on 16 September 1891, her parents inserted a short advertisement in the local newspaper, the *Evening Post*, which was a thinly disguised plea for her return. It read:

Missing friend. Nina Falleni, aged 15, left her home in Newtown, early on the morning of Monday 14th instant, and has not since been heard of. Information is anxiously sought by her father and mother.

Although she returned to her family, Eugenia began what was to be an enduring practice of working as a man. An account of this part of her life was provided many years later by Olga Falleni, the wife of Eugenia's much younger brother Louis:

She was a beautiful woman who wanted to be a man and had dressed like a man. She went down to the West Coast. She drove four dangerous horses, she was the best coachman of all. She loved riding horses; she was a better horseman than any of the men. She worked in the brickworks as a man, she dressed herself as a man in the morning and in the evening she went home and dressed as a woman. Only Rosie and Emily knew – aunt Rosie and aunt Emily, two of the older ones. They would go on the same train at night, Rosie and Emily, and she would say, if you tell Dad, you know what will happen to you. So she would dress again in women's clothing before she went inside. She would drive a horse and cart down the West Coast and work as a bricklayer in Miramar – it's a hard job. She must have been a good actress, very clever, to do this.[3]

From her daily contact with her many brothers and their friends during her childhood, Eugenia was able to effortlessly interact with young men. In her adolescent years, even though she kept her hair very short, Eugenia was considered by young men in Wellington to be a most intriguingly beautiful young woman. Her disdain for any approach from them only enhanced their desire for her affections and caused them to redouble their efforts. Some of these men were from her own Italian community, and her father spent endless hours trying to understand why she so readily rebuffed romantic approaches from these eminently eligible prospects.

Finally, on 14 September 1894, when Eugenia was nineteen, her father, thinking that it would make his daughter 'normal', forced her into a marriage in Wellington to an Italian man by the name of Braseli Innocente. It was clearly a marriage that she did not want, and one can imagine that she was horrified to have a stranger and a male forced upon her by her father. Unsurprisingly, it ended in disaster. Her new husband turned out to be a scoundrel who already had a wife and another family in Auckland. He took Eugenia to Auckland, but she immediately escaped and made her way back to Wellington, where she shunned contact with the family that had tried to force her into a traditional, stereotyped straitjacket.

At this traumatic stage in her life, Eugenia decided that her true identity was as a male. All the years of struggle finally convinced her that she had been born into a body of the wrong gender. She only felt comfortable when she put on men's clothing. She only felt normal and authentic when she adopted the walk and talk of a man. She was happiest when she was in men's company and doing the kind of hard manual work that only they were permitted to do. She was most at home in a pub with the rough, working-class men of Wellington, drinking pints of beer and smoking cigarettes. Her irrepressible need to live life as a male was not something she chose, but was rather an imperative of her real, underlying self. Most of her life thus far had been spent resisting her inner voice, which had been crying out for recognition, and trying to conform to her family's expectations, but eventually the emotional price of living a monstrous lie was too high and she bowed to the inevitable.

In the 1890s, nobody knew of the concept of 'gender identity disorder' – a state in which a person believes that they have been born into a body of the wrong gender. Crossing the gender barrier was a social anathema beyond comprehension, let alone acceptance, while feigning an identity as a person of the opposite gender was considered a serious moral sin and a crime under the law.[4] It was mistakenly viewed as a form of homosexuality, which was viewed by many people as a gross aberration of nature and an evil to be avoided like the plague. Although male homosexuality was a crime, for quaint historical reasons female homosexuality was not.[5]

Eugenia took on the identity of a young man, Eugene Falleni. Her hair was already cut short with a masculine style, and she began dressing in the clothes of a typical working-class man. Her slight but wiry build helped considerably in enabling her to accomplish this transformation and she concealed her negligible bust by tightly wrapping bandages around her chest. The tone of her voice was sufficiently androgynous, so that it did not reveal her true gender. She found work as a manual labourer in a drainpipe factory in Wellington. However, after a week or so, her true identity was exposed when a friend of the family came to the factory, recognised her, and promptly informed the boss, who immediately dismissed her. By this stage, her parents had completely given up and wanted nothing to do with their errant daughter – so great was the shame that she had brought upon their family name. In desperation and without any means of support, Eugenia went to live for a period in a Salvation Army hostel in Wellington.

The work of the Salvation Army had commenced in New Zealand in 1883. With New Zealand in the 1880s beset by economic depression, unemployment, drunkenness and rampant crime, the Salvation Army quickly recruited a ready band of officers and soldiers, intent on implementing the Army's philosophy of 'soup, soap and salvation' and drawn by the exuberance and novelty of its open-air meetings, marches and signature brass bands. By 1890, the Salvation Army had emerged as a recognised part of New Zealand's benevolent and religious scene, with over 270 full-time officers serving throughout the country. Over the course of the 1890s, the Army established a maternity hospital for unmarried mothers, a workman's hostel in Wellington offering food and shelter in exchange for occasional labour and, in 1894, the Salvation Army Rescue Home for women, popularly known as the 'Paulina Home' after Major Annette Paul. In these many significant ways, the Salvation Army in New Zealand performed a critical role during the 1890s in assisting the most vulnerable and marginalised people in society, who would otherwise have been beyond the reach of traditional institutional aid. One such person was Eugenia Falleni. She was accepted by the Salvationists into the Paulina Home, and was even seen by one of her relatives playing the tambourine in one of the Army's traditional brass bands.

On several other occasions, Eugenia tried to secure employment as a male using various pseudonyms, including Lena Salette, but inevitably someone recognised her or realised that she was not a male, and she lost her job. On several occasions, she was brought before the courts on a charge of vagrancy, which was the simplest charge that the police could bring against someone who was desperately trying to lead life as a member of the opposite sex. In August 1896, she was brought before the Magistrates Court in Masterton, a hundred kilometres from Wellington. The local *Poverty Bay Herald* reported that she had a 'rather becoming appearance', and provided the following information:

> She came to Masterton from Wellington on Thursday last, ostensibly in search of work. Being unsuccessful in her efforts she dressed herself in men's clothing and on Saturday applied to Mr T. Duncan, secretary of the Benevolent Society, for work. She was attired in the clothes of a stable boy. Her hair was cut short and her voice resembled that of a boy of 17. She also smoked a cigarette.

Eugenia sobbed as she told the magistrate that she was willing to go back, and if let off would never do it again. She was discharged on promising to go back to Wellington.

Finally, in 1896, at twenty-one, still spurned by most of her family, Eugenia decided to escape the suffocating environment of Wellington, where she was known by too many people, and to leave behind all the restrictions that had been imposed upon her by a family and a society that had no understanding of her needs. Assuming the identity of her male alter ego, Eugene Falleni, she obtained employment as a working seaman on a merchant ship and left Wellington without telling anyone that she was going. After years of suffering humiliation at her hands, it was with relief that her parents discovered that she had disappeared. In time, their anxiety over her fate was replaced by anger at what she had put them through and a fear that one day she might return to cause them further anguish. Over the next eighteen months, Eugenia worked as a seaman on a variety of vessels, until the final, fateful voyage on the Norwegian barque that resulted in her being forced to disembark in the town of Newcastle on the east coast of Australia.

CHAPTER 3

PARENTHOOD

Destitute, in despair and pregnant, Eugenia knew nobody in the port city of Newcastle, where she had been compelled to leave her ship.

The brutal rape and resulting pregnancy forced her, for a while at least, to abandon what she believed to be her genuine, true identity as a male and to revert to her forced, superficial identity as Eugenia – the female aspect she had fought so hard to abandon for much of her adolescent life. She felt as much of a genuine male as any other man. Her female bodily attributes were like having an unwanted, additional limb attached to her body that she overwhelmingly felt did not belong to her. She had hidden them for so long that in a sense they had become separate from her. Her genitals were, for her, like a man's nipples – an ancient vestige of a common human ancestry, but not serving any useful, present-day purpose.

At this time of great need, with a new dependent life due to be born, Eugenia reverted to what was familiar. Her Italian family in Wellington had sometimes spoken about an Italian couple in Sydney by the name of De Angelis.[1] Her parents had remarked how kind and generous Mrs De Angelis was, and how unfortunate it was that she and her husband, Ludovico, had been unable to have their own children. They had also mentioned that Mr and Mrs De Angelis had done particularly well for themselves and that they lived in very comfortable circumstances in an affluent part of Sydney. Surely, she thought, this couple would give her succour and support, at least until the baby was born.

Thus it was that Eugenia found her way to the home of Mr and Mrs De Angelis, a large suburban residence known as 'Tevere'[2] at 131 Pelham Street in Double Bay – one of the exclusive eastern suburbs of Sydney.[3] Mr and Mrs De Angelis had heard about Eugenia for many years before she arrived on their doorstep. They knew about her tomboy ways as a child, her reluctance to be married, her failed marriage, her arrest for impersonating a man, the period she had lived in a hostel run by the Salvation Army in Wellington and about her unannounced departure from Wellington in 1896.

Despite knowing so much about Eugenia's troubled past, Mrs De Angelis readily accepted the young woman into her home. Living up to her reputation as loving, kind, gentle and motherly, she relished the opportunity to care for someone who needed her so desperately. News of Eugenia's arrival in a pregnant state at the De Angelis home in Sydney found its way to Luigi and Isola Falleni in New Zealand. Her parents had long since given her up for dead. The scandal of her multiple arrests, her failed marriage and her short-lived attempts at finding work as a male made the news of her being alive somewhat bittersweet for her parents. In addition, they found it hard to forgive her for having disappeared so precipitously. Apart from the news of Eugenia being alive, in Sydney and pregnant, they were also told that the father of her unborn child was a sea captain who had deserted her. So great was the dishonour that Eugenia had brought upon her family before her departure that the threat of further scandal and shame to this strict, conservative, Italian family led them to reject any further contact with her. Even the prospect of a grandchild from their firstborn daughter was not sufficient to overcome their fear of further trauma and disgrace to their family name and reputation.

Eugenia's much younger sister-in-law, Olga Falleni, had this to say many years later:

> When Eugenia went away to Australia she wanted to come back, but they stopped her from coming back. When the father and mother found out about all this [living as a male] they got such a shock they tried everything to stop her coming back. She had never done any terrible thing, but there was the name, the family name. So they stopped her. I know how the old lady [Isola] felt. She did not want to talk about it. She was a very clean living woman, and she did not want to have anything wrong in the family. But I think, with so many children, there would have to be a black sheep, anyway. The others all turned out very good, and married good, and were hard-working. But there would have to be one.[4]

While Eugenia awaited the arrival of her child, she worked in a business owned by Ludovico and his wife, known as the 'Italian Laundry', at 113 New South Head Road, Double Bay.[5] For a short while, Eugenia mused that giving birth – that ultimate act of femininity – might overcome her desire to resume life as a male afterwards. But this was not to be. It was at the De Angelis house in Double Bay that, on 19 September 1898, Eugenia, now twenty-three years old, gave birth to her only child – a daughter whom she named Josephine. The birth was attended by Mrs De Angelis, who swooned at this newborn child who had come into her midst. Eugenia, on the other hand, could not wait to eject the unwanted lump that had steadily grown inside her, and when it finally emerged she had no interest in caring for it. When it was suggested to her by Mrs De Angelis that she should suckle the child, Eugenia was overcome by feelings of revulsion. Within days of the birth, she became resentful of the impositions that the baby represented. Eugenia could barely bring herself to look at the child, let alone to hold her. On those few occasions when, at Mrs De Angelis's insistence, she did hold the baby, Josephine rooted around for her mother's breasts and in disgust Eugenia held her with both arms outstretched – as though she were a sack of dirty potatoes – waiting for Mrs De Angelis to take the child from her.

Eugenia realised within hours of the birth that nothing had changed within her and that she still possessed the restless need to live as a man. What was she to do? If she were to resume her life as a male, it would be impossible to take on the responsibility of caring for Josephine. On the other hand, this defenceless baby was her flesh and blood and in obvious need of nurturing. She knew the pain of rejection by family, and here she was contemplating the same treatment of her own newborn child. Should she go back to New Zealand and try to convince the Fallenis to take care of Josephine? Her conservative Italian parents, who had already suffered so much, had already spurned any contact with her, but would one of her younger sisters take on her child? Should she go to the nuns at the nearby Convent of the Sacred Heart at Rose Bay and hand over Josephine for adoption? Should she leave the De Angelis household, go somewhere distant and anonymously abandon the baby as a foundling, so that she could never be traced back to her?

In the end, it was the childless Mrs De Angelis who solved the problem by convincing Eugenia that Josephine would have the best opportunities in life if she and her husband took over the baby's care. It was also the best solution for Eugenia, she explained, because there would be the opportunity whenever she liked of coming to visit Josephine at their home. After a lot of agonised thought, Eugenia overcame her feelings of guilt at abandoning her newborn child by promising to come and visit her regularly and by pledging to contribute financially to her upbringing.

Several days after leaving the De Angelis household, Eugenia adopted a new male identity: a Scotchman[6] by the name of Harry Leo Crawford – an identity she was to successfully maintain for the next twenty-two years.

There was of course no need for her to assume the identity of a Scotchman. She had, however, worked on ships with Scotchmen and was easily able to mimic their accent. One can only assume that the additional subterfuge about Harry's Scottish origins was an attempt to avoid the prejudice she had encountered for her Italian origins. Eugenia was incredibly comfortable in her new persona as Harry, and, because of that, she was able to effortlessly blend into life as a labouring man in working-class Sydney. By all accounts, and judging from a contemporary photograph, Harry was a well-groomed man with delicate good looks. He had a charming disposition, which meant he had no difficulty acquiring friends, both male and female.

Harry moved from job to job, working as a general rouseabout and labourer in factories, laundries and hotels. His longest employment was at the Perdriau rubber factory in Drummoyne. At one stage, Harry again worked for Mr and Mrs De Angelis in their laundry business at Paddington, driving a horse-drawn cart to deliver the laundered items. One of the customers to whom he delivered laundry was a government pathologist by the name of Dr Stratford Sheldon, who was to play a role in later events of her life.

Harry was particularly attracted to jobs that required a considerable amount of male muscle and the sort of emotional toughness that was common in working-class men at that time. He easily fitted into contemporary, male society and was known as quite a 'lad'. He had a reputation for hard drinking, a penchant to swear like a sailor and a raw fondness for women, although he was not known to have had any serious, long-term relationships. Harry was so firmly ensconced in his identity as a male that he viewed those brief liaisons with women as the product of a perfectly natural attraction felt by a male for a female.

He lived in various suburbs of inner-western Sydney in cheap boarding houses with other single, working men – each in a small, airless, badly maintained single room. A boarding house typically had a small shared kitchen with some basic cooking utensils, several gas jets and an ice chest to store perishable food. There was a common bathroom on each floor and residents had to put money into a meter to obtain hot water for a shower or a bath. A female caretaker would collect the rent each week and keep the common areas in a semblance of cleanliness. For extra money, the caretaker would wash residents' clothes in a 'copper',[7] which was housed in a downstairs laundry. The landlord would hardly ever appear. Harry frequently changed jobs and boarding houses. His charm and bonhomie, as well as his ability to imbibe and swear, earned him many drinking friends. Not a soul challenged his identity as a male.

Only very occasionally did Harry come to the home of Mr and Mrs De Angelis to see Josephine, who grew into a beautiful, dark-haired child. Even more infrequently did he give Mrs De Angelis, who was known as 'Granny', small amounts of money to help defray the cost of caring for his daughter. The fact was that Harry had no emotional connection to the little girl at all. Sometimes when Harry arrived, he would be drunk and become abusive towards them. The rarity of these visits was a product of Harry's constant sense of guilt that he had abandoned Josephine into someone else's care, and his trips to Double Bay were a reminder of that betrayal. After many years of unsuccessfully trying for a child of her own, Mrs De Angelis considered Josephine to be a gift to her from God. She readily agreed, as a condition for the continuation of this informal fostering arrangement, that Harry's identity had to be maintained, and so she kept his secret completely to herself, as did her husband. Granny tolerated the drunken visits as a necessary ordeal and cared nothing for the infrequent payments of support money. In fact she had no need for the financial help at all and she allowed Harry to make the payments only so as to allay his feelings of guilt, but these meagre contributions to Josephine's upkeep did nothing to banish his demons.

Josephine was wonderfully cared for by 'Granny', and for many years Josephine thought that Mr and Mrs De Angelis were her real grandparents. Ludovico De Angelis, however, over some years developed an intense jealousy of his wife's love and devotion towards the child, feeling that the time his wife spent with Josephine was time she did not have to devote to him. He often threatened to return to Italy alone.

As a young child, Josephine was totally confused by the man who would occasionally come to her home, ostensibly to visit her, but who was generally abusive to both her and her beloved Granny. Although this man had told her numerous times to call him 'Father', he did not act in the way she thought a father should. After he had left, Granny would frequently say to her, 'Don't blame him, he can't help it. He has many problems that I will explain to you one day.'

It was when Josephine was barely seven years old that Mrs De Angelis finally felt she was old enough to tell her that Harry was really her mother. Although her Granny tried to explain the situation to her, Josephine was truly confounded by the knowledge that this man, who insisted on being called 'Father', was really her mother. Despite her young age, she understood instinctively that this was not something to be talked about with outsiders, but rather to be kept a secret. This was reinforced on many occasions when 'Father' arrived at the house drunk, and aggressively extracted promises from her that she would always call him that, and never tell anyone anything different. It was also at around the age of seven that Mrs De Angelis told Josephine that her real father was the captain of a sailing ship. When she enquired further about him, her Granny would merely say that he was the captain of a sailing ship with four masts.

Because of Ludovico De Angelis's hostility and coldness towards her, Josephine longed desperately to meet her real father, and she would sometimes walk down to nearby Rose Bay and sit at the water's edge for hours, looking at the ships that sailed past on their way to the wharves at Darling Harbour, counting the number of masts on each one and wondering whether this ship or that ship was the one on which her father was coming to visit her.

CHAPTER 4

LOVE

It was 1912. Just months earlier, the passenger liner *Titanic* had sunk when it hit an iceberg in the North Atlantic Ocean with the loss of more than 1500 lives. The British government established the Royal Flying Corp in anticipation of a possible war with Germany, while in Turkey the world's first bombing from an aeroplane occurred. Two movie studio companies, Universal Pictures and Paramount Pictures, were established in the United States. For the first time, women were included in the Australian team that went to the Olympic Games in Stockholm. One of them, Fanny Durack, won a gold medal in the 100-metre freestyle swimming race.

Harry Crawford's identity had worked successfully for him for fourteen years. So effortlessly did he fit into this persona that not a single person had challenged it. His occasional visits to Josephine at the De Angelis household in Double Bay were a fleeting interlude that traumatically jerked him back to his misunderstood and brutal past – a reminder of an identity with which he felt no affinity and a revisiting of the traumatic events that had led to Josephine's conception. Whenever he did venture to Pelham Street, he would be adamant that Josephine call him 'Father', despite Mrs De Angelis calling him Eugenia. These visits became more and more harrowing and therefore less frequent. He was determined not to allow the short interludes at Double Bay to intrude into his real life as Harry.

Harry's life had a certain comfortable monotony to it. The labouring jobs, the boarding houses and the drinking sessions with his mates seemed to be his whole existence. He had long ago lost any sense of surprise at how easily people accepted him for the person he now was. His good looks and charm made him popular with both men and women. For many years, when women had thrown themselves at him, he had flirted with them, but in abject fear of exposure he had never taken things any further. He found this agonising because deep down he had a great need and desire for physical and emotional intimacy with a woman, but the risks were too great. On one occasion, when his inhibitions had been sufficiently calmed by alcohol and his desire for intimacy felt overpowering, he found that he could not stop himself venturing further with a woman. The experience was quite terrifying, as he was fearful that it would end in discovery, exposure and humiliation. But the woman was quite inexperienced and had no idea in the dark what to expect from him, and she seemed quite content just kissing, hugging and allowing him to fumble at her. His elation afterwards was overwhelming. It emboldened him to go further the next time. He was resolute that if ever he had another opportunity for intimacy with a woman, he had to be in a position to do more to satisfy her, so he decided to equip himself with an implement of pleasure that would enable him to do just that. Having had many younger brothers in Wellington and having lived for several years with fellow sailors in the close confines of a crew's cabin, Harry knew exactly what dimensions and qualities the instrument required.

The dildo as an explicitly sexual object can be traced as far back as ancient Greece. Greek vases dating from the fifth and fourth centuries BC featured dildos being used in graphic sexual activity and during solitary female masturbation. In the mid-1800s, a phallus-shaped apparatus approximating a dildo (known as a 'speculum'[1]) was widely used as a medical device to treat the symptoms of hysteria in women, a commonly diagnosed condition of which the origins were believed to lie in sexual tension. This device was supplanted by the electromechanical vibrator in the 1880s. From the late nineteenth century through to the 1930s, dildos and vibrators were advertised openly in popular magazines and catalogues for home use as a therapeutic tool primarily associated with female masturbation. However, for a dildo to be used to deceive a female recipient that she was with a male was totally beyond anyone's expectation and, in fact, a serious sexual crime.

Harry experimented for a long time in the shed at the back of his boarding house to fashion a device that would feel like the real thing. It had to be strong, but soft. He had to be able to use it with both hands free. Above all else, it had to be secure so that it wouldn't fail him and alert his sexual partner to the fact that it was not part of him. In the end, he fashioned a piece of hardwood into the right shape and size, and attached two leather straps into grooves at the base of the wood so that the top edge of the leather was flush with the wood. He attached the straps with strong flathead screws which he rounded so that they didn't protrude, and countersunk them into the leather. Next, he placed a layer of gauze around the wooden object, the main purpose of which was to provide grip between the wood and the outer layer. He then tightly wrapped around it the best quality leather that he could afford, making sure that it covered the area where the straps were attached to the base, and he sewed the seams of the leather securely together along the bottom edge with the finest, strong cotton. In this way, even with his fingers, he could barely feel the seam and could not sense the straps or the screws at all. He tested it with his hands many times to ensure that the leather was so tightly attached that it would not come off the wooden base and that there was no part of the device that felt rough or unnatural.

The first time that he tried this new device on an unsuspecting woman, he was terrified that it would fail and he would be discovered. He began by ensuring that the woman had had a lot to drink beforehand. He realised that the whole exercise had to be conducted in the complete dark and that he had to make sure that the woman would not touch him intimately, but that was nothing different from what he had done in the past. When his partner was already naked in bed and the room was almost totally dark, he went briefly to the bathroom, still in his upper and lower underclothes and still protected by the bandages that he always kept tightly wrapped around his chest. He took with him a small cloth bag that contained his secret weapon. In the privacy of the bathroom, he applied a liberal amount of odourless petroleum jelly to it and then strapped it on, putting his underpants back on over it. He then returned to the bedroom and slipped into bed. He spent more than the usual time in the preliminaries, until the woman was bursting with desire for penetration. Only then did he remove his underpants, leaving his upper underwear still in place, and guide his manhood with one hand until it was fully inserted into the proper place. As he entered her, she groaned with delight and he felt a great sense of relief. Once this initial step had been accomplished, he was able to use both his hands freely to caress the woman and ensure that her hands did not wander too far down. When they had completed their lovemaking, he made sure that he was the first to go to the bathroom, where he removed his appendage, wiped it down, and placed it back in its cloth bag. Very few women in those days had enough knowledge of sexual matters to realise that there had been no semen emitted during this intimate exchange or to distinguish the lubricant from semen.

Afterwards, his partner was deeply satisfied and praised him for his performance and 'stamina'. Within a few weeks he had tried it a number of times on several women using the same technique and none of them held the slightest suspicion. Quite the contrary – several said what a fabulous lover he was and commented on how he was able to 'maintain himself' for such a long time. By then, it gave him an intense delight that he was able to satisfy them without them having the faintest idea of how he was doing it. It mattered nothing to him that he received no physical pleasure in return. What really mattered was that he was accepted as a male in the full, complete and most intimate sense. It was the ultimate affirmation of his identity as Harry.

Despite this success, a restless emotional emptiness still plagued Harry, which he tried to quell by drowning his feelings in excessive amounts of drink. He knew that beneath his rough exterior was a softness that he ached to show to a woman. But he had never come anywhere near feeling comfortable enough to disclose his secret to any of his occasional girl-friends. The constant need to guard his identity took an enormous toll on his emotional energy. He deeply longed for the opportunity to be open, truthful and relaxed with just one woman whom he could trust to keep his secret, and who would respect him for being Harry – even in the knowledge of his bodily features. Occasionally, he would daydream that a beautiful woman would come up to him and tell him that she knew his secret but that it did not matter, because she loved him for the person he was, no matter what his body looked like under the multi-layered clothing he used for protection. They would go together to a magnificent house and they would undress each other and do things together without any embarrassment, shame or anxiety. It was the constant fear of exposure, accusation, shame, ridicule and prosecution that always jerked him back from this dream to reality – as well as the constant terror of being raped again if he let his guard down in the presence of the men with whom he lived, worked or drank.

In 1912, now thirty-seven years old, Harry decided that he would advance his prospects by completely changing his employment and the circle of people he associated with. He applied for a job as a coachman and yardman for Dr Gother Clarke, a popular young doctor who lived in the distant, leafy, North-Shore suburb of Wahroonga. Apart from being a good and caring doctor, Clarke had distinguished himself as a cricketer, winning a 'blue' while at Sydney University. Harry was thrilled when Dr Clarke accepted him. Employment in Wahroonga took him away from the atmos-phere of the working-class suburbs on the southern side of the harbour and enabled him to work with his beloved horses.

Wahroonga was a veritable Arcadia. The harbour crossing by ferry or punt had preserved the rural atmosphere of the more distant northern suburbs and, as a result, many of the blocks of land there were at least four or five times larger than in other parts of Sydney. It was only a little more than twenty years earlier that the train line had been completed from the harbour at Milson's Point to the distant northern edge of Sydney at Hornsby. This had made it possible to commute by train and ferry to the city and led to Wahroonga's residential development, with orchardists selling off large parcels of land on which many fine mansions were built. Homes consisted of either grand mansions or small, mainly weatherboard cottages. Dr Clarke's house, 'Terranora', was one of the former.

Terranora was situated on two blocks of land on the Lane Cove Road[2] opposite a girls' school and near to the Wahroonga railway station. The Australian eucalyptus bushland was nearby, and occasionally wallabies would venture up to the sprawling lawns to feast on the abundant grass. These expansive estates required substantial staff to keep them clean and tidy, so the owners were often wealthy people who yearned to live in the country but were unable or unwilling to forego the benefits of life in Sydney. Wahroonga, which was much closer to Hornsby than to Milson's Point, did not have many of the modern conveniences that one would take for granted on the southern side of the harbour, such as a sewerage system or an extensive choice of shops. Many of the roads were still made of dirt, which made car ownership undesirable and the traditional coach or sulky much more appropriate. Dr Clarke hired Harry largely because the man showed a great knowledge of horses and the contraptions they pulled, and the doctor had several of both. Harry was expected to look after the doctor's horses, carriage and sulky, and to drive the doctor around on his medical visits.

Within weeks of starting work for Dr Clarke, Harry became aware of Terranora's beautiful live-in housekeeper, Annie Birkett. Annie was a fine-looking, well-groomed, thirty-five-year-old widow with a nine-year-old son, also called Harry. Annie's husband had died after an illness when their boy was barely three, leaving her with no choice but to work. She was a fine housekeeper and had previously been employed by Judge Herbert Curlewis and his wife Ethel Turner[3] at their home, 'Avenel', overlooking Middle Harbour. Wanting the best possible life for her son, Annie had moved to Dr Clarke's mansion at Wahroonga. Within a few days, Harry Crawford was joking with Annie and teasing her in an affectionate way. He was struck by her fine facial features, her luxurious hair and the slim line of her body. She was indeed a fine specimen, as well as a kind and gentle person, and no one had a bad word to say about her. He was in no way put off by the fact that he was 5'4" and she was 5'7".

Harry felt quite differently about Annie than any of the other women he had met. Whenever he saw her, he felt a great sense of joy, and whenever he left work for the day, he felt a sense of loss and longing for the next time he would see her. Within a short period of time he realised that he was very much in love with her and that he desperately wanted to be with her. He knew even at this time that if ever he were to win her over, he would have to steadfastly maintain his masculinity and keep hidden from her those parts of his anatomy that he himself found so distasteful.

Annie was quite chuffed at this charming man who paid her so much attention, but she was in a very secure situation at Dr Clarke's and was completely focused on the needs of her son, Harry Jnr. It had not been a long time since her husband had died and the trauma of that was still with her. She knew perfectly well that, as a widow with a child, her prospects of finding a new marriage partner were negligible. She considered herself fortunate to have this charming and handsome man showing an interest in her and her son, and helping to fill in the spare time she had when not required to work for the doctor. Yet she had heard stories about Harry's heavy drinking, which made her wary. She was determined not to do anything in haste, because above all else she craved security – financial, physical and emotional – for herself and her son, and being at Dr Clarke's had given her that already. She had to admit to herself that she thoroughly enjoyed the company of this man who was so good with the horses, and she was flattered by the fact that he was completely oblivious to the other female domestics, some of whom had shown quite an interest in him. It was clear to everyone that he had eyes only for Annie.

Over many months Harry carefully and skilfully wooed Annie, taking into account and accommodating her concerns about Harry Jnr. He took them both to see Colleano's All-Star Circus, [4] and for long picnics at Middle Harbour, Clontarf Beach and other popular picnic spots, assisted by Dr Clarke's generous offer to let them use his horse and sulky so that they could get to more distant locations. Both Annie and Harry Jnr thoroughly enjoyed these open-air adventures and the sulky trips to get there. When Harry had hold of the reins, Annie felt secure. He also promised her that his hard-drinking days were over.

Harry explored the whole of the North Shore to discover as many enchanting picnic places as he could. One of them was in the Lane Cove River Park, a large bushland reserve that was to play an important part in Harry's life. The Lane Cove River Park was the most popular outdoor area on the North Shore for recreation, picnics, walks, boating and gatherings of families and friends. This particular picnic spot was an isolated clearing well away from the areas that most other people used in a part of the park that was accessed at the end of Mowbray Road, a long thoroughfare that extended from Middle Harbour in the east to the Lane Cove River in the west, and that crossed the main north–south Lane Cove Road at the Great Northern Hotel at Chatswood. It was a region that Harry vaguely knew, because years before he had worked for a week at the nearby Chicago Flour Mills, several hundred metres further upstream. Harry had left the flour mills after only a week because he couldn't stand the terrible smell. To get to work there, he had approached from the south-west by a boat provided by his employer to bring workers from the southern side of the harbour at Glebe, Drummoyne and Balmain directly to the mills. This time, to get to their picnic spot, they approached from the northeast, coming down the main road from Wahroonga to Chatswood, then turning west into Mowbray Road. At the end of Mowbray Road there was a short walk along a bush path, down to a wonderful little clearing surrounded by native trees and large, heavily weathered sandstone rocks, with a distant view of the mangroves in Stringybark Creek, one of the tributaries of the Lane Cove River. In the distance, they could just see the outline of the Cumberland Paper Mills, near the junction of Stringybark Creek and the Lane Cove River.

It was during such a picnic at this wonderful place one day, when Annie's son Harry Jnr had gone off after lunch to explore the bush, that Harry finally felt bold enough to lean over and kiss Annie, expecting her to pull away in abrupt shock that he could take such a liberty with her. He was surprised by how positive her reaction was, so he drew a deep breath and told her that he loved her. She blushed, and did not respond, but he knew from her smile as she coyly turned her head away that he had a chance to win her over completely.

It was only after more than a year of working for Dr Clarke, and coming up with innovative activities that would interest Annie's young son, that Harry's courting of Annie finally achieved its aim – Annie agreed to marry him. His joy knew no bounds. In anticipation of their wedding, they planned the rest of their lives together. Annie had a sizeable sum of money saved up, and so they decided that she would resign from her service with Dr Clarke and with the money she would buy a confectionery and soft drink store at 231 Darling Street, Balmain, which they had seen advertised for sale at a price of £75. Its location opposite Gladstone Park was ideal, because the sporting and leisure activities there each weekend ensured a good customer base. In addition, they would be able to live in the accommodation above the shop. The purchase of the business took place just three weeks before their wedding and Annie initially moved into the shop premises with her son.

Harry felt that he had constructed a future that was almost as good as his wildest dreams. He was marrying the love of his life and their financial situation seemed secure. And yet, he dared not tell his beloved wife-to-be his darkest secret. Would he be able to indefinitely keep the details of his bodily identity hidden from her, as he had kept them from the many casual women he had previously been intimate with? It was one thing to have a brief sexual liaison, and quite another to be in a marital relationship. About one thing he was quite certain. He could never disclose the true facts to his betrothed, as he knew only too well what her reaction would be. To lose her would be an unbearable agony. His love for Annie and his desire to share his life with her were so intense that he was determined to maintain his secret, no matter how much effort and subterfuge it involved.

CHAPTER 5

MARRIAGE

It was 1913. A French aviator, Roland Garros, was the first to make a non-stop flight across the Mediterranean from southern France to Tunisia. The British suffragette Emily Pankhurst was sentenced to gaol for conspiracy to commit property damage. Work commenced on the construction of Canberra, the new Australian national capital city.

The wedding of Harry Leo Crawford and Annie Birkett took place on 19 February 1913 in the Methodist Parsonage in Montague Street, Balmain. Harry was thirty-eight and Annie was thirty-seven. The minister, Mr Hynes, recited the traditional description of marriage as 'the union of a man and a woman to the exclusion of all others, voluntarily entered into for life'. From Annie's point of view, she was marrying a charming and amiable Scotchman whose parents had already died. Harry appeared to be the typical nervous groom. Behind his nerves was an ambivalence that he found hard to define to himself. On the one hand, he was joyous that the day had come when he and Annie would profess their love for each other in a public ceremony. On the other hand, he knew that if ever his identity were exposed, he would inevitably face complete rejection by Annie as well as the full force of the law for having fraudulently entered into the holy covenant of marriage. In a way, he was resentful at the intrusion of the state into the intricacies of private affairs of the heart. In the end, he meekly accepted that he would go along with whatever was necessary for the ceremony to proceed. They exchanged the traditional vows:

'Annie Birkett, do you take this man, Harry Leo Crawford, to be your lawful wedded husband, to have and to hold, from this day forth, for better or for worse, for richer or for poorer, in sickness and in health, to love and to cherish, for so long as you both shall live?'

The wedding was witnessed by Mr Hynes's wife and Annie's sister, Lily Nugent. Josephine Falleni did not attend the wedding. Indeed, Harry made sure that Annie knew nothing about Josephine's existence and that

Josephine had no contact with or knowledge of his new wife and her son. When he signed the marriage register, Harry listed his father as also being called Harry Leo Crawford, a master mariner, and his mother as Louisa Buti. He had told Annie that they were both deceased and that he hardly knew his father, who had often been at sea.

Although Annie's sister Lily attended the wedding and was one of the witnesses, she was in fact terribly against the marriage and didn't hesitate to tell her sister how much she disliked Harry, who drank too much and sometimes swore like a sailor. Lily was apprehensive that Harry was only interested in her sister's money, and she feared that Harry's bad bachelor habits, particularly his drinking, would return soon after the wedding. Previously, the two sisters had been very close and congenial, but once Annie announced her intention to marry Harry, their relationship quickly deteriorated. After attending the wedding, Lily found her feelings of dislike for Harry were so intense that she was not able to be in his presence, and she refused to visit Annie when he was there. The relationship between the two sisters was so deeply affected that they rarely saw each other.

Harry moved into the shop premises in Darling Street, Balmain with Annie and her boy Harry Jnr, who was now ten years old. Balmain was a densely inhabited working-class suburb which for more than 100 years had arguably been one of the roughest neighbourhoods in Sydney, with a reputation for more than the usual level of crime. So bad had the crime problem there become in 1854 that the government built the Balmain Watch House as a police lock-up.[1] By the 1880s, the suburb had no fewer than forty operating pubs. The most rowdy of these was the London Hotel, which had a reputation as the favourite of both ships officers and sailors and as a no-go area for the police. By 1913 the situation in Balmain had hardly improved.

Harry and Annie led a normal, conservative, suburban life, and were often seen in the neighbourhood walking hand-in-hand. Annie was well aware that Harry was painfully modest about nudity to the extent that she had never seen him naked or even baretop. Their lovemaking was always in the dark and with his undershirt on, but that was one of the quirks about him that she just accepted. Whenever she brought up his modesty in conversation, he would joke about it and say something like: 'You try living in cramped quarters with twenty or so other men on a ship or in a boarding house, and you would be modest too.'

From Annie's point of view, their lovemaking was satisfactory, although a little monotonous in that there was only one position that they always adopted, with him on top of her and his arms outstretched holding up his upper body, or sometimes resting on his elbows. This meant that there was never any body-to-body contact above the waist. This was quite different from what had occurred during lovemaking with her first husband. She noticed that Harry always kept his arms underneath hers and, on several occasions when she had moved her hands a little bit lower than Harry's mid-chest level, he had roughly raised his own arms underneath hers and aggressively told her that it was 'out of bounds'. Annie never raised this with Harry, as a lady did not talk about such things, even with her husband. Their lovemaking was always preceded by Harry visiting the bathroom, and once again Annie accepted this strange habit, putting it down to an obsessive desire for bodily cleanliness. What did annoy her, however, was that their lovemaking always occurred at times determined by Harry. On the odd occasion that she would attempt to initiate foreplay, he would roughly push her away and tell that it was not a wife's role to begin such things. Annie's rationalization was that this was typical male fear of losing sexual control and a relic from a bygone age, but no amount of discussion would convince Harry that it was unacceptable in modern times.

What Annie did not know was that Harry had found a suitable hiding place for the cloth bag in which he kept his secret implement. It was in the bottom of a portmanteau[2] that contained his rarely used best clothing, and whenever he planned intimate contact with Annie he would temporarily transfer the cloth bag from the portmanteau into a hiding place in their bathroom. Soon after lovemaking, Harry would transfer the cloth bag back to its principal hiding place in the portmanteau.

Portmanteaux and trunks had long functioned as storage facilities for significant personal possessions within the home, and not just for travelling purposes. They had become a common depository for such household goods as clothing, linen and even reading materials. They also traditionally served as a place of safeguard for money, jewellery and other valuables within the home. With advances in the design and manufacture of personal luggage in the early twentieth century, these sizeable containers were increasingly confined to purely domestic usage and to the protection of life's most valued possessions.

Harry's relationship with his stepson, Harry Jnr, was a strained one, as many step relationships are. Harry believed that Annie was much too soft on the boy, and he attempted to correct this by providing the discipline he thought the boy needed for his development. The boy was understandably jealous of the attention which his beloved mother lavished on her new husband. Although he had no memory of his late father, he resented this recent imposter asserting his authority over him in the manner of a father.

He missed the bush and open spaces of Wahroonga, where he had been free to explore on his own for hours at a time, and, as he had predicted to his mother, once the marriage had taken place, the innovative outings and picnics quickly evaporated.

The following year, 1914, was a shocking one for Josephine Falleni, who by this time had become a rebellious, strong-willed and strikingly beautiful sixteen-year-old. Two years earlier, Ludovico De Angelis had finally carried out his threat to leave his wife and go back to Italy. If anything, that had made Josephine's life with Granny easier. However, early in 1914, Josephine became pregnant to a sailor on a merchant ship who was almost a generation older than her, whom she had casually met and who, to her dismay, promptly disappeared before she even found out about the pregnancy. At around the same time that Josephine discovered that she was pregnant, Granny De Angelis suddenly died from 'dropsy',[3] leaving an emotionally fragile and vulnerable foster daughter who was still a teenager without anyone to care for her or to support her through the pregnancy and birth. A will was found at Granny's home, but it was unsigned, so because neither Josephine nor Harry was related by blood to her, the entire estate went to a distant relative.

Annie still knew nothing about Harry's daughter, so, wanting to ensure that a destitute and desperate Josephine did not turn up at his house unannounced, Harry took control of the situation. He initially placed the girl in the care of a woman by the name of Mrs Keith, who lived in Hoffman's Lane, Balmain, near to his own home. When Josephine's baby was due, Harry took her to St Margaret's Maternity Home in Bourke Street, Darlinghurst where, in September of 1914, she gave birth prematurely to a baby girl whom she also called Josephine.[4] Harry was as indifferent to the new baby as he had been to his own daughter at her birth. Josephine, on the other hand, was a far better mother than Eugenia had ever been, but tragically her baby suffered from a congenital heart defect and died at three months of age on 10 December. Josephine was heartbroken, and deep down she blamed herself and her immorality for the tragedy. The baby's death made her an even more troubled and restless young woman.

Following the baby's death, as Josephine was old enough to work and earn an income, Harry decided that it would be best for everyone if she came and lived with him and Annie, in which case she could contribute financially to their household. The difficulty was that Annie knew nothing about his daughter. Before bringing Josephine into his household at Balmain, Harry made her swear repeatedly that she would never say anything about his true identity. He explained to Josephine that his wife knew nothing about such things, and that it would be catastrophic if she ever did find out. Josephine promised that she would never disclose Harry's secret. They agreed that if Annie questioned them as to the whereabouts of Josephine's mother, as she likely would, they would tell her that she had died of consumption. During these discussions, Josephine warned Harry that one day Annie would find out the terrible truth. Harry's reply to his daughter's prediction was: 'I'll watch it. I would rather do away with myself than let the police find out anything about me'.[5]

It came as a complete shock for Annie to find out that her husband had a sixteen-year-old daughter he had never mentioned before. Harry explained it to her by saying that he had had a very brief relationship with the mother many years earlier and that he had not known that he had a child until the woman's recent death. Initially, Annie was deeply resentful at having to take on her husband's child from another relationship, but eventually she came to accept that she could not refuse Harry's wish that his own daughter come to live with them, especially after the girl's mother had died. Whenever Annie questioned Josephine about her mother, the girl would say nothing, so Annie presumed that she was severely traumatised by her loss and came to accept that she would get no further information.

Josephine's arrival in Harry and Annie's Balmain household caused a complete change to their domestic situation. Although their financial situation improved because they now had three incomes, Annie was completely unaccustomed to dealing with a difficult and tempestuous teenage girl. She made vain attempts to control Josephine's more precocious activities, including going out on her own at night with persons unknown. One of Annie's friends told her that she had seen Josephine late one night arm-in-arm with a navy sailor at King's Cross. However, when she confronted Josephine about this, the teenager denied everything.

Annie's attempts to control Josephine proved quite futile and indeed counterproductive. All they achieved were further arguments between the two of them and Harry. That in turn caused Harry to begin drinking heavily again, and when he was drunk he became verbally abusive, which terrified Harry Jnr and exacerbated the arguments. It was all a vicious circle. It annoyed Annie intensely that Harry seemed unconcerned at the more extreme activities of his daughter and that he took no action when Josephine was rude to her. Above all else, Annie was concerned that some of Josephine's bad behaviour might rub off on to her own beloved son, Harry Jnr. Josephine was intensely hostile toward Annie's attempts to control her, and perhaps also jealous of Harry's love for Annie, when she herself had been so callously abandoned at birth. Because of all this disruption and ill feeling, what had previously been a relatively calm and harmonious household became a most volatile and argumentative one.

Unfortunately, the confectionery shop in Darling Street, Balmain, was not the success that Harry and Annie had hoped for, largely because there were too many other confectionery stores in the vicinity. After about nine months of poor returns, Annie found a purchaser willing to pay £20 – a substantial reduction from the £75 they had paid for it. By this stage, she was so concerned at the atrocious situation in their household that when the shop was sold, she and Harry Jnr moved out of Balmain to live at the home of her sister Lily in Kogarah, south of the city. Naturally, Lily used every opportunity to lambast Harry and to gloat to her sister that she had predicted just such trouble. Within a few weeks, sick of her sister's carping, Annie secured employment as a housekeeper for a Dr Binns in Belgrave Street, Kogarah, and she and Harry Jnr moved into the doctor's home.

In an attempt to convince Annie that they could work out their problems together, Harry promised her that he would reform his drinking habits and improve his behaviour towards her. Eventually, he succeeded in persuading her to resume living as man and wife. They all moved to a house at number 7 and then next door at number 5 The Avenue, Drummoyne – a suburb not far from Balmain.[6] Harry resumed his usual occupations as labourer and general rouseabout, working in various factories and pubs in the Balmain and Drummoyne areas, including once again the Perdriau rubber factory in Drummoyne. Harry Jnr attended the Drummoyne Public School, but then, at the age of about fourteen, left after obtaining full-time employment in a local grocery shop owned by Mr and Mrs Bone, who took a great liking to the boy.

At one stage, Harry secured well-paid employment for both himself and Josephine at the Riverstone Meatworks, between Rouse Hill and Windsor. This was about thirty-five miles northwest of Sydney, but accessible by train via Blacktown. The meatworks had first opened in 1878 as a beef slaughterhouse employing four slaughtermen. By 1900, the abattoir had expanded greatly and was the chief employer in the Riverstone district. As was common in factories of the time, workers in the meatworks faced poor ventilation, overcrowding and an unsafe work environment. Although the *Factories and Shops Act* had been passed in 1896 to improve work safety standards, a combination of judicial laxity, employer hostility and inadequate penalties meant that many factories still had faulty machinery, a lack of safety equipment and a high incidence of workplace injuries.

For Harry and Josephine, although work at Riverstone involved lengthy travel by train each day, the pay justified the cost and time involved. One day, however, when they were both working at the meatworks, Harry caught the little finger of his right hand in an unfenced meatpacking machine. In the flash of an eye, the machine had ripped off his finger. Harry was immediately taken to the sick bay, and Josephine was brought to him. The stub of his little finger by this stage was wrapped in bandages. When he showed Josephine the wound, she begged him to go to hospital to have it tended to. Harry was terrified of doctors generally, and his fear was intensified when those doctors were in a hospital environment. A doctor might insist upon physically examining him or admitting him, which would involve him removing his clothes and putting on hospital garb. A doctor might more easily see through his constructed identity. Despite Josephine's entreaties, Harry insisted on looking after his own wound. Within several days, he was back at work with a bandage where his little finger had once been.

The situation at home continued to deteriorate. Josephine continued to lead a wild and precocious lifestyle, going out at all times of the night to places and with people unknown to Harry and Annie. On occasion she would disappear for days. Harry continued to disregard her antics. Meanwhile, Annie continued to hold grave fears for the moral welfare of her son. Harry, in reaction to the tension at home, readily resumed his heavy drinking. The level and frequency of the arguments between Harry and Annie escalated to the point where the neighbours would sometimes hear them shouting at each other. On those occasions when they were not arguing about Josephine, the relationship would be quite satisfactory, and they would go out together arm-in-arm, to shop or just walk around the neighbourhood. The neighbours liked Harry, who was charming and easy to talk to, and he clearly fitted into the suburb with ease. In comparison, they found Annie rather prim and standoffish and difficult to talk to. She seemed not to fit into the working-class environment of Drummoyne.

During all of this time, Annie never once suspected that her husband was anything other than what he appeared to be. Some unusual things had occurred during their marriage, but she had put them completely aside. One day, before Josephine came into their household, Annie went into the bathroom to use the toilet, and when she lifted the lid she saw a pad of the kind she herself would use during her menstrual periods, covered in what was clearly blood. It was not her time of the month, and so she confronted Harry. Harry told her that he had injured himself at work in a private part of his body and that the nurse in the sick bay had given him a pad and some tape to bandage it. Annie was surprised that he had not told her about such an incident at work and, being a concerned and caring wife, questioned him about it and the extent of his injury. At this point, Harry became quite hostile and belligerent, so she put it down to embarrassment about an injury to his private parts and meekly accepted his explanation. On another occasion, Annie walked into what she thought was their empty bathroom, only to find Harry inside wrapping a long bandage around his chest. He would invariably lock the door whenever he was in the bathroom, but on this occasion he had clearly omitted to do so. On seeing her, Harry immediately grabbed his clothing and held it in front of him. When she enquired what he was doing, he claimed to have fallen at work and broken some ribs and insisted that the nurse had told him that he should bind them to help them heal. She plaintively asked to see his chest, knowing full well that his modesty would prevent it. When he refused to disrobe, she vehemently pleaded with him that such modesty towards his own wife was an aberration and that all her friends had seen their husbands' bodies, at which point Harry became enraged. His face turned red with anger as he insisted that she had no right to challenge his sense of modesty and decency. Again, she accepted his explanation, thinking that these strange standards must have come from his family of origin.

For Josephine, the situation in the household at Drummoyne had become intolerable. She deeply resented the interference in her upbringing by her stepmother, and she found Harry Jnr annoying and intrusive. Her father's non-interference in her social life was a welcome relief, but at the same time his lack of real caring and affection deeply disturbed her and added to the disdain she felt due to his abandonment of her during her childhood. Although Josephine had had a lifetime of coping with a mother who insisted on being 'Father', the pressure of keeping Harry's secret added immensely to the strain of living in the troubled Crawford household. Harry continually harangued her in private with threats of dire consequences for everyone if the truth came out.

Part of the pressure on Josephine came from neighbours and friends who frequently asked her what had happened to her mother, where her mother was, why her father was not living with her mother, and the like. Some of the time, Josephine was able to ignore these questions and just shrug her shoulders. At other times, in frustration, she would give whatever silly answer came into her head at the time. She was aware that the neighbours would compare these different accounts and gossip about what the truth might really be, but she did not care. She occasionally thought to herself: 'If only they knew the truth, they would be truly shocked.'

CHAPTER 6

EXPOSURE

It was 1917. The Great War had dragged on for three long years, and looked like going for many more. The German U-boats had begun taking a terrible toll of Allied shipping in the Atlantic. The Battle of Passchendaele took place near the village of Ypres in Belgium, with the loss of 140,000 lives, including more than 11,000 Australians, for the capture of five miles of territory. A Bolshevik revolution in Russia began with the overthrow of the tsar. In the United States of America, the two-millionth Model T Ford rolled off the production line.

One morning in January 1917,[1] Josephine was feeling particularly annoyed and distressed at her home situation. Harry had come home the previous evening in a belligerent mood, having obviously had too much to drink. They had had one of their usual rows, and in the morning Josephine could not wait to leave the house. Seeking respite, she went to visit a neighbourhood friend – a young woman of about her own age, who lived with a nosey mother, who had been one of those who had been pestering Josephine with prying questions. While Josephine was amiably chatting with her friend, she mentioned that she had had a nasty row with her father the night before. The girl's mother was, as usual, eavesdropping on the conversation and this was all that she needed to renew her incessant questioning of Josephine.

She began by saying, 'It's a pity that your mother wasn't there to back you up. That's where mothers are good to have around, you know. By the way, where is your mother these days?' The woman kept pestering Josephine with questions and would not relent. Finally, in a fit of pique at her inadequate and belligerent father and in utter exasperation at the nosey neighbour's questioning, Josephine pointed towards her own house and blurted out: 'That's my mother, dressed as a man, living over there with Annie Birkett.' As soon as she uttered the words she deeply regretted them. The neighbour, deeply shocked, stood silently for several minutes and then quietly turned around and went into another room to mull over what she had just been told. Was it just the ravings of a silly teenager? Was Josephine mentally unbalanced? Or had the girl inadvertently disclosed a dark secret that she clearly should not have revealed? When Josephine later went home, she decided to say nothing to Harry or Annie about what she had just disclosed to the neighbour, hoping that the woman would dismiss it as just some silliness on her part.

The neighbour must have thought about what she had been told for several weeks, because for all that time Josephine, who was living in dread of the repercussions of her disclosure, heard nothing. She had already planned what she would say if any other neighbours confronted her about it: she would feign great offence and launch into a tirade against whoever had started such a vile rumour. After a few weeks of hearing nothing, Josephine concluded with relief that the neighbour must have dismissed what she had said as sheer fantasy.

However, the reality was quite different. Having thought about it and having analysed Harry in a different light, the neighbour soon concluded that what Josephine had told her might well be the truth. It was all she could do to muster the restraint not to tell all the other neighbours and her own family, but she thought that if she did, they might disbelieve her and think that x ʍ was mentally unbalanced.

The neighbour strongly suspected that Annie had no idea about her 'husband', and so the question she debated with herself was whether or not she should present Annie with this new-found knowledge. After a lot of thought, she decided that she had a moral obligation to ensure that Annie knew that her 'husband' was a woman. Deep down she was also motivated by morbid curiosity to gauge Annie's reaction and learn for sure whether or not the information from Josephine was correct. She went over at a time when she knew that Annie would be on her own. After a few pleasantries, she told her what Josephine had disclosed. Annie's immediate reaction was to dismiss the very idea with a nervous laugh, but the neighbour could detect a small note of doubt in her voice. Having done her duty, the neighbour beat a hasty retreat, resolute that this terrible secret would go no further, at least through her.

Over the course of that day, Annie spent many hours playing over the events of their courtship and marriage. There were so many factors that pointed against what she had been told: Harry's labouring work, his way with horses, his drinking, his foul language, his eye for a good-looking woman. But there were also behaviours, dismissed at the time, which in retrospect caused her to question every assumption she had ever made about her husband, their marriage and her perception of people. Harry's extreme modesty no longer seemed a quaint quirk of his personality, but a deliberate tactic to deceive her. Why would a husband so uniformly insist on changing for bed in total privacy? The incidents in the bathroom when he had claimed to have been injured at work now took on a more sinister significance. His refusal to talk about Josephine's mother suddenly seemed perverse. The constraints of their lovemaking now assumed totally different connotations. Were his pre-coital visits to the bathroom really related to bodily hygiene? Why had he never allowed her to pleasure him when he had so masterfully pleasured her? The realisation grew stronger and stronger in her mind that what her neighbour had told her, and what Josephine had told the neighbour, was the truth. When Annie thought further about their lovemaking, it brought on waves of nausea and feelings of such revulsion that she started to retch. What had he done under the bedclothes to cause her such intense and prolonged gratification?

When Harry arrived home that night Annie initially said nothing. She could barely bring herself to look at him, let alone to touch him. He noticed that she was very distant but put it down to what he assumed was another argument with Josephine. That night, when they were alone in their bedroom, she confronted him. She told him what the neighbour had told her. He initially dismissed it as the ramblings of a sick mind in someone with too much time on her hands. Annie demanded that he show her evidence of his masculinity, insisting that she was entitled to see the man she had been married to for some years. She told him that not one of her female friends had been prevented from seeing her husband's body as she had. Harry turned visibly white as he refused to comply with her demand, claiming rather lamely that there were some things better left unsaid and unseen between husband and wife. But Annie maintained her insistence. At this point, Harry suddenly changed tack and became aggressive, expressing affront at such a humiliating and unjustified questioning of his masculinity. But Annie was quite determined not to be put off.

Behind the mask of feigned affront and anger, Harry was reeling in abject horror at this sudden challenge to the constructed identity he had maintained so effectively for the previous twenty-two years. For all those years, this had been his worst nightmare, and now it had come to pass. He realised only too well that he was facing the disintegration of the life he had built with Annie, and perhaps much more. Would she leave him immediately? Would she tell the truth she had discovered to all her family and friends and the other neighbours? Would she report him to the police? Would he be charged with some gruesome sexual offence? Would there be a huge public hue and cry about the monster who had committed sacrilege against the laws of marriage and the laws of nature? Would he have to go to court and would he end up in gaol? If he were gaoled, would he suffer a similar fate there to the one he had endured on the Norwegian barque so many years earlier? Death would be preferable to such a fate. All these questions raced around in his mind as he and Annie continued to trade verbal blows and counter-blows. Annie repeatedly demanded to see some evidence that, she assured him, would resolve everything by proving he was a man. Just as firmly, he refused to provide such proof. In desperation, she suggested that they go the next morning to see the local general practitioner just around the corner in Lyons Road for him to inspect the evidence. Again, feigning affront, he refused, saying that all doctors were charlatans anyway. It was this last quite unreasonable refusal that convinced Annie beyond any doubt that her neighbour had spoken the truth. After what seemed like hours of verbal sparring, Annie grabbed her bedclothes and left their bedroom, never to sleep there again.

From that moment, Annie slept on a spare bed in Harry Jnr's room. Never again did she and Harry experience the warm intimacy of their bodies being close together. Annie tried vainly to put out of her mind the minutiae of her sexual life during her second marriage, but thoughts have lives of their own, and images of sex with Harry would float unbidden to the surface of her consciousness with monotonous regularity, causing her to experience waves of nausea. Several times she was on the verge of pressing him to tell her what he had done to her, and with what, however she eventually decided that it was best for her sanity not to know.

Out of sympathy for Josephine's plight, Annie did not have the heart to confront her about her knowledge of Harry's identity, or why she had waited so long to disclose anything, or what had possessed her to make a disclosure to a neighbour. Josephine became aware of fresh tensions between Harry and Annie. Although she did not know exactly what it was all about, because nobody had told her, she felt in her bones that it must be related to her inadvertent disclosure to the neighbour some weeks earlier. She decided that, at age nineteen, it was an opportune time for her to move out of home. Neither Harry nor Annie sought to dissuade her from this view. So Josephine moved into lodgings in Kent Street in the city, where she was near to her work as a packer at Parson Bros. This removed a small part of the stress between Harry and Annie, but the overwhelming issues in their relationship remained.

Over the days and weeks after the disclosure, a plethora of feelings arose in Annie. The predominant ones were a profound sense of betrayal and a complete loss of confidence in her own judgement. With these feelings came an intense revulsion towards her 'husband'. It was the kind of feeling that one gets, but tries to rise above, when one unexpectedly comes across a severely deformed person. After that came painful feelings of hurt as she gradually recalled all the lies that had been told over many years. As she remembered each one, she felt a stab of physical pain in her inner core. She felt so foolish that her stepdaughter had clearly known the truth, whereas she had seen nothing. Finally came feelings of self-loathing in which she blamed herself for not realising what now seemed so obvious. The weight of all these thoughts completely inundated Annie and left her emotionally and socially immobilised – unable to engage in normal exchanges with other people, including her sister. She made a deliberate decision not to lean on her teenage son and burden him with this knowledge, as to do that would not help her, and would certainly traumatise him. As a result of all these feelings, Annie felt desperately alone and isolated.

Harry's overwhelming emotion on the night of their heated discussion was one of extreme anxiety at the prospect of losing Annie forever. Afterwards, he was so focussed on the plight of their marriage that he did not confront Josephine about the havoc she had wrought in their lives by disclosing his secret. Harry was still very much in love with his wife and desperate to keep their marriage together. He was prepared to agree to any conditions that she wanted, if only she would agree to maintain their marriage and keep his secret. He was grateful that she did not question him on the details of his sexual technique — not that he would have disclosed them if she had asked. Although he knew that she was fully aware of his identity as a woman and he had ceased trying to convince her otherwise, he could not bring himself to make a direct admission to her. Neither could he muster the courage to explain to her why he had engaged in half a lifetime of subterfuge and deception. At the same time, he was impelled to maintain his identity as Harry. He had been Harry Crawford for so long that he barely knew himself as anyone else. To discard Harry now would be too much of a wrench, and what identity would replace him?

Annie felt intensely ashamed and embarrassed about the situation she found herself in, and she was terribly fearful that if other people found out about it she would become a laughing stock and a social pariah. Every time she walked down the street, she was wary of the stares of her neighbours. She was worldly-wise enough to know that if ever a newspaper found out about their situation, it would not hesitate to publish all the lurid details, and her public shame and humiliation would be complete. She was also very concerned that any disclosure would severely traumatise and ostracise

Harry Jnr. She therefore resolved not to divulge her burdensome secret to any friends. She felt desperately trapped – in her 'marriage', in their marital home, and in the web of deceit surrounding the horrible secret that she knew but could not share with a soul.

Annie became paralysed by these conflicting concerns. Over eight long months, she explored in her mind various options of how to resolve her predicament. They all involved the end of her marriage by divorce or annulment, but also the real risk of severe public and private humiliation and ostracism. In effect, their marriage was already over, because they were hardly doing anything in common, even though they were both living within the four walls of their house. She thought about moving back to the home of her sister, Lily Nugent, at faraway Kogarah, but she did not want to jeopardise Harry Jnr's job with the Bone family. Mr and Mrs Bone were extremely good to him and would sometimes even include him with their own children in private family recreational activities. She also felt reluctant to contact Lily because, since leaving her sister's house to resume cohabiting with Harry, she had had so little contact with her. She really didn't want to have to face her sister's inevitable 'I told you so'. Buying another shop to live and work in was financially not an option, because she had lost a considerable sum of money when she had sold the confectionery shop in Balmain. Months went by without Annie reaching any satisfactory resolution of the situation.

In those eight months of separate cohabitation under the same roof, an uneasy truce gradually arose between Harry and Annie. Annie came to intuitively realise that Harry had not chosen to have these intractable gender-identity issues. Harry came to have sympathy and understanding for Annie's trauma in dealing with the years of lying and deceit that had built up between them. Each of them recognised and silently acknowledged the pain and suffering of the other. In this limbo, Harry and Annie coexisted for many months with a moderate degree of mutual tolerance. They would sometimes eat or occasionally sit together, often in silence, as Annie did some sewing in the lounge room. They were united in their wish not to have their situation broadcast to all and sundry. Each of them felt equally vulnerable to the threat of public humiliation and ridicule. In a way, their shared knowledge of Harry's secret bound them together at the hip.

Harry interpreted the fact of Annie's continued presence in their household as the basis for cautious hope that she would accept his identity and remain in their marriage. He was quite prepared to forego sexual contact, which was really something that he had done for her benefit, rather than his own. As far as he knew, Annie hadn't told anyone about her discovery and he thought that this boded well for a future together without any pretence or deception. Perhaps they could work towards developing a relationship based on complete truth. However, the fact was that some weeks after discovering Harry's secret, Annie had taken the first tentative steps towards reconnecting with her sister, Lily, and telling her what she had discovered. She sent a letter to Lily, whom she hadn't seen in months, in which she suggested a visit. She added:

I have something I want to tell you. I've found out something queer about Harry. I don't know what to do, but I'll tell you about it when I see you and get your advice.[2]

A week or two later, Annie and Harry came to Lily and her husband's home in Kogagah. After a long interval without contact, the sisters were very pleased to see each other. However, the visit raised concerns for Harry that his wife may indeed have initiated it in order to tell her sister what she had discovered. He therefore clung like glue to Annie during the visit. There were only a few moments when Annie and Lily went to the bathroom during which they were able to exchange a few words in private. All Annie could say to Lily was, 'I have found out that Harry is not a man,' before they were interrupted by Harry knocking on the bathroom door, thereby ending their conversation. There was just no opportunity to tell Lily anything more.

Lily had been dismayed when her sister had returned to Harry after their brief separation, and she had decided to have as little to do with them as possible. Since then, she had had contact with her sister only once or twice a year and had hardly ever seen Harry. Lily was quite perplexed by what her sister imparted to her in the few moments they had together in the bathroom. The scant information about Harry was rather ambiguous. What did Annie want to tell her? Did she mean that Harry was just a wimp of a man? Did she mean that he was failing to live up to his husbandly sexual obligations? Was her sister trying to tell her that Harry was one of those men who were attracted to other men? It never occurred to Lily that what her sister intended to convey was the literal meaning of the words she had said. In the end, Lily decided that the most likely explanation was that Annie had discovered that Harry was exhibiting an unnatural attraction to other men. This just added another layer to Lily's reasons for not wanting to have any contact with this toxic couple. This visit was, in fact, the last occasion that Lily saw her sister alive.

Although they had not been able to talk properly, Lily's visit emboldened Annie in her resolve that she could not continue in a state of ostensible matrimony with Harry. She eventually arrived at what she considered to be a solution that would work for both of them. The way forward had to leave her free to remarry in the future if she wished, and it had to be one which would not excite any scandal in the papers or elsewhere. The solution was this: they would have their marriage officially annulled on the basis that they had never consummated it by an act of sexual intercourse, having agreed on an excuse for the sexual failure of their marriage – one that would be acceptable to the court and the church, one that would cast no irredeemable slur on either of them and, most importantly of all, one that would raise no interest in the newspapers. A possible explanation they could use was that on their wedding night Harry had disclosed to her for the first time the existence of Josephine and his relationship with her mother, and that this revelation had rendered Annie emotionally unable to 'cleave to her husband' as she had undertaken to do by her marriage vows. There were other possibilities that Annie felt they could discuss that might justify an annulment of their marriage. Above all else, they would agree never to disclose the secret of Harry's true identity, thereby protecting them both. She thought that he would probably agree to this, because it would mean that after their separation he could continue his life as a male unimpeded by any scandal or threat of police action. They would be able to go their separate ways and lead independent lives without disgrace and humiliation enveloping them both. Annie decided that she needed to have a lengthy, full and frank discussion with Harry to discuss the details of this solution and hopefully to arrive at a timetable for implementing it. What they really needed was to get away from the house to a location where they could discuss the way forward in complete privacy and in a calm and cooperative manner. It occurred to her that a picnic would be the ideal environment for such a discussion.

At the same time, Harry had become cautiously optimistic that he had a chance to convince Annie to stay in their marriage. After all, nothing had changed about him or his feelings for her. If he could convince her to stay, he was sure that they could reach some sort of compromise about their living conditions and, in time, who knew what could happen as she became more accustomed to the idea of his identity?

It was in the context of these wildly differing objectives that the Eight-Hour Day long weekend in early October 1917 approached.

CHAPTER 7

PICNIC

In October 1917, the attention of the world and the newspapers was focused on the progress of the First World War. The German air force, using planes and Zeppelins, was using the clear autumn night skies to drop bombs on London. Meanwhile, in Russia the Bolsheviks were preparing for the first communist revolution after the fall of the tsar earlier in the year. In Australia, the two halves of the Trans-Australia railway across the Nullarbor Plain between Port Augusta in South Australia and Kalgoorlie in Western Australia were joined.

The anniversary celebrations of Eight-Hour Day held a very special place in the hearts of Australians in the early part of the twentieth century. The battle to win an eight-hour working day had been very protracted during the 1860s and 1870s. Eight hours was more than just a number. It signified a logical division of each day into its natural thirds: a third for work, a third for leisure and a third for sleep. The extra leisure hours meant that working-class men could devote more time to their families, their sporting and cultural pursuits and other extracurricular activities that previously had been reserved for the wealthy. The annual Eight-Hour Day march through the streets of Sydney had started in 1871, modelled largely on its older Melbourne equivalent. For the working class, the march was an institution of great significance and solemnity.

In 1917, Eight-Hour Day fell on Monday 1 October, making it a particularly memorable celebration because it provided a welcome long weekend to every worker throughout the country. The annual march through the streets of Sydney on the Monday was particularly poignant and meaningful that year because just three weeks earlier, a massive, month-long general strike had ended. The strike, which began in the Eveleigh railway yards in Sydney and quickly spread to involve over 100,000 workers in every State of Australia, paralysed the nation for its duration. Harry Crawford was one of the people who had been put off work and sent home from the

Perdriau Rubber factory at Drummoyne because of a shortage of materials during the strike.

Apart from the march through the city, there were many other activities organised for the Eight-Hour Day weekend, including an extensive program of sports and a variety of harbour and railway excursions for the public. Eight-Hour Day was also an ideal opportunity for a picnic. The picnic had been a favourite pastime among Sydneysiders since the early days of colonial settlement. The weather and scenery of Sydney and its harbour made outdoor picnics a particularly popular activity for families, friends and work colleagues. As early as 1811, when South Head Road was first built from the eastern end of Sydney to Watson's Bay and The Gap, Sydney residents would pack a wicker basket with food and picnic paraphernalia and ride in their sulkies or on horseback to these locations, which provided an ideal environment to enjoy nature and the wonderful ocean or harbour scenery just a little distance from the bustle of the town. As the years went by, picnics became quite sophisticated affairs, with baskets full of carefully prepared food, blankets, and sporting equipment for cricket and other games. With the introduction of regular and affordable public transport by tram or ferry, coupled with the additional time available after the introduction of the eight-hour day, working-class people in Sydney had ample opportunity for respite from the strains of urban life, particularly in locations such as Coogee, Clontarf, Botany Bay, Manly and Bondi. The picnic gave those who lived in a tight urban environment the opportunity to savour nature's expanses. By the early part of the twentieth century, the picnic was firmly established as one of the favourite recreational activities across the entire social spectrum, leading the *Sydney Morning Herald* in 1907 to declare Australia as a nation of 'picnickers'. [1]

One of the locations that had been particularly popular for picnics since the middle of the nineteenth century was the Lane Cove River Park. With its easy access by water and well-constructed wharves, built many years earlier to service timber mills, the park quickly became one of the more popular locations for picnics on the north side of the harbour. It afforded the opportunity for safe leisure boating and was viewed as a site of great natural beauty with easy access to the city centre, offering a quiet respite to those who sought an antidote to the hubbub of urban life in its bushland terrain. It was here that the next significant event in Harry and Annie's marriage took place.

By 1900, there were a large number of orchards, market gardens and family farms lining the Lane Cove River, as well as several factories. Picnickers and day-trippers would travel up the river by boat, ferry, launch or rowboat, stopping to enjoy fresh strawberries, oranges and other locally grown produce, before exploring the rugged bushland or swimming in the Blue Hole further upstream.[2] In 1908, local residents formed the Upper Lane Cove Ferry Co. Ltd to carry passengers, mail, livestock and merchandise between the wharf at Figtree House (where there were picnic grounds and the nearest road and ferry service available) and Fiddens Wharf at Killara.

In 1909, the Fairyland Pleasure Grounds was opened in a much-frequented area of the park. Apart from picnic facilities, it had an open-air dance hall and play equipment such as boat swings, a flying fox and a razzle-dazzle.[3] Fairyland also offered organised activities such as cricket, dancing, tugs-o'-war, sack races and egg-and-spoon races. The owners of Fairyland purchased two flat-bottom motor launches, Native Rose and Killara, to transport picnickers from Figtree House Wharf at the southern end of the river to their property. The Grounds proved enormously popular, luring visitors from all over Sydney. By 1910, there was already an awareness of the need to protect the area from potentially adverse development, particularly from the two large, polluting factories on the edge of the river in close proximity to the picnic facilities – the Cumberland Paper Mills and the Chicago Flour Mills. The threat of environmental degradation from these factories prompted calls on government and municipal councils for the creation of a formal national park so as to preserve a permanent playground for the people of Sydney.

However, there was also a dark side to the Lane Cove River Park. In the early days of the colony, the area of Lane Cove had developed a reputation as a haven for all types of criminals, particularly smugglers, sly grog dealers and escaped convicts. This was because of its thick bushland and rugged terrain, which made it ideal for clandestine and illegal activities. Over the intervening decades, the occasional discoveries of bodies had added to the mystique of the area.

Harry Crawford not only had the three days of the long weekend off from work, but also the Friday before it. Annie decided that this four-day break was an ideal opportunity to finally discuss with Harry the orderly dissolution of their marriage. Surely, she thought, with calm discussion they could come to an agreement about how it could be dissolved in a way that suited them both and avoided any public disgrace or humiliation. They would have to agree on facts that would justify an annulment to a court, without disclosing the truth. The inflexible matrimonial laws caused many couples to invent fictitious grounds to legally end their marriages: some pretended that there had been frequent low-level violence in the marriage when in reality the husband had long since gone off with another woman and established a new family; while others pretended that the husband had recently left a short note deserting his family to go overseas when in reality he had disappeared off the face of the earth years earlier without any note or warning. These little artifices were the grease that oiled the divorce courts and enabled spouses to get a remedy when the law strictly applied would not provide one. It was not as if Annie had in mind to tell a deliberate lie, because in reality their marriage had not been consummated by sexual intercourse in the usual way between a man and his wife. They were merely going to hide the underlying reasons why that had not occurred. The last thing that either of them wanted was some salacious scandal that would end up in the newspapers and embarrass them both, as well as their two children.

Annie was aware that Harry wanted to maintain their marriage, and so she anticipated that their discussion might prompt days of argument and haranguing. It was particularly opportune then that her son, Harry Jnr, now fourteen, was working at the local grocery store on both the Friday and the Saturday, and was then due to go on holidays with Mr and Mrs Bone and their children to their holiday house at Collaroy for the remainder of the long weekend. This meant that she and Harry had four clear days for their crucial discussions that, she hoped, would resolve all their issues before Harry Jnr came back on Monday evening. When Annie suggested to Harry that the two of them go on a picnic on the Friday, his hopes were buoyed that this might mark the beginning of a new phase in their marriage, and he readily agreed. He suggested that they go to a place that had special significance for them – the picnic spot in the Lane Cove River Park where he had first told Annie of his love for her. Grateful that Harry had agreed to her picnic plan, Annie agreed to his choice of venue, praying that they could arrive at a mutual plan for their future.

On the morning of Friday, 28 September 1917, when most people were getting ready for work, Harry and Annie set off from their home at The Avenue in Drummoyne. Harry carried a picnic basket the size of a small suitcase, holding their blanket, eating utensils and drink, while Annie carried a much smaller Japanese-style wicker basket with the food. They were seen by a neighbour walking up their street towards Lyons Road. As opposed to the first time that they had gone to the Lane Cove River Park, when they had approached it from the north, this time they approached it from the south. This involved taking a tram from Drummoyne to number 8 Wharf at Circular Quay, where they caught the Lane Cove River Ferry to Figtree. At Figtree Wharf, they caught a launch operated by the

Lane Cove Ferry Company up the Lane Cove River, which let them off at a small wharf at the junction of the Lane Cove River and Stringybark Creek. The wharf was generally used by workers at the nearby Cumberland Paper Mills, situated about 100 yards upstream on Stringybark Creek.

From the wharf, they walked up a well-made track along the northern bank of Stringybark Creek, a waterway servicing the Cumberland Paper Mills that had been widened and dredged to allow access for barges. The track went past a lot of mangroves towards the mills, and then veered away from the creek, up a much narrower and less used track that snaked its way up towards Mowbray Road on the ridgeline about half a mile away. Several hundred yards up this narrow track was a small clearing next to a large sandstone rock with a small cave-like indent in it. The clearing was flat and large enough for ten or so people to comfortably have a picnic. All around it were gnarled eucalyptus and angophora trees and smooth blackbutts. The ground consisted of hard, bare earth interposed with jagged sandstone rocks and many tree roots. It was a place that prior to European arrival had been used through the aeons by local Aboriginal inhabitants, who would sit in the shade of the large rock eating the sumptuous oysters they had just prised from the rocks in the nearby river. More recently, it had been used by occasional picnickers, and a large, empty flagon on the edge of the clearing was a remnant of that use.

From the clearing, Stringybark Creek was just visible through the trees. The clearing was sufficiently far away from Mowbray Road to the north and from the paper mills to the south so as not to be seen. This track was rarely used by walkers or picnickers, and the workers from the nearby mills almost always used the wharf on Lane Cove River to get to and from work. In any case, for most people, today was a working day, so Annie and Harry were unlikely to be disturbed. They were both satisfied that they would have sufficient privacy at this clearing to enable them to talk freely and openly about their marriage and their shared secret, just as they had had sufficient privacy when they had been here during their courting days. If people came by, they would just allow them to pass and then continue their discussion.

Each of them was both apprehensive and excited at the prospect of this picnic. Annie was apprehensive because she anticipated that Harry would at least initially resist her plan for the dissolution of their marriage, but she was also excited at the prospect of finally ridding herself of the burden of their union. Harry was apprehensive because he could feel a certain sense of resolve on Annie's part, but he was excited at the prospect that she might be prepared to remain in their marriage, even in the knowledge of his true identity. Thus it was that Annie and Harry found themselves back at the very place where they had first expressed their love for each other.

They both took off their coats, and Harry opened up the folded blanket that had been in the basket, carefully laid it out on the ground, and took the food and drink Annie had prepared at their home and laid it out in the middle of the blanket, with room for them to sit on either side. It was as if the food and drink were to be the chess pieces for their subsequent contest. They both sat down, and Harry poured them some beer into two enamel cups which he had taken from the large basket. They sat in silence as they ate and drank, each of them pondering how to conduct this most important of dialogues. Only after they had finished eating did Annie begin.

CHAPTER 8

TRAGEDY IN THE PARK

There were only two people who knew exactly what happened next in the clearing at the Lane Cove River Park: Harry Crawford and his wife, Annie. Neither of them was in a position afterwards to give an account, for reasons that will become apparent. What follows is therefore a possible version of events, re-created by the author, that is entirely consistent with all the known facts that later emerged, but interpreted with the benefit of today's superior knowledge in the forensic sciences and unimpeded by the considerable prejudice that existed at the time for someone in Harry Crawford's predicament.

Annie felt just a bit affected by the small amount of beer she had drunk while sitting in silence with Harry on the blanket in the clearing, far away from any other picnickers in the Lane Cove River Park. It was enough to embolden her to begin talking, but not enough to dull her senses or weaken her determination. After months of agonising over the risks of scandal and humiliation, she was determined that today would be the day that she initiated the end of their marriage. Harry, as was his want, had had a little more to drink and this had made him all the more enamoured with Annie and determined to convince her to stay in their marriage and arrive at some accommodation of her knowledge about his identity. He was still anxious that if she agreed to stay with him, she might ask him to explain exactly how he had so dextrously pleasured her sexually during their marriage, and he was still resolute that if she asked he would not tell her the truth.

Annie began the conversation by abruptly stating what had been the unspoken, shared secret between them for many months: 'You and I both know that you are not a real man, and that makes our marriage a complete farce.'

Then came the real blow: 'I intend to get it annulled, both with the church and in court, as soon as I can. An annulment is invariably granted where the couple have not had *any* normal sexual relations, which is the case with us. I can't continue to live this charade with you. Harry Junior and I will be leaving as soon as we can. I've already made arrangements for someone to come and pick up my furniture.'

Harry's response had a detectable edge of anxiety to it. 'That might be a good reason to get an annulment, but how do you think you are going to get it without telling anybody why? As soon as you try doing something like that, people will be pressing you for details.'

She had prepared herself for this question. Indeed, she had thought about it for months. 'We can't tell anyone the truth, because it will get into the papers and cause the greatest scandal that Sydney has ever seen. I promise you I'll never tell anyone your secret, so you can go on living as you are for as long as you like, and with whomever you like, but *not* with me. I'm sure we can agree on a story to tell everybody – the minister and the lawyers – why we're separating, so nobody will suspect the real reason.

After a brief pause, during which Harry was totally silent but his mind was plainly racing, she continued. 'You could tell people that Josephine's mother is not really dead but living overseas, and that you've decided to get back together with her so that Josephine will have a proper home with both her mother and father. We could say that you told me the truth about Josephine's mother on our wedding night and that I was so stunned I refused to have sex with you, and I have ever since, or whatever else you think will work, so long as we both say the same thing. We'll both just insist that there's been no intimacy between us for all of our marriage, right from the start – nothing. I've made enquiries, and it's a valid ground for an annulment. So long as we both agree on the same story, everything will be all right. People will just have to accept that we haven't done it – *ever*! Who can prove otherwise? And in a sense, it's true, isn't it? This way, we can both hold our heads up in public. It also means that Harry Junior won't have to deal with the real truth. It'll also make it easier for Josephine, even though she knows the full story.'

Harry's anxious hope was quickly turning to despair as he realised that their positions were so far apart. His voice edged higher as he replied to her. 'Annie, I love you now as I've always loved you. We've been married for over four years and, although we've had our ups and downs, by and large we've had a successful marriage. Why should anything change? You're not a different person from the one I married, and I'm not a different person from the one you married. You may know a bit more about me now than you did then, but I'm still the same person. My inner self hasn't changed since the day I met you, or the day that I first kissed you right in this very spot, or the day that I pledged my life to you when we were married. I'm still utterly committed to you. Surely we can find some way to be together, even if it means that we both have to make changes.'

Annie rounded on him. 'How can you say you're the same person? How can you say you haven't changed? I fell in love with a man and married a man. The minister asked me whether I would take you as my *husband*, and I promised that I would. It turns out you're not a man after all, and as far as I'm concerned you're not my husband. How can I love you when I don't know who or what you are? You're neither a man nor a woman. How can I continue to live with you when for the last four years you've deceived me and tricked me and done abominable things to me in bed that I don't want to even think about?'

Harry had a ready answer for this. 'The sex is completely unimportant. We can love each other without that. What I did to you in bed was for your sake, and not for mine. I won't miss it one bit if we don't have it. But I can't live without you in my life. You're the only person I've ever loved, and my life will have no meaning without you. I beg you to stay with me, and you'll see that we can be happy together.'

Annie slowly got up on her knees, placed a few of the items that were still on the blanket into her wicker basket, closed it, stood up and put on her coat. 'If I had known then what I know now, I would never have fallen in love with you; I would never have married you; and I would not be here with you now, in this terrible situation. And I won't be with you for much longer, because I've already made plans to go and live somewhere else. I don't ever want to have anything further to do with you. I hope you'll just do the right thing and go along with my plans for an annulment, because I couldn't stand the humiliation if it all became public knowledge.'

At this, Annie picked up the basket, turned away and began to walk across the clearing back in the direction they had come. Harry jumped up and grabbed her by the arm that held the basket, yanking her around to face him. She tried to pull her arm away from his grasp, but he was too strong. He was screaming something at her that she could not make out, and she began to cry out in fear as he dragged her back towards the blanket in the middle of the clearing. Still pulling away, with her free arm she went to push him away from her, but just at that instant he suddenly let her go, putting his open hands up in a gesture of acceptance and surrender. As he did so, she jerked away, caught her heel on a tree root, lost her balance and tripped backwards, with the basket swinging upwards in her hand as she desperately tried to regain her balance. As she struck the ground, the back of her head hit a rock and there was a horrid sound like a whip being cracked. Annie lay motionless on the ground.

Harry instantly ran to her and dropped down on his knees, calling out to her in apology and remorse. He clasped her head in his hands and felt the blood oozing out through a wound at the back. He gingerly laid her head back on the ground and looked in horror at her lifeblood on his hands. He placed his face down close to her mouth, hoping for the slightest sign of life. For a few minutes, as he cradled her in his arms, wailing at her to forgive him and not to leave him now, he was sure that he could feel her breath going in and out, but eventually it ceased and he concluded that she must be dead.

Thinking that Annie had gone, Harry slowly stood up and began to pace around the clearing like a madman, alternately muttering to himself, then crying out his woe, anguish, regrets and fears to the imaginary gods in the tree-tops above. Every so often he would return to Annie's body, drop down on his knees and kiss her on the face, pleading with her to forgive him and to come back to him. Many things went through his mind. How would he explain her death? Would people think that he had deliberately killed her? What would Harry Jnr do without his mother? What would their neighbours think? What would Annie's sister, Lily, do when she found out? Overwrought with grief, dejection and emotional exhaustion, Harry began to question in his mind what he should do now.

His initial thought was to run down to the nearby paper mills and raise the alarm. He reluctantly left Annie's body in the clearing and ran down to the bank of Stringybark Creek, but as soon as he got close to the mills, he looked down at his bloodied hands and clothes and saner thoughts came to him as he realised that no one would believe that Annie had accidentally fallen. He sat down on a rock near the creek to try to calm his racing mind sufficiently to decide what he would do next when, in a state of abject grief, he noticed a woman approaching him on the track from the wharf to the mills. As the woman came nearer to him, she said something, but in his woe he was unable to understand her, let alone respond. She kept walking towards the mills, and he then got up and walked back up the narrow track to the clearing and Annie's body.

By this time, there was a swarm of flies, mosquitoes and other insects feasting on her, attracted by the copious amount of blood on her head and the ground beneath. What was he to do? In a state of panic, Harry realised that if the body were found in its present state, a police investigation would inevitably focus on him, and he would be blamed for Annie's death. Surely, someone on the tram, the ferry or the launch would identify him as having been with Annie that morning as they travelled to the park. As the afternoon wore on, Harry's fears grew. If a police investigation focused on him and he was arrested, would they take him to a men's gaol? Even if he was able to maintain his male identity at the gaol for a while, he ran the risk of eventual discovery. Harry shook with fear as he had a flashback to the horror that had been perpetrated on him by Captain Martello on the barque twenty years earlier. That trauma was still a raw, open wound in his psyche and he shuddered with the memory of it as if it had only occurred the previous week. He could not run the risk of it happening again.

In his precarious mental state, he decided that he had no option but to dispose of Annie's body so that he would not be unfairly blamed for her death. He grabbed a big stick from the bush and poked it into the ground in various places, thinking that the obvious solution was to bury her, but it was so hard that it would not yield to his prodding at all. If he had had a shovel with him, he would have had a chance of digging a grave, but he didn't. Her body was much too heavy to carry any distance, and if he just secreted it in the bush, animals would inevitably uncover it. He had no rope to tie it to something heavy to sink it in the nearby waterways. He realised that if he carried the body further down the track, he was at considerable risk of being observed by people from the mills, such as the woman who had seen him earlier.

Without having the tools to bury her, Harry eventually came to the conclusion that he did not have the means of disposing of Annie's body so that it would never be found. However, what came to his mind at this time of madness and fear was a way to deflect the course of any police investigation away from himself. It involved burning her body beyond recognition, as well as her clothing, and removing any items from the scene that could be linked to either of them. That way, when then body was inevitably found, the police would not know who it was. He planned, when he got home, to tell everyone that Annie had walked out on him, leaving him for another man, and he thought that most people would accept this explanation for Annie's disappearance. The police would then not be in a position to link the body with anyone who had been reported missing. Even if someone did report Annie missing, there would still be no way to positively identify the body as hers. It was not as good a solution as burying the body, but it was the next best option and, more importantly, it was within the means that he had at his disposal.

He built a makeshift fireplace with stones, close to the large sandstone rock at the edge of the clearing. He collected some of the plentiful firewood that was in the area, placed it in the fireplace, and lit it. He then dragged her body to the fireplace and placed her head directly over the fire. The crackling sound of her hair catching alight shocked him to the core. Within a few minutes, her face had become distorted from the heat as her facial fat dripped through the cracks of her skin onto the fire, causing the flames to flare up. After her head was completely blackened and unrecognisable, he pulled her upper torso, still clothed, onto the fire. As each section of her clothing was consumed by the flames and that part of her body blackened, he moved her so that eventually her whole body down to her knees and all her clothing except her shoes had become completely blackened and unidentifiable.

This whole exercise was intolerably repugnant and distressing to him and took much longer than he had expected, as everything burned so slowly. It seemed like an eternity, but it was probably only took two or three hours. In that time, he packed all their picnic paraphernalia into his large basket, but he deliberately left one of their enamel cups on the ground near to the empty flagon, to make it look as if the deceased person had been drinking heavily. Harry thought it would look very strange for him to be carrying two baskets back to Drummoyne, so he left her wicker basket at the clearing with nothing inside it, thinking that it was so very plain and commonplace that nobody could link it to them. He failed to notice, as he burned Annie's body, that a small kidney-shaped greenstone pendant, which Annie had been wearing that day on a chain around her neck, had come off and was lying in the embers of the fire. He considered that he did not need to remove her shoes, which were unburned, because there was nothing distinctive about them. He completely forgot that several weeks earlier he had stuck some patches on her shoes to repair them. He left on her body her diamond engagement ring, which he could not bring himself to remove, and the remains of a cheap brooch she had been wearing on her now carbonised coat. By the late afternoon, when there was still plenty of light, he had finally completed his odious task.

Having rendered Annie's body unrecognisable, in a completely dejected state, Harry left the clearing with the fire still burning and walked down the track, past the mills, back along Stringybark Creek to the Lane Cove River, from where he was able to get a launch back to Figtree. The fire that Harry had lit continued to smoulder. Over several days, it slowly crept through the leaf litter on the ground. By Monday mid-afternoon, three days after Harry had lit it, the fire had spread to the edge of the clearing, when the wind picked up and fanned the flames, causing them to spread into the undergrowth and catch properly alight. The smoke from this fire was seen that afternoon by a woman in a nearby house and by a watchman employed at the Cumberland Paper Mills.

By the time Harry arrived back at his home in Drummoyne, it was already dark. Sitting in his kitchen, completely alone for the first time in years, he opened a bottle of whisky and bemoaned the terrible fate that had befallen him.

CHAPTER 9

DISCOVERY IN THE PARK

On the morning of Tuesday, 2 October 1917, a young lad named Ernest Clifford Howard, who was an engineer's apprentice at the Cumberland Paper Mills, was walking along a track from the mills to the manager's residence at about 10 am, when he noticed traces of a fire a short distance from the track. On investigating, he discovered the charred remains of a human body over a makeshift fireplace in a clearing. The arms were bent across the chest and the right leg was drawn up against the torso. He immediately notified his employers and the police were informed.

Later the same day, Sergeant Maze and Constable Walsh of Chatswood police station attended the scene. From the thighs upwards, the body had been so badly burned as to make recognition impossible. Although the body was clearly female, there was nothing on it or in the vicinity to identify who she was, and any facial recognition was impossible. The body had been so badly burned that on the left side of her chest that the heart and lungs were exposed. All that remained unburned were the shoes, the lower portions of some black stockings, and a small piece of gabardine material beneath the buttocks.

On the northern side of the body, the fire had spread for a distance of about 125 yards, and a small tree in this area had been completely destroyed, showing the extent of the blaze. However, on the other side of the body, the fire had made very little progress. On top of the embers was a full set of upper false teeth and a partial set of lower false teeth.[1] Too little of her clothing had survived the fire for that avenue of identification to be unavailable. The police located a lock of her hair in the ashes and found a small brooch nearby. On the body was an unremarkable diamond ring of the kind found in any jewellery shop. The only items that was sufficiently untouched by the fire to assist in her identification were her black, lace-up shoes. While the shoes themselves were quite unremarkable, they had recently been crudely half-soled and had small, homemade patches on the side of the soles. The police took possession of them in the hope that perhaps someone could identify the distinctive patches.

Within the clearing was an empty quart-sized whisky flagon, an enamel mug, a cheap picnic basket, a blue-headed hatpin, and the wire skeleton of a wide-brimmed hat – all of which were taken by the police. The body was removed and delivered to the Sydney Morgue for a forensic autopsy.

The Sun newspaper reported the following day:

At present the police declare their inability to express an opinion of the mystery. Some of the circumstances suggest that the woman fell asleep alongside the fire and was burnt to death, while others point to a second person having been present.

The day following the initial police search, Detective Inspector Campbell and Detectives Ferguson and McKnight of the Criminal Investigation Branch attended the scene and conducted a further inspection of the scene, including a more thorough search of the fireplace. In the ashes beneath where the body had been they found a small kidney-shaped greenstone pendant attached to a fine metal chain. They also found two metal buttons and a number of false teeth from the body's lower jaw. In some bushes about six yards away these police found a small whisky flask, which contained about a spoonful of kerosene. This caused the police to engage in speculation that this might have been a case of suicide, in that the woman could have poured the kerosene over her clothing and set it alight.

Already, at this very early stage of the investigation, there was conjecture as to whether the body might have been a vagrant woman living in the bush, who had ingested too much alcohol and, in a drunken state, been unable to save herself when she fell into the fire. Such accidental deaths of inebriated people by fire were quite commonplace. The problem of vagrancy in Sydney had been exacerbated by the severe economic depression of the 1890s, during which hundreds of homeless men and women had been forced to seek shelter under old newspapers and loose wrappers in public parks, including the Sydney Domain. Many bush areas near to suburban populations had long-term vagrant residents camping in caves or under makeshift tents. Even by the 1910s, with public housing policy in New South Wales being still quite basic, vagrants and homeless people retained a distinct presence in Sydney and its suburbs.

An autopsy was conducted on 3 October by government medical officers Dr Arthur Aubrey Palmer and Dr Stratford Sheldon at the Sydney Morgue, situated below the Coroner's Court at 102–104 George Street, The Rocks. In 1913, Doctor Palmer had been appointed as the States first government medical officer for Sydney. The view of both doctors was that the deceased female was aged between thirty and forty years and that she had probably died about two days prior to her body being found. Her stomach contents indicated that she had eaten chicken shortly before her death. Surprisingly, in light of the flagon that had been found at the scene, there was no evidence of alcohol ingestion.[2] Apart from the burns, her body did not show any signs of any illness or injury. They examined the skull and found no abnormalities, noting that the skull was 'thick'. They concluded that there were 'no definite signs of violence' to the body and concluded that the cause of death was that she had 'burned to death'. Dr Palmer was of the opinion that the deceased had *probably* been alive when she was burned. This was because of some blisters on the legs at the junction of the charred portions with the unburned portions. These blisters contained thick fluid, and they were surrounded by a red margin of skin. On opening the blisters, their base was also red. Dr Palmer wrote this in his own handwriting in the Register of Post-Mortem Examinations:

Reaction from burning around left knee and down front of right leg: redness and blistering. The skin of legs smooth, elastic and of good colour. Legs firm. Figure probably slipped. Feet had rather bad corns. Feet otherwise not deformed. Stockings much darned (?cashmere). Organs somewhat cooked – on left side of chest some ribs burned through.

The *Evening News* reported that the post-mortem examination earlier that day had 'done much towards clearing up the murder theory'. A local man came forward to inform the police that over a period of some weeks he had seen a half-witted woman in the neighbourhood who wore a hat and carried a suitcase like those found near the body. The *Evening News* on 4 October reported as follows:

It is stated that for about a fortnight or so a woman has been observed in the vicinity of the paper Mills, and on Thursday last a carter saw a woman trudging along Mowbray Road. He offered her a lift but she stared vacantly ahead and ignored his offer. As a set off against the assumption that the dead woman is identical with the person, the Government Medical Officer has reported that the woman's stomach contained a quantity of chicken, apparently eaten just before her death. This points to a picnic party of more than one person.

On 16 October, a photograph of the patched shoes was published in a number of prominent newspapers, and the police were hopeful that someone would recognise the distinctive patching and come forward to identify them. The *Evening News* on that day published the photograph of the shoes and reported as follows:

> *The detectives engaged in clearing up the mystery surrounding the death of a woman on Eight-Hour Day, whose charred remains were found in the bush at Chatswood, have arrived at a dead end. The work of the police is made more difficult by reason of the fact that the woman's identity has not yet been established. The fire destroyed practically all traces that might have led to identification, with the exception of the woman's shoes, as shown by the accompanying illustration. It will be observed that the shoes had recently been repaired by two small patches being placed at the side of the soles. The police would like to hear of anyone who effected the repairs.*

No one came forward to identify the patching on the shoes.

On 22 October 1917, the Acting City Coroner held a formal Inquest into the death of the woman whose body had been found near Mowbray Road. The Coroner was less convinced than the two forensic pathologists there were no signs of violence. His findings were:

> *That the said woman, name unknown, was found dead in the bush off Mowbray Road, Lane Cove, in the District of Sydney on 2 October 1917, with certain marks of violence appearing upon her body. And I further find that she died on about the 1st of October 1917 at the same place from the effects of burns caused through her clothing catching fire, but whether accidentally or otherwise, the evidence adduced does not enable me to say.*

After the Inquest, the unidentified body was buried by a government contract undertaker in an unmarked grave in the paupers section of Rookwood cemetery. The few items that had been found at the scene were placed in an exhibit box and kept in storage at the Chatswood police station. The police investigation was unable to progress any further and lapsed.

CHAPTER 10

ANGUISH

Harry returned from the picnic in the Lane Cove River Park a broken man. He was inconsolable at the loss of the love of his life. Added to this burden was a deep sense of guilt that he was to blame for the accident that had led to Annie's death. Had he been too rough with her? Had he berated her too severely? Should he have refused to go on the picnic at all? He was convinced that people would never believe him if he told them what had really happened to Annie – that her death had been accidental – and that if the police ever identified her body, he would immediately be suspected of having murdered her. He harboured fears that his measures in the park to prevent identification of the body and to divert the police investigation away from a murder theory might not have been sufficiently broad. In particular, he was anxious that someone may recognise Annie's engagement ring, and he regretted that he had not removed it. He anxiously awaited the inevitable discovery of Annie's body – he believed it could take days or even weeks for someone to stumble upon it. There would then undoubtedly be some note about the burned woman in the newspapers, although, being illiterate, he would have to rely on someone else to read it to him. Then he would need to allow time for the police enquiries to take their course before he would know whether or not they were able to link the body to him. What would happen after that was impossible to predict.

Over the long weekend, Harry languished in his kitchen over a bottle of whisky, agonising about what would become of Annie's fourteen-year-old son, and indeed himself, without Annie. When the boy returned from his long-weekend holiday at Collaroy with the Bone family, how was he to break the terrible news to him that his mother had gone off without telling him or even leaving a note, leaving him with his stepfather? He felt great sorrow for this boy who had lost his father when he was very young and who now faced being informed that his mother was gone.

Harry Crawford was possessed by an overwhelming desire to move away from their Drummoyne home, which was now a constant reminder to him of Annie's absence and the terrible circumstances of her death. And so, over the next three days, Saturday, Sunday and Monday of the long weekend, he packed up all of his and Annie's worldly possessions and separated them into items that he would keep, those that he would sell, and those that he would give away. He spoke on the telephone to a dealer, Joel Hart, who was known to buy used furniture and other items, and arranged for him to come to their home to view their possessions. The dealer agreed to buy the furniture for a meagre ten pounds and arrangements were made for him to pick everything up and cart it away on Wednesday 3 October. All this time, Harry anguished over how he was going to tell Harry Jnr that his mother was gone. His whisky drinking was unremitting.

By the time Harry Jnr came home from the weekend at Collaroy on the night of Monday 1 October, Crawford was in a very fragile and inebriated state. He felt completely unable to deal with the boy in this condition, so when Harry Jnr asked him where his mother was, he voiced the first thing that came into his mind: 'We had a tiff. Your mother has gone to North Sydney with Mrs Murray and her daughter.' Mrs Murray had been a distant friend of Annie's whom they had not seen for over a year. Harry knew that the boy had no way of getting in touch with her. Harry then directed his stepson to go to bed, hoping to delay until the morning when he would be more sober any further discussion about where Annie had gone, and why, and for how long.

That night, Crawford didn't go to bed, but kept drinking on and off all night, managing to get short, intermittent intervals of disturbed sleep with his head and arms resting on the kitchen table. By the next morning, more than three quarters of the bottle had disappeared. When the boy got up, Crawford was fully expecting him to intensively enquire what had happened to warrant the grave step of his mother leaving the house, why she had gone with Mrs Murray and her daughter, where in North Sydney she was residing, and how he could get in touch with her. Amazingly, it didn't happen. The boy seemed content with the flimsy explanation that he had been given the previous night. That day, Tuesday, was a normal workday, and the boy went to the shop as usual to work for Mr and Mrs Bone. When he returned from work that evening, he addressed no questions to his stepfather as to his mother's whereabouts.

In the meantime, Harry began to give away Annie's personal items to friends and neighbours, telling them that Annie had left him. He had trouble keeping up with all of the stories that he told people about where and with whom she had run off. One of the neighbours who enquired about his wife was Mr George Smith, who lived in nearby Bush Street. Mr Smith's wife had become ill and he came to enquire whether Annie might come and attend to some domestic tasks to help them out during her illness. Crawford said to him, 'Oh, you are too late. She has cleared out with a plumber from over in Balmain.' Naturally, the neighbours began to gossip about Annie's disappearance, and to compare the different versions that Crawford had given them. Some of them expressed deep misgivings about her sudden departure, but none of them felt inclined to report their suspicions to the police.

Most of the time, Harry Crawford sat at the table in the kitchen of their Drummoyne home, where Annie had spent so much time over the previous three years until their fateful picnic in the Lane Cove River Park. Never again would he see her sweet face and hear her gentle voice in that essential room of their family life where they had passed so many hours together. Crawford felt overwhelmed by waves of emotion, especially grief, guilt and fear. His future was so uncertain and so fraught with danger that he did not know how he was going to cope. He faced the prospect of venturing out into a cruel and uncertain world without Annie. Would he ever be able to live without constantly taking care not to disclose too much about himself, and without the relentless fear of discovery and rejection? He firmly believed that he would never love again as he had loved Annie.

The person who was the least surprised that Annie had left Harry was Josephine Falleni. When she had lived with them in Drummoyne, Josephine had witnessed a household filled with arguments and hostility, so she fully accepted that her stepmother had finally decided that she had had enough. Josephine believed that one day, when Annie was settled, she would come for her son.

As the days wore on, Crawford's ruminations became progressively darker and he descended into a hellhole of grief and depression, which he was unable to relieve despite the voluminous amounts of whisky he was consuming. He had considerable difficulties falling asleep, and even when he did slip into an exhausted doze, he achieved no respite, as he constantly dreamed of Annie drowning in a deep pool of water, desperately calling out to him for help, while he stood by helplessly, paralysed with fear. His other dream was of three burly policemen suddenly appearing at the door of a room where he was seated in a deep lounge chair. As soon as they came into the room, they surrounded him, shouting obscenities, but he couldn't understand their language and they didn't seem to be able to understand him. No matter how much he pleaded with them that he had done nothing wrong and that they should leave him alone, they still stood there shouting.

After several days, Crawford felt that he was losing control of his mind and he seriously contemplated going to an asylum and asking to be admitted. But his fear of hospitals and doctors, and what they might discover about him, prevented him from doing that.

On top of everything, Harry now had the responsibility of looking after Annie's son, Harry Birkett, who was too young to live independently. He felt incapable of assuming any long-term parental or pseudo-parental responsibilities for the boy, and his mind was taken back to the time, now nearly twenty years earlier, when he had had to decide what to do with the newborn Josephine. He had agonised over that decision for so long – without the additional burden that he carried now of the grief, the guilt and the anxiety over Annie's death. Would he have to go through a similar period of agony with his stepson? Harry felt barely able to cope with his own dark feelings, let alone deal with the needs of an adolescent.

Over the next few days, Harry Jnr failed to ask him anything at all concerning Annie's whereabouts. Crawford just could not understand how the boy could meekly accept the paucity of details of where his mother had gone, and why. By then, Crawford had told so many people different stories about Annie's departure that he could no longer recall exactly what he had told his stepson. By the morning of Wednesday 3 October, Harry Crawford was so deeply distressed and depressed that he decided the only way out of his pain was to end his own life. In his disoriented and inebriated state, he decided that the kindest course of action was to take young Harry's life at the same time as his own, so that the orphaned boy would not be left to fend for himself without any support.

When Harry Jnr got up that morning, Crawford told him that he should not go to work at the Bone's grocery. The boy seemed quite happy with this. Crawford took Harry Jnr to the home of a Mrs Parnell, who was the proprietor of a boarding house known to him, where he paid for the boy to have a fabulous, last breakfast, while Crawford paced around outside. Crawford went back inside about an hour later, and then took the boy by tram to Circular Quay. At Circular Quay, he purchased two single ferry tickets to Watson's Bay, as he was not planning on either of them returning. When the boy enquired why he was not buying return tickets, he had to hurriedly think of an excuse, and told him, 'We'll return by tram.' They caught the next ferry to Watson's Bay – a, golden sandy beach about eight miles from the city on the promontory that extends to the South Head of Sydney Harbour. On arrival, they walked up the steep hill away from the harbour towards the magnificent towering sandstone cliffs in Gap Park overlooking the Pacific Ocean.

Gap Park is bordered on the eastern, seaward side by the steep cliffs of The Gap, with its dramatic view of the Pacific Ocean and the waves breaking on the rocks more than 100 feet below. At that time it had already been a popular destination for tourists, picnickers and sightseers for more than 100 years. The park had been dedicated as a public recreation reserve in 1887, but it was not until the extension of the tramline to the Signal Station at Watson's Bay in 1903, and the further extensions to Gap Park in 1909, that it achieved greater accessibility and even more popularity. However, The Gap has also held a very dark place in Sydney's history, as it has long been a popular place where desperate, anguished and depressed people have taken their own lives by jumping off the top of the cliffs onto the jagged rocks below.[1] Its sinister attraction for suicide was and still is due to its easy accessibility at the extreme edge of the city, the flat wavecut ledge on the other side of an easily climbable fence, and its exceedingly beautiful and dramatic aspect.

Once at The Gap, Crawford stood with the boy for a while, pretending to admire the view, then climbed over the waist-high, three-rail fence and approached the edge of the cliff-top overlooking the rocks and sea below, and began throwing stones into the water. His plan was to entice the boy over the fence near to the edge of the cliff, and then to grab him by the hand and tell him that his mother was dead, before running to the edge of the cliff and jumping over, dragging the boy with him. With this in mind, Crawford urged his stepson to climb over the fence and join him on the rock ledge to throw stones over the cliff and see them fall into the water. However, something innate in the boy alerted him to the undesirability and danger of joining his stepfather at such a precarious place. Perhaps Harry Jnr realised how unstable his stepfather's mental state was. Fearful that something was seriously amiss, the boy refused to step over the fence. After about three-quarters of an hour of unsuccessful urging, Crawford finally gave up and, with an ambiguous sense of relief, accepted that his plan was not going to work and that they would both live to see another day.

From Gap Park, they walked south, further up the hill to the Macquarie Lighthouse, with the boy repeatedly asking where they were going and what they were doing, and Crawford deep in thought and not saying a word in answer to the boy's questions. Eventually, they returned to the wharf and caught a ferry back to Circular Quay. By the time they got back to the city, Crawford was elated that he had not gone ahead with his plan – so elated that he bought them some cakes and buns at one of the Sergeant's Tea Rooms.[2] They then walked through the Domain to the Botanic Gardens where they sat down, again in complete silence, and ate what he had bought. After later getting the boy some dinner, they walked to the residence of a Mrs Bannon, another boarding house proprietor that he knew, in Glenmore Road, Paddington, where he left the boy to stay for the night, telling him that he would come for him the following day. He then went back to Drummoyne, where he allowed Joel Hart to pick up much of the furniture, and completed his preparations to move out of the house that he had shared with Annie. The following morning, Thursday 4 October, a second dealer picked up the remaining items of furniture, so that Crawford was free to leave the Drummoyne house he now found so oppressive.

Later that same day, Harry Crawford and Harry Birkett moved to live together as lodgers in the residence of a German couple, Mrs Henrietta Schieblich and her husband, a piano teacher, at 103 Cathedral Street, Woolloomooloo. Harry told his stepson that the move was because they could not afford to stay in the Drummoyne home now that Annie was no longer there. The boy accepted this explanation without question. On their second or third night in their new home, there was a furious storm over Sydney during the evening, with lightning and thunder. By this time, Crawford's mood had again deteriorated and he once more became possessed by thoughts of suicide and what he considered to be the mercy killing of the boy. In his madness, he decided that the storm was a sign that the deeds had to be done that night. Crawford borrowed a raincoat from another lodger, obtained a short-handled shovel, and told his stepson to come out with him. His landlady, Mrs Schieblich, told Crawford that it was pitiful to take the boy out on such a night, and this caused Crawford to become enraged at her presumptuousness to know what was best for the boy. In anger as he went out the door he said to her: 'I am going to kill the young bugger.'

The two Harrys walked together to King's Cross and then got the tram to Ocean Street, Woollahra. From there they walked to Bellevue Road, up a hill and some stone steps to a vacant piece of land covered in scrub.[3] There Crawford led Harry Jnr into a small clearing encircled by trees and not visible to any nearby houses. The storm was still crashing around them, and the rain was pelting down, absolutely soaking them. Crawford took up the shovel and began digging a hole about four foot square and three foot deep. His plan after completing the hole was to hit the boy over the head with the shovel, and then, after making sure that he was dead, to bury him in this makeshift grave. After that, he was planning to get a tram to Gap Park where he would throw himself off the cliff. When Crawford got tired, he asked the boy to dig for a while. The boy did not ask him what the hole was for, as he was fed up with receiving no answers from his stepfather and preoccupied with the lightning and thunder crashing around them, but he too soon grew tired and stepped out of the hole. Crawford then dug out a few more shovelfuls. All this time, Crawford was taking nips from a bottle of brandy to bolster his fortitude to do what had to be done. However, when it came to the crunch, he was unable to do the foul deed, as the thought of hitting the boy with the shovel just seemed so preposterous and barbaric, and he thought it was quite likely that the boy would not die immediately, necessitating hitting him repeatedly in order to make sure that he was dead. He was just not prepared to do this.

Instead of killing the boy, Crawford took him wandering around the bush for some time, whereupon he once again became convinced that the storm bespoke ominous psychic messages, and he was once again consumed by thoughts of killing the boy, so he started digging a fresh hole on a sandy flat. All this time, the lightning and thunder were crashing around them, while the wind was driving the rain straight through their clothing. Finally, Crawford decided to bring the evening to an end, and he threw the shovel into some bushes so that he could not change his mind again, and took the boy home.

Mrs Schieblich was so concerned at what Crawford had said when he had left the house with Harry Jnr, that she waited up for them. It was nearly eleven o'clock when they finally returned with their clothes completely soaked and full of sand. The only explanation that Crawford gave to her was, 'Oh, Harry's a coward. He started crying and would not go to his auntie.'

During their second week at Mrs Schieblich's something occurred that was to have profound consequences nearly three years later. On 16 October *The Evening News* published an article accompanied by a photograph of a pair of oddly patched shoes. Harry saw the photograph but, being illiterate, was unable to read the article. He brought the paper home to the boarding house, placed the open page on a table in front of Harry Jnr and asked the boy to read the words of the article to him. Harry read him a report about an unrecognisable and unidentified, burned body that had been found nearly a fortnight earlier, just after the Eight-Hour Day weekend, in the bush at Chatswood. The article reported the following:

Chatswood Mystery
Woman not yet identified
Who patched the shoes?
The detectives engaged in clearing up the mystery surrounding the death
of a woman on the eight hour day, whose charred remains were found in

the Bush at Chatswood, have arrived at a dead end. The work of the police is made more difficult by reason of the fact that the woman's identity has not yet been established. Fire destroyed practically all traces that might have led to identification, with the exception of the woman's shoes, as shown by the accompanying illustration. It will be observed that the shoes had recently been repaired by two small patches being placed at the side of the soles. The police would like to hear of anyone who effected the repairs.

Harry Jnr noticed that his stepfather didn't say anything after the article was read to him, but he seemed to have an unusually emotional reaction to it. However, not even this was sufficient to raise the boy's suspicions about his mother's whereabouts and there was nothing about the photograph of the shoes that caught his attention or raised his concerns.

Over the ensuing months, Harry continued to tell people various different stories about where Annie had gone and with whom she was living. Sometimes she had gone with a plumber, sometimes with other men. Sometimes she was living on the North Shore, sometimes in other locations. To many people, he said that they had had a tiff, and that she had stormed off, vowing never to return. To Mrs Schieblich, Harry added the rather alarming detail that: 'I had a jolly good row with her, and I gave her a crack on the head, and she cleared out.' To many people, he said that after he had sold their furniture, she had returned to claim part of the money. To some, he claimed to have unexpectedly come across her recently in George Street outside the Palais de Danse, an establishment where single people would congregate to meet and socialise.[4] He said that she had requested money from him and that he had refused her request and walked off. The clear implication was that she was leading a wild and furious lifestyle as a single woman on the hunt for men.

Despite these varying stories, all of which described behaviour that was quite out of character for Annie, nobody thought of reporting her as a missing person. Harry Jnr, who was only fourteen at this time, meekly accepted that his mother had gone to live elsewhere and religiously went to work at various jobs, some of which were found for him by his stepfather. He was so preoccupied by his day-to-day survival that for two and a half years it never occurred to him to question what he had been told about his mother's disappearance. Perhaps he felt that her life with Harry Crawford had become so intolerable over the last few months of their marriage that she chose to leave. Perhaps he felt that she had so suddenly left without leaving any contact details or a message for him in order to prevent Harry

Crawford following her and badgering her to return, as he had done before. Perhaps the boy thought that she had left him at Drummoyne because he had such a good job and prospects with Mr and Mrs Bone. Ultimately, it remains inexplicable that the only son of such a devoted and caring mother would meekly accept that she had suddenly left him, without saying goodbye or leaving any forwarding address. Whatever the reasons, Harry Jnr accepted that his mother had gone to live elsewhere and he either did not hold any suspicions or, if he did, he did not act on them. In fact, at the time nobody reported Annie as a missing person.

Mrs Schieblich was suspicious of what had befallen the wife of her strange lodger, but she also did not go to the police, explaining, 'I would have gone to the police, but on account of us being German, and I had my husband in the Concentration Camp and my boy was five years in the camp and I could not do it.'[5]

The person most likely to report Annie as a missing person was her sister, Lily Nugent. Due to the decline of their relationship since Annie's marriage to Harry, however, when Lily failed to hear anything from her sister after October 1917, she thought nothing of it beyond that her sister must have foregone contact because of the antagonism between Lily and Harry. Of one thing Lily was certain: her sister had a very close relationship with her son – wherever her sister was, Harry Jnr would be with her.

Harry Crawford and Harry Birkett remained as lodgers with Mrs Schieblich for about six weeks until November 1917. By that time, Harry was fed up with the presence of this dependent boy and desperate to find a solution that would relieve him of responsibility for his stepson. He was anxious to find a place for the boy to live that was sufficiently far away from himself, in case he was ever overcome by the kind of feelings that had led to the trips to The Gap and Woollahra.

The solution that he adopted was, in many respects, similar to the one he had chosen in desperation nearly twenty years earlier after being put off the barque in Newcastle when he had gone to the home of Granny de Angelis – although this time the solution was fraught with a hightened danger of exposure. He went to see a kindly Italian woman, Mrs Marcellina Bombelli, who spoke little English, lived at 156 Cathedral Street, Woolloomooloo, and who Harry had known for about ten years.[6] Although she had only seen Harry in men's clothing, Mrs Bombelli knew perfectly well through her Italian connections that traced back to his family in Wellington that Harry was a woman. She knew him as 'Nina', one of the nicknames his family had used in his early life in New Zealand. Harry told Mrs Bombelli, in Italian, that the boy's father was dead and that his mother was ill in hospital with consumption. Being a soft-hearted and generous woman, Marcellina Bombelli agreed to take the boy into her home. So keen was Harry to find a place for the boy and relieve himself of the burden of looking after him that he was prepared to ignore the obvious risk of placing his stepson with a woman who knew his secret. Mrs Bombelli had never been indiscreet about his identity in the past, and Harry hoped that she would not be so now. However, by placing him in her home, Harry accepted the risk that one day his stepson might be told his secret. Harry Jnr had no objection to replacing his strange and morose stepfather with a motherly and emotionally outgoing landlady, even if there was a language problem.

After moving out of Mrs Schieblich's accommodation, Harry Crawford resumed the itinerant and irregular lifestyle that he had lived prior to meeting Annie. He lived in a succession of boarding houses and worked at a series of unskilled labouring jobs. It was a period of regressive unhappiness and turmoil as he drifted from job to job, often drinking to excess. He would frequently lose his job due to erratic and unreliable behaviour. However, through it all, the identity of Harry Crawford remained intact and unchallenged. Several months after Annie's body had been found, with no approach to him by the police, Harry assumed, quite correctly, that the investigation had disclosed nothing to link him to her death, and he began to lose the fear that he might be blamed for her death. By then, people had stopped questioning him about where his wife had gone, and with whom. However, he incorrectly assumed that nothing further would happen in the future to connect him to the body that had been found in the park.

CHAPTER 11

LIZZIE

It was 1919. The Treaty of Versailles, between the major combatants of the First World War, was signed, formally marking the end of the conflict. The Spanish flu pandemic, that had swept the world from early 1918 and was exacerbated by the demobilisation of massive numbers of soldiers after the war, was slowly dying down, after having killed between 50 and 100 million people worldwide. The Prohibition era, involving a regularly flouted ban on alcohol, began in the United States of America. The innovative Bauhaus architectural movement was established in Weimar in Germany. In Milan, a man by the name of Benito Mussolini founded a political movement known as the Italian Fascists.

For two years Harry Crawford laboured under the burden of his lost love. He repressed his depressive thoughts, often involving self-harm, through tough physical work and hard drinking. Even so, he was left with an enormous sense of loss and a fear of the future. He had always had a tendency to remain apart from others and to keep any personal information close to his chest. Now he had even more reasons to shut off his emotions from the outside world and, as a result, he had numerous drinking buddies, many acquaintances and even several women with whom he had fleeting dalliances, but not a single person he would call a true friend – and so he felt quite isolated and alone. When, late at night, he would get back to his boarding house, he would immediately retire to his own room and shun any attempts at conversation by other residents.

Then, without any warning, he came across Elizabeth (Lizzie) King Allison. Lizzie was working in the office of the same hotel where he was working as a general hand. She was most unlike the kind of people who would ordinarily befriend him. For a start, she was six years older than him, however because of her youthful good looks they looked about the same age. More importantly, she was smart, educated and had a sophistication and refinement that he lacked. She had remained a spinster all her life – not because of any shortcomings in her appearance or personality, but rather, as she readily told others, because she had just not met the right man. Lizzie engaged Harry in conversation whenever he ventured into the office, and seemed genuinely interested in his stories. She would notice when he was depressed, and would jolly him out of it with empathetic humour and genuine concern. Before long, he was frequenting the office whenever he could, feeling as though he was grabbing hold of her steady hand and pulling himself out of a mire of black quicksand.

Before long, Harry spruced himself up by buying a new suit and being much more careful about his appearance, behaviour and language. He curtailed his drinking, which from the time of Annie's death had been excessive, and slowly, under the influence of her caring empathy and charm, his mood lifted and he began to appreciate life once more. Within a short time, against every expectation, he fell in love for a second time and, against all odds and expectations, his feelings were reciprocated. Why at the age of fifty Lizzie decided that forty-four-year-old Harry Crawford was the right man for her, he never quite understood. Perhaps she was attracted to a man who had a real need for her emotional support. Perhaps it was just the thought that, at her age, this was her last chance at marriage. Perhaps their common Scottish origins also played a part.

After a whirlwind romance, Harry and Lizzie were married at the Canterbury Registrar's Office on 29 September 1919. He declared himself to be a bachelor marrying for the first time. With a name as common as 'Crawford' and the state of public records at that time, he was not at risk of his previous marriage being discovered from official sources. After the wedding, Harry and Lizzie took up residence as man and wife in a house at 47 Durham Street, Stanmore. Their lives together were far more harmonious than during his marriage to Annie. Not that Harry had told his new wife about his previous marriage to Annie or about his daughter, Josephine, who was leading a completely independent life. It was as if he had begun life afresh, making a clean cut with the past. From Lizzie's point of view, she had married a confirmed bachelor with no children. At forty-four, Harry was more sedate in manner and more appreciative of his wife than he had been in his previous life with Annie. They rarely argued and Harry's drinking had moderated considerably because he no longer needed it as a crutch. Neither did he require the drink to engage in social chitchat with strangers in a bar, because he was quite content to go home and be with Lizzie. He hardly ever gave a thought to what had happened in the Lane Cove River Park two years earlier, because it felt as though it had happened a lifetime ago to someone else.

Harry had kept his pleasure-giving device after Annie's death, and had even used it several times in the intervening years whenever a woman he casually met suggested a dalliance. Harry was so practised at the use of it that he had little nervousness when first using it on Lizzie. He believed that his new wife, despite all of her intelligence and learning, lacked the sexual experience of most women her age and therefore would not notice anything amiss – and he was right. If anything she was more accommodating of his modesty and his frequent visits to the bathroom than any woman he had previously known. Lizzie seemed to relish their sexual contact immensely. In fact, her capacity for sexual enjoyment was greater than that of most of the women with whom he had been intimate. It was as if she was making up for the lost years of her spinsterhood. He still kept the device in a cloth bag buried beneath a lot of clothing in the large portmanteau in a spare room of their house, moving it to the bathroom each time he intended using it. When deploying it, he had become so confident that his technique would not be discovered that he allowed her more freedom of movement during lovemaking than he had permitted Annie, confident that she would respect his wish not to be touched 'down there'. He had long since lost any fear that the bandages wrapped around his chest and covered by his undershirt would fail him.

In the same portmanteau, Harry kept an old revolver, which years earlier had been provided by the owner of a hotel where he was employed, to take with him in a bag when he took the day's takings to the bank. One day, after delivering the money, he forgot to return the weapon, and only realised when he got home that it was still in his possession. Noticing that the weapon had live bullets in four of its five chambers, he decided to keep it, thinking that it would be good to have for self-protection if ever a group of men at one of the boarding houses discovered his secret and attempted to do to him what the captain had done on the barque so many years earlier. When the owner of the hotel questioned him the next day, he insisted that he had returned it to the drawer where it was normally kept. The owner initially seemed to accept this explanation, but a few days later Harry was informed that his services were no longer required. Many months later, he took the revolver to a bush area near Hornsby to test it and see how it worked, firing off two of the four live rounds. Not wanting to attract attention by buying more ammunition, he returned the still partially loaded gun to his portmanteau, where it remained unused.

Meanwhile, Harry Birkett remained at the home of Mrs Bombelli for about six months, and then, in mid-1918, went to live with her son, Frank Bombelli, in Sans Souci. He had long since ceased to think about his former stepfather, Harry Crawford, until one day in early 1920 when the younger Harry, now seventeen, happened to stop by a hotel where the older Harry was working. Harry Crawford was surprised and alarmed by this unexpected intrusion into his new life and so, when the young man suggested that they have a drink after work, fearful that he may want money from him, Harry fobbed him off by suggesting a meeting at the hotel the following day when he knew he would not be there. Harry Birkett readily agreed, and when he arrived at the hotel the next day there was no sign of his former stepfather.

Josephine had only very occasional contact with the person she called 'Father' but knew as 'Mother', and 'Father' was quite happy with that. At twenty-one, she was independent and living her own life, and had little wish to meet up with the parent who had been the source of so much grief. In any event, after spending years of her childhood imagining a meeting with her 'real father' – the man whom Granny De Angelis had described as the captain of a four-masted ship – Josephine had a new relationship with a seaman in the Royal Australian Navy, Arthur Whitby. Arthur Whitby served on HMAS *Sydney*, a Chatham Class light cruiser with four funnels. He had been on-board on 9 November 1914 during the First World War when the *Sydney* sank the German Cruiser SMS *Emden* off the Cocos Keeling Islands in the Indian Ocean about 1700 miles northwest of Perth. Although Josephine and Arthur were unmarried, they were living together as man and wife in Pyrmont. Just as Harry Crawford had deliberately not told his new wife about his daughter, his daughter had not told her new partner about her unorthodox parent.

In May 1920, when Harry and Lizzie had been married for about eight months, Lizzie noticed that she had missed her usual menstrual period. For all her adult life she had been as regular as clockwork, so, when she missed this first period, she became cautiously excited, but said nothing to Harry. A month later, when she again missed a period, she decided that she must be pregnant. Thinking that she was still fertile, she was not surprised at this, because she and Harry had been engaging in a regular and vigorous sex life without any contraceptive precautions. After the second missed period, she decided that she couldn't keep the good news from Harry any longer.

Lizzie chose her time to tell Harry the good news very carefully, because it was such an important announcement. She was sure that he would be thrilled, because it would be a further bond in what was proving to be a singularly satisfying and supportive marriage and, from her point of view, neither of them had any children. She chose an evening when she knew beforehand that he would be home from work early. She prepared a particularly sumptuous dinner for him, lit a candle and placed it on the table between them, which was something she usually only did on special occasions. When Harry arrived home and saw her preparations, he wondered whether he had forgotten an anniversary of some important event in their lives, but could think of nothing. During the meal, Lizzie gleefully announced to Harry that at the ages of forty-five and fifty-one God had blessed them with the prospect of their first-born child.

When Harry heard this news, he was immediately thrown into a storm of confusion. Knowing perfectly well that she could not be pregnant to him, his immediate concern was that she had engaged in intimate relations with another man. The few seconds that it took him to dismiss such a base thought seemed to Lizzie a pause of inappropriate length. She had expected him to be instantly rapt with unadulterated delight, as she was, so when he initially looked puzzled and concerned at her news, she was perplexed. Harry quickly recomposed himself and unconvincingly muttered some innocuous, rather formal expression of feigned delight. Lizzie decided that he was just a typical man, who was more concerned about his own claims on her time and attention than with the promise of a new life in their midst.

Within a week, Lizzie was out and about feathering her nest in preparation for the addition to their family. Her face acquired a rosy glow, which was accompanied by a delicious but uncomfortable feeling of warmth emanating from her whole body. A month later she began to notice that she was putting on weight. She did not mind this, and indeed increased her intake of food, because now she was 'eating for two'. When her interest in sex declined, she put it down to the natural hormones of pregnancy. She marked in her diary that at the beginning of August she would need to see a doctor who would care for her during the latter stages of the pregnancy and attend at the birth. She would often quiz Harry how he felt about the forthcoming addition to their family, and he would answer with mild and meaningless platitudes. She again attributed this apparently uncaring attitude to a concern that she might have less time for him once the baby was born. In fact, Harry was growing increasingly anxious about what would happen to their relationship when this pregnancy was unmasked for whatever it was.

What had been a clear sky for Harry and Lizzie Crawford was becoming increasingly threatened by approaching storm clouds as the time came nearer for Lizzie's visit to the doctor. Little did Harry and Lizzie know that even darker and heavier clouds were looming unseen just over the horizon and racing towards them at breakneck speed, destined to drown them in a deluge of tears the likes of which they could never have imagined.

CHAPTER 12

INVESTIGATION AND ARREST

For two-and-a-half years, Harry Birkett had been too preoccupied with the demands of daily existence to concern himself with searching for his mother, who had vanished from his life without warning during the Eight-Hour Day long weekend in October 1917. After spending a few weeks following her disappearance living in boarding houses with Harry Crawford and a few months at the home of Mrs Marcellina Bombelli, in mid-1918 Harry Jnr went to live with her son, Frank Bombelli, in Sans Souci. It was in Frank Bombelli's home in about April 1920 that Harry Jnr was told something so extraordinary that he was finally prompted to enquire into what had happened to his mother. Frank Bombelli told him that Harry Crawford was really a woman called 'Nina' dressed as a man, and that Marcellina Bombelli knew Nina's Italian family in New Zealand. Frank had known this information for a long time, having been told years earlier by his mother, but when the fourteen-year-old boy first moved into his home he had thought that it was inappropriate to tell him such scandalous details. However, by the time Harry Jnr was seventeen, Frank considered him old and mature enough to be told the truth.

When Harry Birkett was finally given this astounding piece of information about his former stepfather, he was seized by a sudden panic about his mother's fate. He thought back to the last eight months of their family life before his mother's disappearance in 1917, and he could now see that there had been an abrupt change in her attitude to her husband during that time. His mother's actions made more sense to a young man than they had to an adolescent boy. He was overwhelmed with guilt that he had meekly accepted the pathetic explanation that his stepfather had given him on that first evening after he had returned from Collaroy. He vividly recalled the extraordinary journeys to The Gap and Woollahra that his stepfather had dragged him on in the first week after his mother's disappearance. In a moment of sudden, shocked revelation that hit him like an unexpected punch to the solar plexus, he abruptly remembered when Harry Crawford had asked him at Mrs Schieblich's lodgings to read an article about an unidentified, burned body that had been found in the Lane Cove River Park some days earlier, and he replayed in his mind the strange emotional reaction he had witnessed in his stepfather. Over some days, Harry Birkett became utterly convinced that his mother had been murdered by Harry Crawford over the Eight-Hour Day weekend and that the body that had been found near the Cumberland Paper Mills was hers. He became determined to uncover his mother's fate, no matter what it might have been, and, if she had been murdered by his stepfather, to bring him to justice, whether he was a man or a woman.

With this in mind, Harry Birkett sought out his aunt, Lily Nugent, whom he had not seen in about three years. He went to see her at her home in Kogarah to tell her of his grave suspicions. Lily was very pleased to see her nephew after such a long absence, but when he informed her that he hadn't seen or heard from his mother since the beginning of October 1917, Lily became terribly distressed and concerned about the fate of her sister. Harry Junior told his aunt of his suspicions, and each of them disclosed to the other what they had heard about Harry Crawford's gender. Harry Jnr told Lily that he had heard from the Bombelli family that Harry Crawford was really a woman called Nina from an Italian family living in New Zealand. Lily told Harry Jnr that during a visit by Lily to Drummoyne shortly before the disappearance, Annie had told her that Harry was 'not a man'. As Harry Jnr and Lily discussed Annie's disappearance, they fed off each other's suspicions until Lily quite independently came to the same view as her nephew – that her sister must have been murdered by Harry Crawford.

Harry Jnr and Lily determined then and there that they would report Annie to the police as a missing person, that they would tell the police of the suspicions they harboured about Harry Crawford, and that they would inform the police of the strange facts they had been given about his gender, his Italian origins and his New Zealand family.

In May 1920, Harry Birkett and Lily Nugent attended the Criminal Investigation Branch of the New South Wales Police, which was situated on the upper floors of the multi-storey Central police station in Central Street, Sydney,[1] to report Annie Crawford as a missing person. They were interviewed by Detective Sergeant Stewart Robson, who assumed the role of chief investigator. Harry Jnr told the Detective Sergeant as many of the circumstances as he could recall about the strange fortnight after his mother had disappeared. This included mention of the article in the newspaper about the body that had been found in the Lane Cove River Park around the time his mother had disappeared and his strong suspicion that the body could be his mother's. Harry Birkett and Lily Nugent also told Detective Robson what they had heard about Harry Crawford's real gender and his origins in an Italian family in New Zealand. Detective Robson was naturally intrigued at this extraordinary information, and resolved that, if it was true, he would use it to his advantage during the investigation. He asked them both to come back to see him several weeks later, by which time he would have been able to ascertain what evidence still remained from the original police investigation in 1917, and they could then make formal written statements.

It was an easy task for Detective Sergeant Robson to locate the police documentation about the investigation in 1917 of the body that had remained unidentified. He simply called for the file and exhibits, which had been retained at the Chatswood police station. In mid-June, several weeks after their initial visit, Harry Jnr and Lily again attended the Criminal Investigation Branch, where Detective Robson showed them the jewellery, shoes, enamel cup, picnic basket, and the small piece of gabardine material that had been recovered from the park. Each of them was able to readily identify various items as having belonged to Annie. Harry Jnr told the detective that not only were the shoes similar to ones that his mother had owned, but that the patches were very similar to ones that had been applied to his mother's shoes by his stepfather.

At long last, more than two-and-a-half years after Annie's death, there was sufficient circumstantial evidence to conclude that the body was hers.

Detective Sergeant Robson took formal statements from his two witnesses. He deliberately did not include in their written accounts the information about Harry's gender and origins, but kept this up his sleeve so that he could use it as a potentially powerful investigative tool. He would later present it in an unduly self-complimentary way that suggested it had only emerged because of his comprehensive and exemplary skills as a detective.[2] He also created the impression that it was excellent investigative work by the police that had linked the finding of the body in 1917 with the 1920 report of Annie Birkett's disappearance, rather than attributing this connection to Annie's son.

The task of further investigating Annie Birkett's death now fell to the police under the leadership of Detective Sergeant Robson. The sergeant had available to him the information that had been presented to the Coroner in 1917, including the autopsy report that stated that there were no signs of violence. Despite this finding, it does not appear that the police engaged in any further enquiries before deciding to arrest and question Harry Crawford. For Detective Sergeant Robson, the information he already had from Harry Birkett and Lily Nugent was sufficient to make the decision to arrest Harry Crawford. Robson thought that there was a good chance that, on being confronted with what the police already knew, Harry Crawford might confess to the murder of his wife. The decision to adopt this course of action – trying to prompt a confession from their suspect – was made in the belief that if Harry did admit to the murder, it would make the police investigation much more straightforward and require far less laborious police legwork. This was a common approach by the police to the prospect of an involved and protracted investigation. A calculated decision was therefore made to delay any further police investigations until after Harry Crawford had been interviewed.

At about 11.30 am on Monday 5 July 1920, two men in dark suits and grey felt hats went to the Empire Hotel on the corner of Parramatta Road and Johnston Street in Annandale, where Harry was working as a general hand. They came up to the licensee's office, where Harry was sitting during a break, and Robson began: 'I am Detective Sergeant Stewart Robson and this is my colleague Detective Watkins. What is your name?'[3] Although Harry did not initially know the purpose of the visit by these two officers, any confrontation with the police was sufficient to raise his level of stress and fear. As a highly experienced police officer, Sergeant Robson immediately detected that rise in tension and his instinct was to exploit it to his advantage.

After asking his name, the sergeant asked, 'How long have you been working here?' to which Crawford replied, 'A few weeks.'

Sergeant Robson then asked him, 'What nationality are you?' This was ostensibly a strange question for Robson to ask at this early stage, but understandable if one knew what Harry Jnr had told him.

Crawford's response was to ask the detective, 'What do you want to know that for?', to which the policeman replied, 'I believe you are an Italian.' Crawford said, 'No, I am a Scotchman and was born in Edinburgh.'

Robson said, 'I have my doubts about you, and I am going to take you to the Central Court or the Detectives Office to make further investigations.' The moment that Harry Crawford had dreaded for so many years had finally arrived.

In a legal sense, Robson was deliberately vague as to whether or not Crawford was then under arrest, although his suspect would clearly have thought he had no option but to accompany the police to wherever they wanted to take him. The law provided that if Detective Sergeant Robson was going to arrest Crawford, he was under an obligation to take him to the

Central Police Court at the 'earliest reasonable opportunity'. At this hour, around the middle of the day, there was clearly no impediment to meeting this requirement of the law, as the Central Police Court in Liverpool Street, contiguous to the Central police station, would still have been in session. However, instead of taking Harry Crawford to the court, Detective Sergeant Robson took him to the Criminal Investigation Branch offices at the Central police station.[4] No doubt, if Robson had been queried about this diversion, he would have asserted that Crawford was not under arrest and had voluntarily accompanied them to the police station for questioning.

The Central police station in Central Street functioned as Sydney's police headquarters. It was situated in the Haymarket area about a mile from the business district of the city. Although Haymarket was not the commercial centre of Sydney, it was definitely the retail centre. Within two blocks of the police station, there were two enormous emporiums or department stores: Anthony Hordens and Mark Foys.[5] Several blocks further away were Sydney's two main produce markets: Paddy's Market and the markets of the Queen Victoria building. A mile away on Broadway, past the Central Railway Station, was the Grace Brothers Department Store.

The main entrance to the Central police station was through a grand archway, which incongruously faced onto Central Street, an unimpressive, narrow laneway between George Street and Pitt Street. The police station, which backed onto the rear of the Central Police Court in Liverpool Street, consisted of a central courtyard where police vehicles could load and unload prisoners who were due to appear in the adjoining courts, surrounded by a multi-storey building which housed the Criminal Investigation Branch and numerous other specialist police departments. When one came through the impressive main entrance, there was a public enquiry room on the left side. On the right side, behind a locked door, was the 'charge room' where police would process those who were charged with committing crime. Above ground, the station consisted of a multi-storeyed series of police offices, corridors and interview rooms. Below ground, and accessed via the charge room, was a rabbit warren of underground cells that connected to the adjoining Central Police Courts in Liverpool Street. When one entered the Central police station through the grand archway, one crossed into a totally alien environment that had its own processes and protocols.

Harry Crawford was escorted to the third-floor offices of the Criminal Investigation Branch. He was introduced to Superintendent Bannan, who was the officer in charge. With the authority of his office and his superior age supporting him, the Superintendent said to Crawford: 'These officers, Robson and Watkins, have been enquiring for some days about a matter which we think concerns you a great deal. And what I want to know is whether you are willing to make a statement setting out your social relations with different people since you have been here, where you have been working, and people that you know generally. You will be taken out to the top room and you can make your statement there. But, before you do go, I wish you to thoroughly understand that the statements that you do make shall be absolutely voluntary.'

Crawford replied, 'All right.'

Crawford was then taken to one of a series of small interview rooms on the top floor of the police station. A formal statement was then typed out by a police typist based on Crawford's answers in response to Sergeant Robson's questions. After the statement had been completed, Sergeant Robson invited Crawford to read it. Despite the fact that Crawford was illiterate, he gave the appearance of reading the document, and then signed it. The statement contained numerous lies about his origins and personal history and, most importantly of all, stated that he had been a single man all his life until marrying Lizzie Allison in September 1919.

Following the making of the statement, Sergeant Robson left the interview room for five or ten minutes and then returned to inform Crawford for the first time that he had interviewed Harry Birkett and Lily Nugent and that he had reason to believe that Crawford had married Harry Birkett's mother some years earlier. Sergeant Robson also told Crawford that he proposed to produce Harry Birkett in his presence, and he gave Crawford the option of an identification line-up with other people if he wished. Crawford declined the offer, saying, 'I don't want to be lined up with a lot of other people. I have got enough worry on my head at present.'

There then followed a most extraordinary exchange between Sergeant Robson and his unsuspecting and disadvantaged suspect, who did not know the extent of the Sergeant's knowledge about his identity. Sergeant Robson skilfully used the information he had been given by Harry Birkett and Lily Nugent to unbalance his suspect and to push him into a corner from where, Robson hoped, he could only escape by making admissions. According to the police, it went like this:

> Robson: You still say that your name is Harry Crawford and you were born in Scotland?
> Crawford: Yes.
> Robson: Have you any marks about your body that will assist in identifying you as a Scotchman and where you say you were born?
> Crawford: No.

Robson: Strip off a little and let me see.

Crawford: No, I object to that.

Robson: Very well, the government medical officer is in this building –
Dr Palmer. Would you care to go before him?

Crawford: I do not mind.

Robson then took Crawford to Dr Palmer's office, nearby in the same complex. By this stage, Harry Crawford was in a complete panic. He had no idea what evidence the police had to link him to Annie's death. Unbeknown to him, there was in fact very little. Robson was playing a very nimble game of cat-and-mouse. Crawford had a flashback to the time many years earlier when, as a sailor on the Norwegian barque, he had been caught out and exposed, and he shuddered with horror at the memory of the terrifying ordeal that had followed. He was fearful that the police were intending to charge him and that he would be sent straight to a men's gaol where he would again be viciously raped. He was prepared to do anything to avoid a repetition of the terrible, violent invasion of his body suffered all those years ago. However, when confronted with Dr Palmer, Crawford could not bring himself to disrobe, and so he objected to the doctor examining him. Robson then took Crawford back to the interview room, and their conversation continued:

Crawford: I suppose now I will have to go to gaol?

Robson: I am not quite sure about that yet, at the present juncture.

Crawford: What do they do with you when they take you to gaol?

Robson: Well, I'm not quite familiar with their methods, but I think they
first give you a good bath and a change of clothes.

Crawford: Well, I want to go into the women's ward.

Robson: Oh, not quite. No chance of that.

Crawford: Come here. I want to tell you something (calling Robson away
from the typist). I want to tell you that I am a woman and not a man.

Robson: Well, I can only take you as you appear to be, dressed as a man,
and that is a matter entirely for the doctor.

Crawford: Is the doctor here now?

Robson: Yes, he is still there.

Crawford: Well, can I go and see him?

Robson: Yes.

Robson again took Crawford to see Dr Palmer and, in Robson's quite intrusive presence, Crawford disrobed a little and told the doctor that he was a woman. After an examination that required a mere second or two, Dr Palmer declared that Crawford was indeed a woman. Robson and Crawford then returned once again to the interview room, where the conversation continued:

Crawford: This is a terrible thing for me, and the worry of my life.

Robson: Well, we are going out to your place now, where you say your wife is, and I am going to make a little search.

Crawford: (desperately pleading) I do not want you to let her know anything.

Robson: What, do you mean to say that she has not found out anything since you have been living with her?

Crawford: No, she does not know anything.

At that point, Robson brought Harry Birkett into the room. The young man immediately identified Crawford as the man who had married his mother years earlier, and promptly left the interview room without the slightest acknowledgement of his stepfather. Robson then offered to read Harry Birkett's statement to Crawford. After reading it to him, their conversation continued:

Robson: How is it you never mentioned anything to me about this first wife, that is explained in the statement?

Crawford: Oh, you have it all now. You have got as much as I could tell you. I did not want to say anything about it. She had been drinking a great deal, a source of worry to me, and she had been going with other men.

There then followed several further questions about the circumstances of Annie leaving home in 1917. Robson then informed Crawford that he and the police would go to where he was living with his present wife, in order for the police to conduct a search. Robson at this stage still maintained a deliberate obfuscation about whether Crawford was under arrest and whether he was compelled to accompany them to his home. Crawford had still not formally been placed under arrest, but neither had he been told that he had a choice whether or not to accompany the police to his home.

By this stage, Crawford was feeling quite terrified and thoroughly confused at his predicament. He was horrified at the thought that Lizzie, whom he dearly loved, might discover his true identity and the reality of their lovemaking. He firmly believed that if she did find out, their relationship would disintegrate, just as had the one with Annie. More than anything else, he wanted to protect Lizzie's feelings.

Detectives Robson and Watkins then took Crawford to his home at 47 Durham Street, Stanmore. When they arrived, Detective Robson introduced himself to Lizzie, told her that they were investigating a murder and informed her that they were going to search the house. Lizzie began to cry, and continued crying for the whole time that they were there. The two police officers, with Crawford in tow, went into the main bedroom, where the police commenced to search. Crawford felt completely defenceless and overwhelmed by his overriding concerns for Lizzie, who was crying in another room. In one corner of the bedroom there was a large, handsome, solid leather portmanteau inscribed in gold letters with the initials 'HLC'.

Detective Robson walked across the room as if to open the portmanteau, when Crawford interrupted him:

Crawford: Let me open the bag and I will give you something that is in it.
Robson: No, I could not do that.
Crawford: Well, don't let the wife see it.
Robson: What is in the bag?
Crawford: You will find it, something there that I have been using.
Robson: What is it? Something artificial?
Crawford: Yes, don't let her see it.
Robson: Do you mean to say that she doesn't know anything about this?
Crawford: No, and I do not want you to let her know.

Robson then opened the portmanteau and searched through it. He found a pair of well-tailored trousers of a blue cheviot serge material,[6] braces, shirts, sleeve links, sleeve suspenders, collars, socks – in fact a complete masculine outfit. Robson also found a revolver that contained two live rounds, two empty fired cases and one empty chamber. Hidden underneath, he found a cloth bag. He opened the bag and in it he found the object Crawford had so carefully fashioned all those years before and with which he had so surreptitiously but successfully pleasured many women, including both his wives. With a furrowed brow, Robson gingerly removed the object from the bag and in front of Crawford held it up by the strap between two fingers, as though it were the tail of a decomposed rat that the cat had brought in. The conversation continued:

Robson: Is this what you referred to as having used on your wife?
Crawford: Yes.

Robson: Did your first wife know that you were using anything like this?

Crawford: No, not until about the latter part of our marriage. Not until about the latter stages of our married life. I think somebody had been talking.

By this stage, Robson clearly thought that he had sufficient evidence with which to charge Crawford. The police took him from the house at Stanmore, telling Lizzie only where they were taking her husband and leaving her in a state of complete ignorance about what had just occurred. They proceeded directly back to the Central police station to charge their suspect with the murder of Annie Birkett.

In the space of just a few hours, the persona of Harry Crawford, which had been so carefully crafted and successfully maintained for twenty-two years, had abruptly disintegrated, as he was forced to revert to his original identity as Eugenia Falleni. Harry felt as though his inner soul had been ripped from within him. Eugenia was an alien presence that had 'passed away' years earlier and now she had been forcibly resurrected.

CHAPTER 13

LIZZIE'S DISCOVERY

It was July 1920. The Panama Canal opened, allowing shipping to pass from the Atlantic Ocean to the Pacific Ocean, and vice versa, without rounding the southern tip of South America. The first world Scout Jamboree was held near London.

When Eugenia Falleni was taken back to the Central police station at about 3 pm on 5 July 1920, she was escorted into the charge room and seated in 'the dock', a small area surrounded by waist-high wooden panels, signifying that the person was officially in custody. She waited there while the formal police paperwork required for charging her and for her first court appearance was being prepared by Detective Sergeant Robson. This entailed the preparation of a typed charge sheet and a summary of the facts alleged against the prisoner, as well as the filling out of the huge leather-bound charge book maintained by the station sergeant. It also involved the taking of a formal police photograph and the fingerprints of the prisoner. The process would be concluded by the station sergeant's formal reading of the charge to the prisoner, after which he or she would be removed and placed in one of the underground cells. This process could take an hour or even more, during which time the prisoner would have to sit patiently in the dock. While Detective Sergeant Robson and Detective Watkins were busily preparing the documents relating to Eugenia's case, other police at the station were milling around, performing their own duties. One of those was Constable Lillian Armfield. Five years earlier, Constable Armfield had been appointed a probationary special constable, making her the first policewoman in Australia.

About half an hour after Robson, Watkins and their prisoner had arrived back at the Central police station, a police officer came and told Detective Robson that there was a Mrs Harry Crawford at the front enquiry desk, wanting to see her husband. Robson consulted with Watkins and they both decided that it would be best if a female police officer dealt with Mrs Crawford. Robson went over to Constable Lillian Armfield and asked her if she would speak to Mrs Crawford. He explained to the constable what had happened during the course of that day. Constable Armfield then went into the enquiry office and spoke to Lizzie Crawford. Detectives Robson and Watkins were listening in the background. The conversation proceeded as follows:

Lizzie: (in a whisper) Do you belong to the police? (Armfield nodded) I want to see my husband. They have arrested my husband. I'm Mrs Harry Crawford.

Armfield: I'm afraid you are in for a terrible shock. The person you married can't be your husband.

Lizzie: (staring incredulously and speaking with dismay) You mean he's a bigamist?

Armfield: No. The person we have locked up under the name of Harry Crawford is a woman.

Lizzie: (staring at the police woman as though she was out of her mind) How can you say he is a woman? I'm his wife. He is my dear and loving husband.

Armfield: Your husband has been examined by the government medical officer, and he is definitely a woman.

At this juncture, Lizzie Crawford started to swoon and it looked as though she was going to collapse in a dead faint. Constable Armfield came around the counter and supported her as she stumbled towards a chair in the public waiting area. Detectives Robson and Watkins, who had been hovering in the background, quickly came over to help Constable Armfield, who was asking another constable to get the poor woman a glass of water. Robson then spoke to Lizzie.

Robson: We can understand her deceiving other people, madam, but we can't understand how she could deceive you and the other woman she married and murdered.

Lizzie: Murdered?

Robson: Yes, murdered.

Lizzie: I don't believe it. I want to talk to him.

Armfield: (to Robson) We'll have to let her see Crawford and talk to him ... her.

Constable Armfield then went and spoke to Eugenia in the charge room. She told Eugenia that her wife was in the waiting room wanting to speak to her. Eugenia became very distressed and started shaking uncontrollably. Fighting back tears, she said to Constable Armfield, 'I can't possibly face her. Please tell her that I love her, but I can't possibly speak to her right now. I don't want her to see me here like this.' Armfield asked her if she was sure about it, and Eugenia stated that she was. Armfield then returned to the waiting room and the following conversation took place.

> Armfield: *I'm very sorry but she's not prepared to see you at this time. She asked me to tell you that she loves you, but she just can't speak to you right now.*
> Lizzie: *(wailing bitterly) I just don't believe what you've told me. What have you done to my husband?*
> Watkins: *(to Robson, but audible to everyone) I think you'd better show her what was in the suitcase. It's the only way you'll convince her.*

Robson went back into the charge room, retrieved the cloth bag he had found in the portmanteau and brought it into the enquiry room. Without removing the object, he held the cloth bag wide open in front of Lizzie, who tentatively peered inside it and then, without another word to the police, got up in a huff, walked to the door and left the station, ignoring the sympathetic words offered by Constable Armfield.

Once in the laneway outside the police station and safely out of view, Lizzie burst into copious tears. How could they say such dreadful things about her much-loved husband? How dare they show her a revolting apparatus fit for a bordello? Although she had been a spinster until her marriage to Harry, and he was the only man that she had fully 'known' in a sexual sense, she considered herself sufficiently worldly-wise to know that the pleasure that he had given her did not come from an artificial device. She was confident that she knew the truth, and that was that her husband must be a man, because she was pregnant to him. She did not feel the need to tell the police this piece of private information, because she did not have to justify or prove anything about the manhood of her husband. She had the living proof growing inside her.

Back inside the police station, about half an hour later, the police photographer came to Eugenia and took her downstairs to a large, below-ground room, which was used on occasions as a prisoner exercise yard, in which the ceiling was open to the air above and covered by wire mesh.[1] Here the police photographer took two photographs of her with a six inch by four inch glass plate camera, using a blank wall as a backdrop.[2] There was no need for a flash because there was plenty of light coming through the open ceiling. Eugenia was still in the clothes in which she had been working at the Empire Hotel. The photographer then went to his small darkroom in another part of the station, processed the two glass negatives, made contact prints from them, wrote on the prints *234 E. Falleni* and scratched *Eugene Falleni* on the edge of the negatives. He then placed both the prints and the negatives in a paper sleeve on which he wrote *Falleni Man/Woman*. Another junior constable then took her back upstairs to the charge room to take her fingerprints. Sometime later, the station sergeant wrote up her personal particulars in the charge book:

Name: Eugenia Falleni
Sex: female
Age: 45
Address: 47 Durham Street, Stanmore
Occupation: General useful

and the formal charge:

On or about 1 October 1917 at Lane Cove in the State of New South Wales Eugene Falleni did feloniously and maliciously murder Annie Crawford, also known as Annie Birkett.

For some reason, the station sergeant used the male version of Eugenia's name in the charge book, possibly because he was unfamiliar with the female version, thereby ensuring that this was the name that was used thereafter during the legal proceedings and the aftermath. The station sergeant then read the charge to Eugenia and told her that she would remain overnight in the underground cells at the police station, so that she could appear first thing the next morning in the adjoining Central Police Court. She was also told that the Legal Aid office in the Attorney-General's Department had been informed of her charging and that they would probably provide a solicitor for her to speak to in the morning. At around 5 pm, when all the formalities had been completed, Eugenia was taken downstairs and placed on her own in a cell.

Alone in an underground cell, Eugenia bemoaned the terrible turn that her life had taken in just a few hours, but she was grateful that at least for tonight she was not at risk of any violent invasion of her body. Her almost forgotten fear that she would be linked to Annie's death had been realised. If only she could wake up in the morning, safe in Lizzie's arms, to find that the day's events had all been a bad dream. She was not to know that the nightmare had only just begun, and that it would get worse – much worse.

The following morning, Eugenia was listed to appear in the Central Police Court. Someone had alerted the press, because there was a swarm of them hovering around the courthouse. Press photographers avidly took her photograph as she was needlessly paraded in public, accompanied by Sergeant Robson, on the way into court. It would have been much simpler to adopt the usual practice of taking her via the underground passageways that connected the police station to the court complex. For a private person like Eugenia, being in the spotlight was sheer agony. The knowledge that these people were gawking at her, that they would publish her photograph and write about her in the newspapers made her feel excruciatingly uncomfortable. Her public exposure, still in male clothing, was designed to serve two purposes. Firstly, it highlighted Sergeant Robson's profile as the lead investigator. Secondly, it was part of the police plan to encourage further witnesses to come forward.

After a brief appearance in court, Eugenia was taken in a prison van to the new gaol at Long Bay, near Malabar, and admitted to the Women's Reformatory. She was not given a bath, as Robson had suggested she would be, but was issued with a set of prison clothes that she had to immediately change into, so that the guards could take possession of her civilian clothes. It was the first time that Eugenia had worn female clothing in more than twenty years – not that anyone would have classified the prison garb as particularly feminine. It consisted of a shapeless, loose-fitting, ankle-length, tunic-style dress in a heavy coarse material, probably wool, buttoned up the centre front, with a wide, falling puritan collar set well back from the centre. After years of dressing as a male, it seemed utterly foreign to put on female clothing. She felt as though she were one of those performing monkeys dressed by its keeper in mock human clothing for a circus performance or as an assistant to an organ grinder.

Several days later, on Thursday 8 July, the police spoke again to Lizzie Crawford at police headquarters. She told them that she had been 'so pestered by calls and sensation seekers since the arrest of her husband that she has been forced to change her address'. Her visit to the police headquarters somehow became known to the press and soon a large crowd had drawn up outside the office. She appealed to the superintendent in charge of the CIB for 'police protection against the activities of those who seek to have a word with her about the case'. She firmly adhered to her belief that Harry Crawford was her loving husband, insisting that he had been an ideal partner and that they had had a very happy married life. She told police that she had 'an indelible passion and affection for her husband'.

The following week, Lizzie Crawford, in a state of dismay and confusion, attended on her local general medical practitioner. The doctor examined her and informed her that she was not pregnant, but undergoing the early stages of 'change of life'.[3] Within a day, she had packed up all her belongings from their home at Stanmore and left Sydney, determined to avoid the press scrum that had greeted Eugenia's first few Court appearances. Lizzie was never to see or speak to her husband again. When the police tried to locate her several weeks later to serve a subpoena to give evidence at the committal proceedings in the Police Court, she was unable to be found.

CHAPTER 14

EXHUMATION AND SECOND AUTOPSY

Despite the fact that Eugenia Falleni had been charged with the murder of Annie Birkett, the police, in fact, had very little evidence against her. In reverse of the usual course of an investigation and in anticipation of a trial, Detective Sergeant Stewart Robson and his team set out *after* her arrest and charging to obtain as much further evidence as possible. As previously mentioned, the publication in the newspapers of her photograph in male attire was a part of this plan. Right from the start, the police did not hesitate to create a prejudicial atmosphere about the whole matter by referring to it as 'the man-woman case', a term readily picked up by the newspapers and thereafter invariably used by them in their headlines.

The *Daily Telegraph* reported on Wednesday 7 July, the day after her first appearance in court, that 'police investigations on a most detailed and searching scale are being continued day and night'. The further enquiries included an application by the Inspector-General of Police, Mr J Mitchell, for the exhumation of Annie Birkett's body at the Rookwood cemetery. The precise location of the grave was not determined for some days. On Friday 9 July, *The Sun* newspaper reported:

> *Under the direction of superintendent Bannan, head of the Criminal Investigation Branch, Detective Sergeant Robson and Detective Watkins are continuing their enquiries into the cause of the death of Annie Birkett at Chatswood in 1917. They have interviewed nearly 100 persons, and have many sheets of statements from people who knew Mrs Birkett.*
>
> *The woman's grave has been located at Rookwood. Application will be made by the police next week to have the body exhumed, and if it is granted, the remains will be examined by government medical officers.*
>
> *Superintendent Bannan wants to hear from the dentist who made a set of teeth for the upper jaw and some single ones for the lower jaw for Mrs Birkett early in 1914.*

The assertion that nearly a hundred people had been interviewed was a gross exaggeration. Detective Robson decided to use the massive coverage of the case in the newspapers to encourage any potential witnesses to come forward. On 8 July, the *Daily Telegraph* published a request from the police under the heading *What the Police Want*:

> *The police are particularly anxious to obtain information regarding one important phase of the story. They want to know and to get into touch with any person who saw the dead woman and the accused either at North Sydney or at Drummoyne, or in the vicinity of either place, on September 29, 1917, or any approximate dates.*

On the same day, the *Sydney Morning Herald* reported:

> *The police are anxious to hear from any person who saw Annie Birkett, or Mrs Harry Crawford, after September 29, 1917.*

The publication of the police request for assistance proved very fruitful, and a number of people came forward who claimed to have seen a man fitting the description of Harry Crawford in the vicinity of the Cumberland Paper Mills around the Eight-Hour Day long weekend in October 1917. Of course, this was assisted by the publication of Eugenia's photograph in the papers after her first court appearance. Several former neighbours of Harry and Annie Crawford at Drummoyne also came forward claiming to have seen both of them leave their home, or having seen Harry arrive back in Drummoyne alone, on that same weekend.

One of those who came forward was Mr James Hicks, an employee of the Cumberland Paper Mills, who, in an amazing feat of memory, claimed to have seen a man acting suspiciously on the Sunday morning of the Eight-Hour Day long weekend nearly three years previously. Mr Hicks had carefully looked at the photograph of Eugenia as a male in *The Sun* newspaper before he contacted the police. After Hicks came forward, Detective Robson organised a farcical pretence of an identification parade. On 22 July 1920, at the Central police station, he placed Eugenia, dressed as a male, in a line-up with fifteen to twenty men, and then brought in Mr Hicks who, as would be expected after seeing her image in the press, identified Eugenia as the person he had seen at the Mills in 1917. As if this charade was not a sufficient travesty, Detective Robson then took Eugenia (still dressed as a male) with Mr Hicks and two other police officers to the vicinity of the Cumberland Paper Mills. Detective Robson then asked

Mr Hicks to indicate where he had seen the man in 1917. Mr Hicks pointed to a spot near the mills and said to Eugenia, 'That is where I saw you on that morning,' to which Eugenia made no reply. She was then asked by Detective Robson whether she knew the locality, and she replied, 'I have never been here in my life.' A little while later, however, she informed the police that many years earlier, as Harry Crawford, she had worked at the nearby Chicago Flour Mills for a week. This was considered by Detective Robson to be an inadvertent disclosure by Eugenia of her familiarity with the area. The reality was that to get to the flour mills from the south, one did not need to go past the paper mills, which were several hundred yards up Stringybark Creek.

On 7 July 1920, Detective Watkins travelled to Hay to visit a dentist, Mr Harry Vernon, who had previously had a dental practice in Lane Cove Road, Wahroonga, in the same premises where Dr Gother Clarke practised. The police were seeking to ascertain whether Mr Vernon had made either of the two dental sets that had been found with Annie Birkett's body in October 1917. According to the *Evening News* on 8 July, Mr Vernon remembered Annie Birkett, but could not say for certain whether he had done any dental work for her.

The Truth on 18 July reported that:

> *The upper set of false teeth found near the charred remains discovered off Mowbray Road, Chatswood, on October 2, 1917, have been identified by Mr J.J. McManus, a Balmain dentist, as having been made by him for a Mrs Birkett in 1913.*

Contrary to the earlier newspaper report, *The Truth* on 18 July also reported that:

> *Detective Sergeant Robson interview Dr Vernon, of the T & G buildings, who identified the lower set of teeth as his work. Detective Robson stated yesterday that the police enquiries were almost complete, but tomorrow and Tuesday they expected to glean some important information from enquiries that were afoot.*

At around this same time, the police interviewed the dealer who in October 1917 had bought most of the furniture from Harry Crawford's home at Balmain.

Despite the fact that Harry Birkett and Lily Nugent had told the police about Josephine Falleni's existence, it was not until 14 July that Detective

Watkins managed to locate her living in Harris Street, Pyrmont. She was described by the *Evening News* as 'a slight, pleasantly spoken, and good-looking young woman'. The police were hopeful that the discovery of Eugenia Falleni's daughter would yield them much important information. The newspapers disclosed to the public the sensational information that Josephine Falleni had known for many years that Harry Crawford was her mother.

On 14 July, during one of Eugenia's many appearances in the Central Police Court, the police prosecutor requested an adjournment, stating, 'The police have yet a number of enquiries to make in the matter.' What he was referring to was an application to the City Coroner for the exhumation of Annie Birkett's body, which was heard on the following day when Superintendent Bannan informed the court that 'facts had come to the knowledge of the police that made a more comprehensive examination of the body desirable'. The City Coroner, Mr Jamieson, issued a warrant authorising the exhumation of Annie Birkett's remains.

The exhumation took place on Wednesday 21 July. The coffin, bearing the inscription *The body of an unknown woman* was transported to the City Morgue in The Rocks and made available for a further forensic examination by the very same doctors who had conducted the first autopsy in 1917: Drs Palmer and Sheldon. However, on this occasion, as opposed to 1917, the police prefaced their request for a further autopsy with the information that they suspected foul play.

Once the coffin had arrived in The Rocks, in an unwarranted act of gross insensitivity, police took Eugenia Falleni from Long Bay to the Morgue, placed her in a nearby room where she could hear the hammering of the coffin being opened, and then ushered her into the autopsy room where she was shown Annie's degraded remains, now nearly three years old, and informed by the police: 'This is the woman you murdered.' If the reason for this bizarre episode was that the police were hoping for Eugenia to break down and make a solemn confession, they were sorely disappointed. She barely looked at the scant remains and kept silent throughout, realising that the police were anxious for her to incriminate herself. *The Truth* on Sunday 25 July blandly reported that after the exhumation, 'Falleni was taken to the Morgue and saw the remains'.

When the coffin was opened at the Morgue, the body was understandably very decayed. None of the charred sections remained. Prior to the second autopsy, a Dr Edwards attended at the Morgue to take X-ray photographs[1] of Annie Birkett's body to see if any bullets had been missed during the first autopsy. This had been prompted by the finding of the revolver with two fired cartridge cases during the search of the portmanteau at Harry and Lizzie Crawford's house in Stanmore. Because the body had been burned, it was thought that the original autopsy may have missed any bullet wounds, and the decayed state of the body now certainly prevented any such wounds being evident. However, the X-ray photographs did not reveal any bullets. Samples from the body were taken for analysis to detect any poisons, but none were found.

Drs Palmer and Sheldon conducted the second post-mortem examination on 22 July 1920. Dr Palmer noted their findings, again in his own handwriting, on the same pages of the Register of Post-Mortem Examinations as the original 1917 report. He wrote:

> This body was exhumed, brought to the morgue and the coffin opened in Dr Palmer's presence on 21 July. As previously arranged with Dr Sheldon, a number of X-rays were taken by Dr J.S. Edwards and on the 22nd the parts were examined in more detail by Drs Sheldon and Palmer.
>
> The body was wrapped in a blanket (?) or cloth. The soft parts of the body were caked in adipocere[2] which was either separated or could be easily separated from the bones. The skull, from which the calvarium[3] has previously been removed, was practically bare except in one orbit.
>
> On the right side behind at right angles of the lambdoidal suture[4] there was a linear crack through the parietal bone – 1 inch from the squamous – two and a quarter inches long on the outer surface and about one and three quarter inches on the inner surface (no section of this made at this stage). The lambdoidal suture below this was apparently more open than on the other side. Just before reaching the jugular process, the crack extended into the foramen magnum.[5] No displacement or fragmentation along the cracks.
>
> In the cranial cavity there are three cracks in the body of the sphenoid bone,[6] and one in each mascella,[7] etc. – probably due to the burning of the body. The rest of the body showed nothing of note and portions were forwarded to the government analyst for examination.

Having found 'no signs of violence' during the first autopsy, Drs Palmer and Sheldon found no fewer than seven fractures in the skull during the second autopsy. They were quite convinced that six of these were due to the heat of the fire, however, both of them were suspicious about one of them. It was a linear crack in a thick portion at the back of the skull towards the right side. Dr Palmer was of the view that this fracture 'was undoubtedly due to violence'. Dr Sheldon believed that it 'was more likely to have been caused by violence'. Both doctors still thought that death had been caused by burning. The clear inference from the second autopsy was that Annie Birkett had been violently struck on the back of her head, rendering her unconscious or senseless, and then killed by being burned alive in the fire. This was to have very significant consequences at Eugenia Falleni's subsequent trial for the murder of Annie Birkett.

On 24 July, the remains of Annie Birkett were reinterred at the Woronora Cemetery. This time, a proper funeral was held, attended by her son Harry, her sister Lily, other family members and friends. Eugenia, naturally, did not attend. She was preoccupied with her incarceration in the Women's Reformatory at Long Bay and the prospect of committal proceedings in the Police Court that had been fixed for three weeks hence. She was also anguished that Lizzie had not been to visit her or even sent her a letter. Eugenia had seen some of the newspaper articles about her arrest and the police investigation and concluded, correctly, that Lizzie had fled Sydney and abandoned their relationship.

PART II

LEGAL PROCEEDINGS

CHAPTER 15

THE PRESS

Eugenia Falleni's arrest caused the press to engage in a feeding frenzy of unrivalled proportions, as though she were a recently discovered hominoid species that had never been seen before and was now on public exhibition at the zoo. The press reports created an enormous amount of interest in her case throughout Australia, as well as in New Zealand[1] and as far away as Italy. At her first court appearance on 6 July 1920, journalists went quite feral, focusing almost exclusively upon her appearance and attire. The *Daily Telegraph* reported that 'not an inch of space was to spare in the portion of the court set apart for the public'.

Eugenia was represented in the committal proceedings in the Police Court by Edward George (Maddocks) Cohen, a private Sydney solicitor practising in Elizabeth Street, Sydney, whose services had been retained on her behalf by the Legal Aid Office. Legal Aid would pay for a solicitor while a murder matter was before a magistrate in the Police Court, and then if it was sent to the Supreme Court for a trial by jury they would pay for both a barrister and solicitor.[2] The committal proceedings are very important, because they are an opportunity for the defendant's legal representative to test the strength of the prosecution case, and if it is found wanting, a good advocate might convince a magistrate to dismiss the charge rather than sending it for trial. The magistrate therefore acts as a gatekeeper to ensure that only matters in which there is sufficient evidence go to trial by jury in the superior courts.[3] Even if a matter is sent for trial, it is an opportunity to get some good answers that can later be used at the trial during cross-examination of Crown witnesses.

Maddocks Cohen was born in 1867 into a Jewish family in Launceston, where his father, Lewis Cohen, was an auctioneer. Maddocks's grandfather, Henry Cohen (1790–1867), was a Jewish tailor and clothing salesman from London, who in 1833 had been convicted on dubious evidence of receiving stolen promissory notes and sentenced to fourteen years transportation to

New South Wales. In August 1833, Henry boarded a 'bay ship',[4] arriving in Sydney after a journey of 114 days. His wife and ten children arrived aboard another ship three days later. Henry was sent to Port Macquarie, where he was assigned as a servant to Major Archibald Clunes Innes. Henry was granted a ticket-of-leave[5] seven years later in 1840, and he and his wife moved to Sydney in 1845. By the 1850s, the Cohen family owned two schooners plying trade between Sydney and Port Macquarie. Henry died in Sydney in 1867. His son, Lewis, who had been born in London, remained in Port Macquarie after his parents left for Sydney. Lewis, his wife and twelve children moved to Launceston in 1856. In 1871, Lewis and his family moved to Sydney, where Maddocks received his education at Sydney Grammar School[6] and Sydney University. Maddocks was admitted as a solicitor in 1891 and married Mary Jane Hopgood in 1898. They had five children. Maddocks was a very dapper man, with a beautifully coiffured moustache which he kept in place using pomade.[7]

Having been admitted as a solicitor, Maddocks Cohen set up a legal practice. He also formed a company with some partners to patent certain articles to be used in the sheep and cattle industry. The company borrowed money at high interest rates and the business eventually failed. On 2 February 1902, Maddocks Cohen precipitously left Sydney without telling his staff. He travelled to Valparaiso in Argentina where he worked for eight months as an accountant, bookkeeper and English-language teacher. While he was overseas, his assets were sold and he was normally put into bankruptcy owing £2772. A payment of five shillings in the pound was made to his creditors.[8] Maddocks returned to Sydney in March 1905 where, because of his lengthy absence, he had to reapply to the Supreme Court for permission to practise law. At the Supreme Court hearing, the Chief Justice was concerned that Cohen may have absconded overseas to defeat his creditors, but the solicitor representing Cohen stated that he had departed before any bankruptcy proceedings had commenced and that his fare overseas had been paid by his father. By that stage, all of his creditors had accepted the payment of five shillings in the pound and the Bankruptcy Court had approved his release. Still harbouring reservations, the Chief Justice stood the matter over until the following year, when Cohen was finally given permission to resume his practice as a solicitor. By the time of Eugenia Falleni's committal proceedings in 1920, Maddocks Cohen had already amassed considerable experience in the Police Courts. Indeed, he had appeared in 1914 for one of the three defendants in the committal proceedings in the famous Eveleigh Holdup case.[9]

When Maddocks Cohen appeared in court on 6 July 1920 for the first mention of Eugenia Falleni's matter, never before in his many years as a lawyer had he seen such a commotion. He felt incredibly distressed for his client. He informed the magistrate that he would be making no application for bail, and the magistrate adjourned the proceedings until 14 July.

The Sun reported the first court hearing the same afternoon:

The accused woman was strangely interesting. She bore an extraordinary resemblance to a man, for facially she is masculine, and she wore a man's clothes. In the dock she appeared distinctly nervous. With her left-hand she wears a gold band ring on the little finger – she 'fiddled' with the dock rail. In her right hand she carried a grey felt hat. Her hair is almost black, clipped short, of course, and neatly brushed in part on the left side. Her head and face are remarkably small. The face, particularly around the mouth, is considerably wrinkled, and suggests that she is older than her stated age – 45. Her complexion is sallow, and her small eyes are brown.[10]

The strange woman's clothing consisted of a well-worn dark grey cloth sac suit, a white tennis shirt, and neatly tied green Broadway tie. Her well-polished boots seemed about size 6, and were of patent leather, with dull uppers. She is of medium build.

The *Evening News* on the same day carried her photograph in male attire, which, as previously stated, played a sinister role in encouraging sighting witnesses to come forward and identify her as a person in male clothing whom they claimed to have seen in the Lane Cove River Park back in 1917.[11] The *Daily Telegraph* carried her photo the following day, noting that 'the woman is facially masculine, though a close scrutiny betrayed feminine characteristics'.

On 8 July, the *Evening News*, under the heading 'Strange Attachment', reported on Eugenia's relationship with her current 'wife':

A feature of the case, fascinating in its revelation of the eccentricities of human nature, is the apparently sincere attachment which exists between Falleni and the woman who now passes as her wife. This woman has protested passionately to the police that Falleni is her dear and loving husband, and nothing will shake that statement. She protests an affection for Falleni which is astonishing in its strength and would be so even between man and wife.

The following day, the *Evening News* added this prurient detail of her story, which no doubt came from the police:

She says Falleni has been an ideal husband, and tells of a very happy married life. The woman has been so pestered by calls and sensation seekers since the arrest of her 'husband' that she has been forced to change her address.

The press took a remarkably superficial approach in their reporting of Eugenia's apparent reasons for leading life as a male. This report in *The Truth* on 11 July exemplified the shallowness of contemporary understanding of her gender issues:

Her hands were rough like a man's from the work she had been doing, and she said, according to the detectives, that her reason for assuming the personality of a man was that she thought it better to give up life as a woman, because they worked long hours for a small wage. She was quite competent to do the work of a hotel useful and other manual labour, and did it, working fewer hours for better money than she would have received had she 'remained' a woman.

It is stated Falleni is an inveterate cigarette smoker, and is very fond of cigars. It is alleged that she is also a whisky drinker, being particularly fond of 'Johnnie Walker'.

On 14 July, at the second hearing before a magistrate, the police were not ready to proceed and applied to have the matter adjourned until 22 July. Maddocks Cohen was furious that his client was being paraded in front of the public and the press each time there was a court appearance. He was determined to spare Eugenia as much trauma as he could, and so he implored the court not to adjourn the matter to the date that the police were seeking because he claimed that they would not be ready. He unequivocally stated that his client 'did not wish to be paraded before the court in the meantime'.

The most atrocious article of all was in *The Sun* on 14 July. It stated:

If Eugenia Falleni, who has been designated the man-woman, were taken into the forum like the Romans were in bygone days, probably the whole of the metropolis would turn out to get a glimpse of her. This was the impression conveyed by the huge crowd that assembled at the Central Police Court this morning.

What *The Sun* failed to add was that the Sydney press was metaphorically doing to Eugenia what would have been done in Roman times – feeding her to the lions.

The committal proceedings of Eugenia Falleni for the murder of Annie Birkett took place at the Central Police Court in Liverpool Street on 16 August 1920. Mr Roderick (Rod) M Kidston, a prosecuting officer in the Crown Solicitor's Office, appeared for the Crown. Mr Maddocks Cohen appeared for the defendant. The proceedings were heard before Magistrate Mr Gale.

One of the witnesses who gave evidence at the committal proceedings was Acting Inspector Maze, formerly a sergeant stationed at Chatswood. He gave evidence of the finding of the body near the Cumberland Mills. In answer to Mr Kidston, he said that there were a number of tracks in the locality and that it was a place frequented by picnickers. He said that the spot where the body was found was only a little distance off one of those tracks. In answer to questions from Mr Cohen, this officer admitted that there were no signs of a struggle and that at the Coroner's Inquest he had said that he thought that the deceased woman had either deliberately or accidentally set fire to herself, and that it was more likely accidental.

Harry Birkett, Annie's son, gave evidence that back in 1917, shortly after his mother's disappearance, the accused, who couldn't read, showed him a newspaper photograph of a body that had been found in the bush with some shoes, and asked the boy to read the words of the article to him. Kidston produced a copy of the *Evening News* from October 1917 that contained a photograph of some shoes that had been found on the body in the Lane Cove River Park. Harry Birkett said that the shoes in the article were similar to ones that had been owned by his mother. He told the magistrate that he couldn't remember the date of the newspaper article which the accused had asked him to read, but he was shown a copy of the relevant day's paper by Mr Kidston and said that the photograph in that issue was similar to the one that he had seen in 1917.

Two days later, on the second day of the hearing, 18 August, Mr Kidston recalled Harry Birkett to give further evidence about the same newspaper article. During this further evidence, Kidston and Cohen almost came to blows, demonstrating vividly how heated the atmosphere had become between these two opposing lawyers. The *Evening News* reported the interchange between them:

> Mr Kidston (*reading from the newspaper that had previously been shown to Harry Birkett*): 'It was on page 2 of the issue of —'
> 'I object,' shouted Mr Cohen, *and snatched the paper from Mr Kidston's hand*. 'He was going to read the date out. I have strong reasons for objecting to it.'

Mr Kidston: 'You've got strong hands. I don't know what your reasons are, but there is no reason to resort to violence.'
(Mr Gale admitted the newspaper into evidence.)

One of the many witnesses to give evidence at the committal proceedings was Mr George Smith, a box-maker who had previously lived near Harry and Annie. It was an important part of the prosecution case to prove that the relationship between the couple had deteriorated in 1917 after Annie had discovered that Harry was not a man. George Smith described them in this way.

Mr Smith: The Crawfords seemed to be two extremes. One day they would be jangling,[12] and the next day they would be on the veranda, as affectionate as a young couple.
Mr Cohen: On the whole, they lived on affectionate terms?
Mr Smith: I suppose every couple has a jangle now and again.'

On the third day of the committal proceedings, 19 August, Eugenia's daughter, Josephine, was called to give evidence. Her arrival at court aroused a great deal of attention. As the only person who had known Eugenia's identity all the way through, she was seen as having a unique insider's perspective on this strange case. However, the newspapers were disappointed if they thought they would get some good photographic opportunities from her. She wore a grey veil over her face while she was at court – even while giving evidence. Josephine clearly found the whole experience traumatic and she cried literally the whole way through her evidence. It was clear that she was a reluctant witness against her mother and that the whole experience was traumatic, although it was equally apparent that there was no closeness between mother and daughter, as they exchanged not even a single glance while Josephine was in the courtroom.

The *Evening News* on the same day reported Josephine's appearance in this way.

The principal witness in the Falleni murder case today was the man-woman's daughter. She remained veiled in court and sobbed profusely while giving her evidence. She was led into court sobbing by another woman, and given a seat in front of the witness box. She was smartly dressed in a dark blue costume, trimmed with fur, a small black hat and a grey motor veil. This she carefully kept down over her face all the time, so that not a *glimpse of her features could be obtained. She sobbed all the time she was giving her answers, and her replies were difficult to understand.*

One part of Josephine's evidence in the Police Court was of particular significance. It was an important aspect of the prosecution case to prove that Annie Birkett had found out Harry's true identity, because the risk of Annie exposing Harry as a woman was alleged to be the motive for the killing. The evidence from Annie's sister, Lily, was insufficient to prove this knowledge. Josephine, however, was reluctantly able to provide the missing link. The *Daily Telegraph* reported her evidence:

In 1917 I met my mother, and my mother told me, 'Everything is unsettled now and upside down. Annie has discovered I am a woman. We are going to sell out, and I am going my way, and Annie is going her way.' My mother seemed very agitated and upset.

Another witness to give evidence in the committal proceedings was the government medical officer, Dr Palmer. He, of course, had conducted two autopsies on Annie Birkett's body, separated in time by three years, from which he had given two different opinions about the cracks in the skull. As previously stated, his original opinion had been that the body showed no signs of violence. Mr Kidston, exhibiting a level of fairness that probably exceeded his duty as a prosecutor, elicited the doctor's previous opinion and sought to explore the ramifications of it. The newspapers reported these important questions by Mr Kidston:

Mr Kidston: Q: Would it have been possible for the woman to have fallen asleep and caught fire?
Dr Palmer: A: I think it would have been.
Mr Kidston: Q: Did you notice any signs of a struggle?
Dr Palmer: A: I was not so much interested in that aspect.

After three days, the committal proceedings concluded with the Magistrate committing Eugenia Falleni for trial in the Supreme Court on the charge of murder.

Following the committal proceedings, the media frenzy about Eugenia Falleni's case died down to a large degree, due to the risk of prejudicing her impending trial by jury. If any of the newspapers had published material that could prejudice the jury, they faced the prospect of being prosecuted for contempt of court. This was a huge dampener on what they could publish. What had been a 'free for all' before the committal proceedings became dignified silence after. All the press could do was to wait patiently for the trial.

CHAPTER 16

JUDGE, CROWN PROSECUTOR AND DEFENCE COUNSEL

The system of criminal justice, which the Australian States inherited from England, is called the 'adversarial system'. It is based on the premise that the best method for ascertaining the truth is to have two opposing barristers – one representing each side – with each one calling their own witnesses and testing the witnesses of the other through cross-examination. Sitting above both barristers is the impartial judge, who plays no role in the presentation of evidence or the ultimate verdict, but who acts as an umpire in the event of any differences between the parties and also informs the jury of the applicable law. The ultimate decision is made by a randomly selected jury of twelve citizens who base their decision on the evidence that is presented and tested in front of them by the parties. This is the essence of the adversarial system.

The efficacy of the adversarial system to arrive at the truth is predicated upon what is called 'equality of arms'. As in a joust or duel or military campaign or boxing match, the concept of equality of arms refers to the two opposing parties having a rough equivalence in the forces at their disposal. In the courtroom context, this means that the two opposing barristers should be somewhat evenly matched in terms of their ability and experience. This is not always easy to achieve, especially if there is a disparity between the financial means of the parties. For legal aid to be effective, it must provide representation for an accused person at a level that is appropriate for the seriousness of the charge and sufficient to match the representation that has been allocated to the case by the prosecution.

The principal participants in the trial of Eugenia Falleni, apart from the accused and the twelve men of the jury who judged her,[1] were the judge who presided over her trial, the Crown Prosecutor who presented the case against her and the defence counsel who represented her. Each of these men played a pivotal role in her trial and its outcome. As this trial attracted so much press attention, these three key players were very much in the public eye for the duration of her trial.

The judge presiding over the trial of Eugenia Falleni was none other than the Chief Justice of New South Wales, Sir William Portus Cullen KCMG LLD. Sir William was without doubt the most highly regarded jurist of his day. An entirely self-made man who had risen to great heights from very humble origins, he was universally respected and admired. William (Bill) Portus Cullen was born in 1855 at Mt Johnstone near Jamberoo. Despite his father's attempt to curtail his education so that he could be put to rural work, William insisted on walking miles each day to the nearest school, at Kiama, where he excelled in his studies. He left home at age twenty to enter the University of Sydney on a scholarship. In 1880, he graduated BA with first-class honours in classics. Two years later, he was awarded an MA degree and three years after that he obtained his bachelor of laws degree.

Cullen initially decided to pursue an academic career and, in furtherance of that ambition, in 1887 he obtained his doctorate of laws. Amazingly, he then applied for a lectureship in mathematics at the University of Adelaide. When he was rejected for that position, he gave up his plans for full-time academia and decided instead to pursue a career at the New South Wales Bar. He was admitted as a barrister on 30 April 1883.

In December 1891, Bill Cullen married Eliza Jane White at Carrington on Port Stephens. They set up a household in what was then the new Sydney harbourside suburb of Balmoral, where they built a stately home they called 'Tregoyd'. At this home, William was able to pursue his interest in growing Australian native plants and wildflowers. Bill Cullen entered politics in 1891, when he was elected as a member of the New South Wales Legislative Assembly for the electorate of Camden. He was defeated at the next election in 1894, however in the following year he was appointed a member of the Legislative Council, a position he retained for fifteen years. He was a very strong advocate in favour of the Australian Federation and, prior to its achievement in 1901, he lost no opportunity to express his views supporting it. After Federation, he was a keen proponent of the creation of the High Court of Australia and, unusually for the mainly conservative lawyers of his day, he favoured the abolition of appeals to the Privy Council in London.

Cullen had a solid, long-term association with Sydney University. He was a member of its Senate for many years. He was Vice-Chancellor of the University from 1908 to 1910 and, at the time of Eugenia Falleni's trial in 1920, he had already been Chancellor for six years. Cullen was appointed a King's Counsel (KC) in 1905. After this appointment, he regularly appeared as counsel in the High Court. The first Chief Justice of the High Court, Sir Samuel Griffith, regarded him as one of the finest barristers then practising before that court.

Bill Cullen was appointed as the Chief Justice of New South Wales on 14 February 1910. He was the first Australian-born occupant of that office. His appointment was widely acclaimed, both in the legal profession and the general community. He was knighted in 1911 and appointed KCMG in 1912. As Chief Justice, he was considered to be 'courageous in his judgements and rapid in his determination'. As part of his role, he also served as Lieutenant-Governor in the absence of the Governor. In 1911, as Lieutenant-Governor, he faced a particularly difficult constitutional problem.[2] The Legislative Assembly was evenly divided and the acting Premier requested Cullen to prorogue (dissolve) the House. Cullen initially refused, but finally acceded to the request when he failed to secure the appointment of any Ministry able to govern. The subsequent election produced another deadlock, which was only resolved when an opposition member defected to become Speaker of the House.

By the time of Eugenia Falleni's trial in 1920, Bill Cullen had been Chief Justice of New South Wales for a decade. His position on the bench and throughout the legal community was pre-eminent.

The Crown Prosecutor who conducted the trial of Eugenia Falleni was William (Bill) Thomas Coyle KC. Bill Coyle was born on the Sofala goldfields in 1868. Both his parents came to New South Wales from Ireland. During the gold rush, his father operated very successful hotels at Hill End and Sofala. His parents then came to Sydney, where his father bought another hotel and, for a time, was an alderman on the Redfern Council. William Coyle attended St Ignatius College, Riverview, where he was the captain of the first fifteen, a rower in the school's first crew, and captain of boats. From Riverview, he went to the University of Sydney, where he obtained a double blue in rowing and rugby. This was quite an accomplishment for a young man who was only five-foot-nine in height and weighed only nine-stone-seven.[3] He was one of the founders of the Sydney University Sports Union. He obtained his BA degree with honours in 1891.

There followed a very difficult period for Bill Coyle. At around the time of his graduation from the Arts Faculty, his father suddenly died. He decided not long afterwards that he would go to England to commence his legal studies. Shortly before leaving Sydney, he made arrangements to meet a woman who had been a close friend at university and who was considerably older than he was, in order to farewell her before his departure. When he arrived for their meeting at the appointed time and place, he discovered that she had brought with her a rather suspicious-looking clergyman. Without any explanation or warning, this woman announced to Coyle that the Minister was going to marry them then and there. Coyle firmly declined her offer of instant matrimony and promptly departed, leaving the woman and the clergyman behind. Judging by the woman's actions, one assumes that in some way she felt that Coyle had compromised her virtue. Even in those days of fixed views about sexual propriety and the solemnity of promises to marry, her actions must have seemed quite bizarre. However, the upshot of it was that the woman subsequently initiated an action for breach of promise of marriage, which resulted in Coyle having to appear in court,[4] where her allegations of an engagement to marry were peremptorily dismissed. This episode slightly delayed Coyle's departure for England, but it did not prevent him from ultimately leaving.

Coyle's problems did not end there. After proceeding to England together with his mother, while both of them were overseas, the solicitor handling the estate of his late father misappropriated a very large sum of money. It was perhaps the combination of all these unfortunate events in close proximity to each other that later propelled Bill Coyle in the direction of a career in criminal law.

His mother returned to Australia, and Coyle undertook a law degree in England, becoming a member of the English Bar in 1896. It was said that his genial disposition made him many friends there. In London he met and married his wife, Margaret. He returned with her to Sydney in 1902 and was admitted to the New South Wales Bar in that year. Bill and Margaret Coyle initially settled in a home called 'Selbourne' in Randwick and later moved to 'Woodbridge' at Double Bay. They had five children. Palm Beach was Coyle's weekend and holiday playground. He used to wear ragged shorts and adopt a general beachcomber appearance, which caused great embarrassment to his young daughters.

Over the next eighteen years, Coyle built up a very sound practice as a junior counsel at the New South Wales Bar, mainly in the common law and criminal law jurisdictions. On many occasions in the period 1913 to 1916 he did country circuits as an occasional Crown Prosecutor, instructed by an officer from the Clerk of the Peace Office. Those circuits included Armidale, Grenfell and Albury. It was said that Coyle would sometimes annoy defence counsel with his perseverance and sardonic manner.

The year 1920 was momentous for William Coyle. On 26 August, he was appointed a King's Counsel (KC). Just two days later, he was appointed as the very first Senior Crown Prosecutor for New South Wales.[5] Six weeks later, on 5 October, he commenced what many have called the case of the century – the trial of Eugenia Falleni.

Upon his appointment as the State's first Senior Crown Prosecutor, under the heading *A New Method of Prosecuting*, one of the daily newspapers had this to say:

> *The methods of 'Billy' Coyle, the Mother State's new Crown Prosecutor, have struck the average defending practitioner like a cold douche. Until Coyle's advent it was the custom to 'open' the prosecution's case in the most perfunctory manner. The jury had to glean the facts from the evidence as the case went on. The defender made it his business to prevent continuity in the story. By means of interruptions, objections, arguments, the interposition of witnesses out of their turn, and a score of similar devices, a skilled and determined defender would reduce a tale which in itself was symmetrical to chaos. In the result, the bemused jury, being in doubt, would acquit.*
>
> *Coyle makes a point of 'opening' with precision, at length, and in detail. From the jump, the jury gets a grip of the case that cannot be shaken. As a consequence, many an errant citizen who would otherwise be amongst us, will languish within stone walls.*

Coyle's work ethic as Senior Crown Prosecutor must have been prodigious, leading to newspaper articles like this one, under the heading *The Legal Bulldog*:

> *One who has been before the public eye a great deal lately is Mr W.T. Coyle KC, the Crown Prosecutor in the four sensational murder trials which have been conducted at Darlinghurst during the past fortnight.*
>
> *Of a genial disposition, Mr Coyle is noted for his tenacity of purpose, and once he gets his Bulldog grip on a witness it is not much that the witness can withhold. Nevertheless he is eminently fair-minded, and never yet has he 'put one over' on a witness. Considered one of the cleverest cross-examiners in a prosecution, it never takes him long to get the truth from a witness.*

It is not known whether Coyle's nickname at the Bar – 'Bulldog' – derived from this newspaper article or preceded it. As a Crown Prosecutor, Coyle continued his sardonic ways that had so infuriated defence counsel in the past. One newspaper reported the following:

Darlinghurst Court philosophy is that Mr W.T. Coyle KC, the State's Senior Crown Prosecutor, is most dangerous when he smiles. Yesterday his smiles caused trouble. Rare, indeed, is the day when Mr Coyle does not smile. Mr Coyle really cannot help it. Possibly, he came smiling into a smiling world. But Mr S. Mack KC objects to Crown Prosecutors smiling. He objected yesterday in the criminal court. Mr Mack, without a smile, suggested that Mr Coyle's smile conveyed a sinister meaning to the jury. The novel objection made the Chief Justice smile. Smiling jurymen were told by his Honour that as sensible men they would not decide the case on the smiles of Counsel. Mr Coyle's smile widened. Mr Mack again protested. He thought that the Crown Prosecutor should not smile. But, his Honour, this time without a smile, asked what was the use of Mr Mack objecting to Mr Coyle smiling. 'I cannot watch counsel's face all the time' the Chief Justice assured Mr Mack. With a smile, Mr Coyle said he would try to oblige Mr Mack by not smiling.

Another newspaper feted Coyle as 'the Man of the Week'. After referring to several of his cases, the newspaper noted this:

If they could canvass those who have stood in the dock with Coyle KC prosecuting, they would admit that they have always had a fair deal. Offer no quarter, but just as certainly no trickery to get a conviction. And many a man who has left the dock by way of acquittal, but with nothing and with no prospect of a job, has found a few shillings slipped in his hand by his late 'enemy'.

Because Eugenia Falleni did not have sufficient money to pay for her own private barrister, her defence counsel was assigned to her by an officer in the Attorney-General's Department who was responsible for Legal Aid.

In New South Wales, the *Poor Prisoners Defence Act* of 1907 allowed any person committed for trial for an indictable offence to apply to either a magistrate or a judge for legal aid for their defence. If the judicial officer was satisfied that such person was without adequate means and that it was 'in the interests of justice' that legal aid should be supplied, he would certify accordingly to the Attorney-General, who would then arrange for the accused person's representation and for the payment of the expenses of all defence witnesses. In New South Wales, government-funded legal aid was provided in the form of 'Crown Assignments', which allowed barristers to represent defendants in serious criminal matters for fixed but reduced fees. This assistance scheme had been received with some measure of reticence and hostility by the legal profession, by reason of the meagre remuneration and a fear of the implications of such a scheme on the profitability of the legal sector.[6] The pool of counsel willing to accept these assignments was often limited to those who had the least amount of work.

The barrister who was assigned to represent Eugenia Falleni at her trial was Archibald (Archie) McDonell. Maddocks Cohen, who had done such a splendid job of her committal, was relegated at the trial to the position of McDonell's instructing solicitor. Archibald McDonell was born at Mondrook in the Manning River district of New South Wales on 15 September 1868. He may well have spoken Gaelic, because his two paternal grandparents, Donald and Jane McDonell, couldn't speak English. Those grandparents had come to Australia in 1837 from Knoydart in Scotland, where they were farmers. They first settled at Belltrees near Scone, where apparently there was so much 'trouble' with the local indigenous population that the family soon moved to Narragut (King Island) near Maitland. From there they went to Miller's Forest and then to the Manning River area, where Donald McDonell purchased two blocks on the River at Mandrook. There they engaged in farming activities and became one of the pre-eminent families in the district.

Archibald's parents were Charles Paladius McDonell and his wife Sarah. In 1863, Charles McDonell had a magnificent hotel custom-built in the main street of Taree. He named it the Caledonian Hotel[7] and he owned and operated it for ten years. It was known as the finest hotel in the region – so fine that the famous bushranger known as 'Captain Thunderbolt'[8] used to stay there before he became widely known. The Earl of Belmore,[9] when he was Governor of New South Wales, also chose to stay there when he visited the region and a grand vice-regal ball was held in his honour in the upstairs portion of the hotel. Archibald McDonell's parents were therefore important members of Australia's equivalent of the British landed gentry – later called the 'squattocracy' – who were large landowners, many of them from upper and middle-class English and Scottish families, with extensive pastoral interests, an elevated socio-economic status and often an involvement in the breeding and racing of horses.

Charles Paladius McDonell owned a racehorse by the name of Zulu, whose short body and over-long legs hardly impressed the experts. His early racing career, from his maiden run at the Clarence River races in July 1880, was confined to the Northern Rivers district of New South Wales, where his record was quite mediocre. But Charles McDonell never lost faith in his horse. In 1881 he was brought down from the country to race at the Randwick Autumn Carnival, where he made a miserable showing.

Although he had absolutely no form to warrant his nomination, Zulu was entered in the Melbourne Cup of that year and awarded the minimum weight of five stone seven pounds. The weekend before the Melbourne Cup, Zulu finished second-last in the Essendon Stakes. What interested the bookmakers and bettors most was that when he pulled up after the race he appeared to be lame. Many fans could actually see the swelling in his offside fore fetlock. That night, Zulu's odds in the betting for the Cup quickly diminished to 100/1. What only Charles McDonell and trainer Stan Lamond knew was that every time the horse ran, the swelling would come up, followed by a rapid return to normal after a rest. They allowed rumourmongers to spread the word that Zulu was virtually a cripple and could safely be written off as a possible Cup winner. On the day of the Melbourne Cup, nobody noticed that at the last minute there was a huge betting splurge in which Zulu was quietly backed, reducing the odds from 100/1 to 50/1.

The race got underway normally, with Zulu and his stable mate, Wheatear, both towards the back. Both of them began a swift move forward, when suddenly a dog ran under the fence in front of Wheatear, causing him and two other horses to fall and pushing another horse heavily against the fence. The jockey on this last horse was crushed against the rails and became the first jockey to be killed in a Melbourne Cup race. At this point, Zulu left his rivals labouring under their heavier weights and came charging down the outside overtaking all the other horses to win the race.[10] Afterwards, he limped off the course, however only half an hour later as the horse was being led away from the sheds all trace of the limp had disappeared. The newspapers nicknamed him 'the horse with the educated limp'. The Manning River district, particularly the towns of Cundletown, Wingham and Taree, went wild with excitement at the win by their horse. The following weekend Zulu broke down in the Victorian Racing Club handicap and was then walked home to Taree. After that, he raced only a few times locally around Taree and was used to pull a cart into town on market days.

It was at the Caledonian Hotel at Taree that Archibald McDonell was born in 1868. When Archie was five, his parents sold the hotel to the Bank of New South Wales and moved to the family property at Mandrook on the Manning River. Archie went to Mandrook Public School and in 1886 was sent to St Ignatius College, Riverview, in Sydney for the last three years of his secondary education.[11] He showed early promise as a student and in his second year at Riverview was dux of his class. He became a member of the four-oar rowing crew and was an active member of the rifle club. He was also a member of the College debating society where it was said of him that 'his logic and sound reasoning gained for him special renown and the forecast that he would go a long way in the public life of the world in which he lived'.[12]

Immediately after finishing his secondary education, Archie returned to Mandrook and took over the management of the family's estate, where he was known as 'Silent Mac', a rather unusual nickname for a man who later chose to become an advocate. He was known as a very modest, rather shy and scrupulously honest man. While managing the property at Mandrook, he entered into a formal agreement with his older brother, Charles McDonell Jnr, a solicitor in the Sydney firm of McDonell & Moffitt, to look after all the livestock and horses, including the now ageing Zulu. This arrangement lasted for several years, after which the family decided to subdivide the property and sell it. It was only then that Archie McDonell, having moved back to Sydney, began to study law at the University of Sydney.

Archibald McDonell was the ripe age of forty-two when, on 5 May 1910, he was admitted as a barrister of the Supreme Court of New South Wales. By that time, his mother and half of his siblings had died of tuberculosis. His sister Annie was a Good Samaritan Sister at Tempe and another sister Mary was also a nun. At the time of Eugenia Falleni's trial, Archibald was unmarried and living in an upstairs bedroom in 'Arundel', the stately home of his brother, Charles, in Victoria Square, Ashfield. It was said that Archibald had the invariable practice of retiring early each evening to read in his upstairs bedroom at Arundel, his favourite reading topics being criminology, psychology and psychiatry. He had a large library of scientific and medical books, including recent literature on the new field of sexology. He was said to have a good knowledge of metallurgy and the preparation of bones for cupellation[13] when making fire assays.

Smith's Weekly reported on another area in which McDonell was considered knowledgeable and erudite: the subject of 'sexual inversion', which was a very early, crude sexual classification that conflated homosexuality and transexualism:

No man at the NSW bar is a closer student of criminology than Mr A. McDonell. He has made a special study of 'inversion'[14] and has a remarkable library on this recondite subject. For years he was in touch with Sir Neville Howse, VC,[15] from whom he acquired a wide knowledge of anatomy and physiology.

This pre-existing knowledge of science, medicine, cupellation and the curious state of 'inversion' provides a clue as to why the Legal Aid office chose Archibald McDonell to represent Eugenia Falleni at her trial.

If Archibald McDonell was Zulu, then William Coyle was Phar Lap.[16] Viewing the trial of Eugenia Falleni as a boxing match, the two opposing counsel were in vastly different weight divisions, with McDonell being in the lightweight category while Coyle was a superheavyweight. The Crown Prosecutor was a highly skilful and experienced senior counsel, while the barrister representing the accused can only be described as pedestrian and unremarkable. People were saying behind McDonell's back that his lacklustre approach was no match for the razor-sharp advocacy of Coyle KC. The disparity between the two counsel was described in *Smith's Weekly* in this way:

> *To marshal evidence against Falleni, the Crown selected Mr Coyle, a most experienced barrister with an unsurpassed reputation as a successful prosecutor. To weaken the evidence in its doubtful phases, and to prove 'the benefit of the doubt' for the accused, the Crown chose Mr McDonell, a junior barrister, with no special reputation in the defence of persons charged with serious crime. There are ways in which the Crown can give a fairer run to persons on trial for their lives.[17]*

A review of the transcript of Eugenia Falleni's trial reveals frequent examples of the disparity between Coyle and McDonell. Maybe that is the reason why Eugenia Falleni's trial was replete with tactical errors and lost opportunities by her counsel. If McDonell had been the prosecutor and Coyle her defender, there is little doubt that the trial would have been conducted in a very different manner. The legal aid office failed to provide Eugenia Falleni with representation that was appropriate for a complex murder trial or which matched that of the prosecution. This demonstrates the undesirability of the situation in 1917, where the legal aid office was housed within the Attorney-General's Department – a department that was by nature more closely aligned with the prosecution than the defence.[18]

Rather than being provided with equality of arms, Eugenia Falleni was afforded a quantity of alms. The consequences for her were disastrous. Critical issues that should have been ventilated in evidence and in counsel's addresses were ignored. Too much attention was focused on vainly attacking the strongest parts of the Crown case. Prejudicial evidence that should have been objected to was allowed to go before the jury without challenge. While her counsel skilfully cross-examined the main expert witness about the cause of death, an area where the lawyer had much scientific knowledge, he unwisely sought to portray his client as a 'true sexual invert', thereby demonstrating that his understanding of her gender issues was just as meagre as that of the public. Eugenia Falleni was sent to trial against a background of highly prejudicial press coverage. She was represented by a barrister who was out of his depth in a trial for a murder that may never have happened.

CHAPTER 17

THE TRIAL BEGINS

William (Bill) Coyle KC sat back in his chair at the Bar table in the Central Criminal Court at Darlinghurst with the ease and confidence that came from twenty-two years of practice as a barrister at the New South Wales Bar, reinforced by his recent appointments as a King's Counsel and the State's first Senior Crown Prosecutor. His silk robes had only been purchased several weeks before when his appointment as a KC had been publicly announced. He was a short but lean and muscular man, with a determination in his eyes that could instil fear or confidence, depending on which side you were supporting. Although he had conducted many prior trials as a part-time prosecutor on country circuits, nothing he had previously done had fully prepared him for the trial of Eugenia Falleni, which was about to begin on this day, 5 October 1920.

Eugenia Falleni's defence counsel, Archibald (Archie) McDonell, had nowhere near the confidence and gravitas of Coyle KC. McDonell constantly checked his papers and occasionally consulted with his solicitor, Maddocks Cohen, who knew everything about the matter, having conducted the committal proceedings in the Police Court on his own. Maddocks had Eugenia's trust and confidence, and he had had to explain to her why he could not appear for her in a Supreme Court trial,[1] but he had reassured her that he would be there instructing their counsel who was the right man for the job.

The two knocks on the wood-panelled door behind the Bench heralded the entrance into the courtroom of Sir William Portus Cullen KCMG LLD, the Chief Justice of New South Wales, preceded by his tipstaff carrying the Royal Staff. Everyone stood as a mark of respect and waited for him to bow and sit down behind the raised Bench before they, in turn, bowed and sat down.

Sir William surveyed the overcrowded courtroom and called for the accused to be brought from the cells below, up a set of steep stone stairs directly into the dock in the middle of the courtroom. As Eugenia Falleni emerged from the underground complex of cells beneath the court, every single pair of eyes was trained upon her, followed moments later by suppressed gasps from the press and the public gallery. Eugenia had chosen to wear female clothing for her trial, no doubt on the recommendation of her counsel that there was no need to unnecessarily antagonise the jury. The press reported that Eugenia wore a white linen dress with a collar turned out over a black woollen coat, and black buttoned boots with brown cloth tops, with her closely cut hair hidden by a velvet black hat. Eugenia's demeanour had deteriorated markedly since her first court appearance, a mere three months earlier – due no doubt to her incarceration whilst on remand at the Women's Reformatory at Long Bay. With a few angry stares from the judge, there was soon a hushed courtroom, but the feelings of distaste towards the accused were palpable. A uniformed female prison officer sat in the dock a few feet away from her, and another one sat on a chair between the dock and the door at the back of the courtroom.

'Yes, Mr Crown,' said the judge, and Coyle rose purposefully to his feet. Next to Coyle sat Mr John Gonsalves, his instructing officer from the Clerk of the Peace Office. At the other end of the Bar table was Archie McDonell and his instructing solicitor, Maddocks Cohen. 'I present an indictment against Eugenia Falleni, your Honour,' said Coyle in a voice that let the whole room know that he was a King's Counsel who had earned his nickname of 'Bulldog' during years of practice in the higher courts. He handed over the traditional blue indictment which he had signed that morning to the uniformed court officer, who approached the bench and handed it to the judge's associate, who swung around and handed it to the judge. The judge carefully scanned the indictment and handed it back to his associate. Prompted by her counsel, Eugenia stood up.

The judge's associate stood up and read out the charge of murder. 'How say you: are you guilty or not guilty?'

'Not guilty, your Honour,' said Eugenia in a voice that hardly anyone in the gallery could hear. With these formalities, the trial had begun.

During the selection of jurors, McDonell challenged eleven of them and Coyle challenged only one. Once the twelve men[2] had been chosen and sworn, the judge spent the next ten minutes or so explaining the solemnity of the task before them and the need to approach the case dispassionately and without being influenced by family or friends, who were not there to listen to the evidence. The Chief Justice reminded the jury that the accused was on trial for murder and not for sexual perversion. He asked them to put aside any feelings of sympathy or prejudice for anyone associated with the trial and instructed them that they should totally disregard anything in the press that they may previously have read or might read during the trial. This was indeed a tall order, as the press had extensively reported the arrest of Eugenia Falleni and her committal proceedings in the Police Court. The whole of Australia knew about the 'Man-Woman case'.

Coyle quietly surveyed the twelve men chosen to serve on this jury and thought that he was not going to need his considerable powers of persuasion to convince this lot to overcome their natural reticence about convicting someone for murder, which would inevitably lead to the judge imposing the mandatory death sentence. Coyle had experienced other Supreme Court juries over the years agonising about whether or not they were going to convict an accused person, with that dreadful knowledge of what was likely to be the consequence. Not that many of the death sentences had actually been carried out in recent times, as the vast bulk of them had been commuted by the government to life imprisonment. In fact, not a single woman had been executed for more than three decades.

Coyle knew that this case had already excited an enormous amount of attention in the press throughout Australia, and even as far away as New Zealand and Italy. He knew that, despite the Chief Justice's warnings, the jurors would probably bring that background knowledge with them into the courtroom. This placed an extra burden on him as the Crown Prosecutor to make sure that he used language that was tempered and calm, and to rely entirely upon the forces of logic and rationality, rather than on any emotional appeal. In a case like this, the jury would be incensed enough at the evidence that he would be calling, so he would not need to appeal to their passions.

The main difficulty for the prosecutor in this case would be to convince the judge to allow all of the Crown's evidence to go before the jury. Coyle considered it fortunate that Sir William Cullen was presiding over this trial, as the Chief Justice was sure to bring his sound legal mind to bear on any tricky legal issues. Coyle knew Cullen quite well, from when Cullen had been a barrister himself. The New South Wales Bar was quite small, with only about a hundred and fifty barristers, of whom only roughly a hundred were regularly practising. The Chief Justice, he knew, would not permit the throng of press reporters, which had come from every part of Australia and which was now crowded into their special box in the courtroom, to turn this hearing into a circus. Coyle also knew that if any member of the public at the back of the courtroom got too excited and started disrupting the proceedings, Sir William would immediately have them thrown out. The object for both of them was to run this trial with dignity and professionalism and hopefully in a way that would not later be criticised by the Court of Criminal Appeal.

Coyle viewed with distaste the ghoulish members of the public, mainly female, who had queued for hours for one of the seats in the public gallery. For them, this was like a visit to the zoo, with an opportunity to view and glare at the main attraction: the accused Eugenia Falleni a.k.a. Harry Crawford. Never before, to his knowledge, had there been a case in New South Wales of a female who had lived undetected for so many years as a male, or the reverse for that matter.

In the absence of Mrs Lizzie Crawford, the accused's second 'wife', who had disappeared and so could not testify as to the convincing nature of Crawford's charade, Coyle knew that one of the difficult tasks for him would be to convince the jurors that this accused had lived with Annie Birkett in a state of full matrimony for some years without his wife having the slightest realisation of his true gender. How could either wife not have known? How could he explain to the members of the jury the technique that the 'husband' had used to engage in intimate sexual relations with his wife, without running the risk of scandalising everyone in the courtroom? This aspect of the case had not previously been mentioned in the press – not out of a sense of propriety, as the press had little enough of that, but because it had not been led in evidence at the committal. The eminently fair Mr Kidston had considered that it was highly prejudicial and hardly probative, and unnecessary to secure a committal for trial.

The main peril that he feared was that some of the jurors might mistakenly think that the deceased wife must have known all along about the true gender of her husband and been complicit in this unnatural, distasteful and illegal pantomime of marriage, and so acquit the accused out of a sense of distaste for the victim. If they formed this view, it would also remove the motive that Coyle was relying on to explain the murder – that Annie had been killed after she discovered her husband's true gender to prevent her exposing the sexual fraud perpetrated upon her by the accused. Coyle liked to be able to put himself into the mind of the accused, so that he could explain to the jury exactly what the motive had been for the crime. But the facts of this case were so bizarre and so outside the experience of ordinary members of society that he realised he was going to have considerable difficulty conveying to the jury the sexual passions that had existed in this irregular relationship and the complex emotions that had prompted Harry Crawford to murder his wife Annie.

Coyle fully realised that the main shortcoming in the prosecution case was that he was not in a position to be able to prove to the jury exactly how the deceased, Annie Birkett, had come to die. The evidence suggested that she may well have received a heavy blow to the back of her head, but whether or not this blow was capable of killing her, or even rendering her unconscious, was a matter of doubt. Because the body had been burned on a makeshift fireplace, much of the forensic evidence that could have disclosed the exact cause of death had been destroyed. There were only two important facts that Coyle was confident he could easily prove beyond a reasonable doubt, which was the standard of proof required in all criminal cases. The first was the identity of the body that had been found in the Lane Cove River Park. The second was that Eugenia Falleni, as Harry Crawford, had had a convincing motive to kill Annie Birkett in order to prevent her exposing his true identity as a female and the sexual deception that had been practised by him upon her during their marriage.

Another task that Coyle knew he would confront during the trial was to explain the very complicated, technical and scientific evidence that the government forensic pathologists would be giving. Jurors were always a mixed bag, and some of them would only have had two or three years of secondary schooling, so their scientific knowledge would be limited to basic facts like the boiling point of water or the names of the eight planets of the solar system.[3] How could he convey to them the evidence he was going to call about blunt force trauma to the human skull, and the findings you would expect when a body is burned, and how to determine whether the person was alive or dead when the body was set on fire? More importantly, how was he going to explain to the jury that the two government forensic pathologists had missed some of the vital evidence when they first examined the body just days after the death, and had come to a completely different conclusion about the cause of death three years later after the remains of the body were exhumed from the grave and her spouse had been charged with murder?

Sir William looked down from the Bench to the Bar table and again said, 'Yes, Mr Crown.' Coyle again rose slowly to his feet. This was one part of the trial that he really loved. The opening address is the first opportunity for the prosecutor to weave a story about the case to the jury. If it is done well, it will leave a lasting impression that will be very difficult for the defence to remove. If one views the jury as putting together the pieces of evidence like the pieces of a jigsaw puzzle, the opening address is like showing the jury the puzzle box with the complete picture to help them to later place each of the individual pieces in its correct position.

Coyle skilfully informed the jury in a factual, no-nonsense way of the evidence that he anticipated he would present during the prosecution case.

Falleni Family, New Zealand, about 1910.

Eugenia Falleni in Sydney about 1910-1912.

Eugenia Falleni at the Central Police Station on the day of her arrest, 1920.

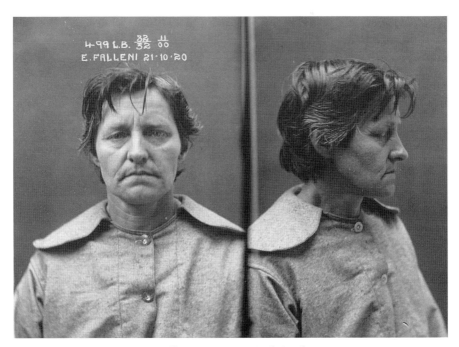

Eugenia Falleni in Long Bay Gaol, October 1920.

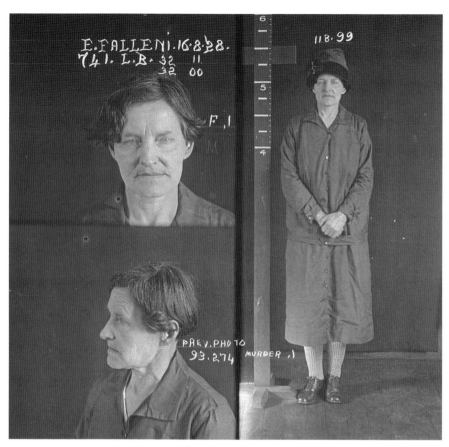

Eugenia Falleni in Long Bay Gaol 1928.

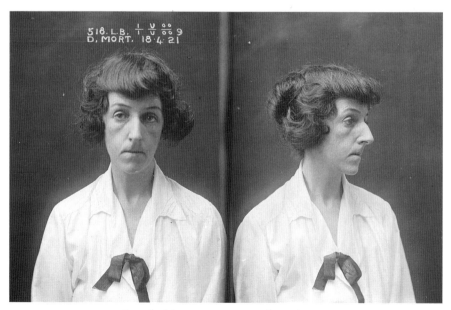

Dorothy Mort in Long Bay Gaol, April 1921.

Annie Birkett about 1910.

Harry Birkett in about 1910.

*Counsel Archibald McDonell
in about 1910.*

William Coyle KC in about 1920, the year he took Silk and was appointed the State's first Senior Crown Prosecutor.

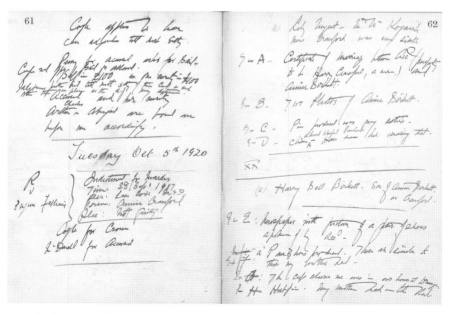

Chief Justice Cullen's handwritten notes during the evidence of Sergeant Robson when the article was tendered and admitted into evidence.

Exterior of Central Criminal Court Darlinghurst 2012.

WOMAN MASQUERADES IN MEN'S CLOTHES.

MARRIES TWO WOMEN.

ARRESTED AND CHARGED WITH MURDER.

The police have arrested a woman at Annandale who has been masquerading in men's clothes. She had married two women at different times, although she had a daughter herself.

She has been charged with the murder of Annie Birkett, the woman she first married.

The remains of a woman which were found near Chatswood two and a half years ago are believed to be those of Birkett.

Newspaper article from the Queanbeyan Age, Tuesday July 6, 1920.

THE MAN-WOMAN CASE.

Eugene Falleni, the man-woman, was committed for trial from the Central Police Court yesterday afternoon on a charge of having murdered Annie Birkett or Crawford on or about October 1, 1917.

Josephine Crawford Falleni, the daughter of the man-woman, gave evidence. She was in a state of great distress and wept bitterly the whole of the time she was in the witness-box.

Newspaper article from the Queanbeyan.

He began his address by telling them that the accused had for years dressed like a man and undertaken the work of a man in factories and other places. 'The story of this crime is a long one,' he explained, 'and I will have to go right back to 1910, when Annie Birkett, then a widow with one child, Harry Bell Birkett, was working for Dr Clarke at Wahroonga. The accused was also working for Dr Clarke as a useful, and was then posing as a man.' He told them how Harry had wooed Annie; about the marriage ceremony in 1913 at the Parsonage in Balmain; and about their lives, together with Harry Jnr, at 5 and 7 The Avenue, Drummoyne. As he was describing the unnatural relationship between these two people, he could see looks of disbelief and distaste on the faces of several of the jurors. At this stage, Coyle said nothing to answer the obvious question in everyone's mind: how did they engage in intimate sexual relations?

During all of this, Eugenia sat in the dock motionless and expressionless. It was as though the prosecutor was talking about someone else she didn't know and didn't care for. Indeed, for most of the trial Eugenia adopted this approach. No doubt, McDonell had told her to remain impervious to what was said in court, which she interpreted as impassive. Her apparent lack of engagement with the proceedings, which was most likely a defence mechanism to enable her to survive this frightful ordeal, could have been mistakenly viewed by the members of the jury as disdain for the legal process, branding her even more as an outlaw and a threat to society.

Coyle then came to Annie's fateful discovery of Harry's true identity, which led into a description of their trip on Friday 28 September 1917, just before the Eight-Hour Day long weekend, to a secluded bush location in the Lane Cove River Park. He told the jury that Harry Jnr had last seen his mother on the Thursday night. The following morning, a neighbour who lived in The Avenue at Drummoyne saw both Harry and Annie Crawford going out, and one of them was carrying a small case.

When it came to what had actually happened between Harry and Annie in the park that led to Annie's death, Coyle was deliberately vague. He explained to the jury how Annie's body had been found in a burned state, and detailed the items that had been found nearby. He told them that there had been two post-mortem examinations done by two pathologists who would give evidence in the trial. When they examined the body, they found that the skull was cracked in many places, but Coyle conceded that, with one exception, the pathologists would say these could have been caused by the heat of the fire. There was one crack, however, on the right side at the back of the head, which both doctors were of the opinion 'could' have been caused by violence. Coyle stressed the word 'could', as he wanted to pre-empt the anticipated defence attack on the two pathologists, and then cautiously qualified this by saying, 'However, seeing that the body was so badly burnt, they are not prepared to say that this fracture could not have been caused by the extensive fire.'

Coyle then added this, which caused everyone in the courtroom to draw breath and recoil in horror: 'In the opinion of Dr Palmer, the government medical officer who conducted the post-mortem, Annie Birkett was alive when her clothing caught fire or was set on fire.' The imputation was quite clear: Annie Birkett had been killed by being burned alive.

Coyle had realised that there was a serious flaw in the Crown case. If all the cracks on Annie's head could be attributed to the effect of heat, then there was no evidence of any act of violence to her, and nothing that could have rendered her unconscious. How, then, did she come to be burned alive? If the opinion that she had been burned alive was wrong, then there was no evidence whatsoever as to how she had died and therefore no viable case for murder. Coyle was surreptitiously suggesting to the jury that the one skull fracture that the pathologists were unsure about must have been caused by violence and must have rendered her unconscious or in a condition in which the accused was able to burn her alive. The difficulty with this proposition was that neither of the two pathologists was prepared to definitively express an opinion that any one of the cracks in the skull had been caused by violence. So how could the jury ascertain beyond a reasonable doubt the way in which Annie had come to die, or that she had died a violent death at all? Coyle realised that the defence counsel, Archie McDonell, might easily expose these shortcomings in the Crown case.

Coyle continued his opening address by telling the jury that after the first post-mortem examination the body had been buried, but the police had kept the remains of some clothing, items of jewellery, and both upper and lower false teeth until mid-1920, when Annie Birkett's sister and Harry Jnr had immediately recognised some of these effects as having belonged to their sister and mother. The two dentists who had made her false teeth were able to identify the handiwork as probably their own. Coyle was so confident that the jury would accept that the body must be Annie Birkett's that he said to the jury: 'Altogether, there are so many things that were found round the poor, charred body that the Crown can say, without hesitation, that you will come to the conclusion that the body burned there was the body of Annie Birkett.'

Coyle then went on to describe the witnesses who had seen a person, whom they later identified as the accused, dressed of course as a man, in the vicinity of the Cumberland Paper Mills around the Eight-Hour Day weekend. Coyle told the jury that he anticipated evidence would be given by a male neighbour of the accused in The Avenue, Drummoyne. The neighbour's wife had been indisposed, so he had gone to the accused's home on the night of Friday 28 September to enquire whether Mrs Crawford could assist his wife in some domestic duties. The neighbour had found the accused at home on his own. When the neighbour explained why he had come, Harry Crawford informed the neighbour that his request was 'too late, because she has bolted with someone else'. The neighbour noticed that many household items in the accused's home were packed up as if for sale. The following morning, Saturday 29 September, arrangements were made by the accused to sell the furniture to a dealer named Hart.

Coyle informed the jury that Harry Jnr had not returned to the home until the Monday night, after spending the long weekend at Collaroy. He found the accused sitting in the kitchen over a whisky bottle which was three-quarters full. When Harry Jnr asked where his mother was, he was told by the accused that she had gone to visit some friends at North Sydney. He was told to go to bed. The next morning, the whisky bottle was only a quarter full and the accused appeared not to have slept all night.

Coyle was only too aware of the difficulties he faced with the sighting witnesses. The accused and Annie had been seen leaving their home with what was clearly a picnic basket on the Friday morning. On the Friday afternoon, one of the sighting witnesses claimed to have seen the accused in the Park in an excited and strung-out condition. That night, the accused was seen at his home in Drummoyne by the neighbour, to whom he said that his wife had bolted. The furniture was clearly already being prepared for sale. On this evidence alone, Annie Birkett had already been killed by the Friday night. However, two further witnesses from the Cumberland Paper Mills had seen a man whom they identified as Harry Crawford acting suspiciously early on the Sunday morning, while another witness claimed to have seen smoke from a fire in the park on the Monday.

The various sighting witnesses were clearly irreconcilable, which was unsatisfactory from the Crown's point of view. Coyle sought to conveniently sweep these discrepancies under the carpet by saying to the jury: 'The accused on the Sunday, unable perhaps to get rid of something, came back, the Crown alleges, and returned to the place where this woman was lying dead.' Coyle realised that he was trying to 'have his cake and eat it'. If the fire was not lit until the Monday, then how could it be said that Annie was still alive when she was burned? On the other hand, if Annie was already dead by the Friday night when the accused was preparing their furniture for sale, why on earth would he come back on the Sunday morning and then again on the Monday? Coyle deliberately did not mention to the jury the glaring weak point in his case: that each of these sighting witnesses had identified the accused nearly three years after their observations, and only after they had seen the photograph of her, dressed as a male, in the newspaper after her arrest. Coyle realised that a skilful defence counsel could easily render these identification witnesses valueless.

In his opening address, Coyle listed the many different lies the accused had told various people about where Annie had supposedly gone after she disappeared. They included:

- she was visiting friends at North Sydney
- she had bolted with a plumber from Balmain
- she had cleared out and left him without a penny
- they had had many rows and he had had to do something

and the final version, which was the most damaging, and which Coyle read word-for-word from Mrs Schieblich's statement as he ostentatiously held it up:

- 'We had a jolly good row, and I gave her a crack over the head, and she cleared out.'

Coyle emphatically asserted to the jury that every version that the accused had given was a lie: 'every bit of it – a tissue of falsehood'.

The prosecutor clearly wished to prepare the jury for the fact that he was intending to tender the object with which Harry Crawford had pleasured both his wives, as there had been no previous mention of it in the press. He gingerly broached the subject by saying, 'I will refer to another matter, though it is an unpleasant subject to speak of in the presence of women.' At this point, the Chief Justice interjected and said, 'We must not hesitate for one moment on account of the women. If women choose to come to a criminal court, they cannot be considered.' Clearly, he thought that it was inappropriate for women to have come to hear such a case in the first place. If this was an opportunity for women in the public gallery to get up and leave to save themselves hearing these scandalous details, it failed miserably, because not a single member of the public departed.

Although the admonition of the Chief Justice did not have any effect on the women in the public gallery, it seems to have had an effect on the Crown Prosecutor, because Coyle changed his mind about mentioning the object that had been found hidden at the bottom of the accused's portmanteau; instead, he proceeded to tell the jury that within a year of Annie's death, the accused 'whilst still posing as a man, again went through a form of marriage, this time at Canterbury. The woman who went through the second marriage ceremony was over 50 years of age'. Coyle did not mention that this woman was so convinced of the fact that she was pregnant to her husband that even on being presented with the false phallus, she refused to believe that he was not a man. He could not include this detail because Lizzie Crawford had disappeared and was not available to be called as a witness at the trial. Was Coyle reticent to mention the object that Harry had used to pleasure his wives out of prudishness, or was he teasing the jury by keeping them in suspense and telling them nothing at this stage about it?

Coyle then moved to tell the jury what was alleged to be the accused's motive for the murder. He referred to the fact that there would be evidence that the accused and Annie Birkett had frequently quarrelled during 1917, and then said:

The accused has been through the form of marriage with two women, and the Crown will suggest something like a motive for the getting rid of Mrs Birkett. The accused was so practised in deceit as to deceive these two women into the belief that she was a man. It was only in the end, when that deceit was discovered, that there were quarrels, that the Crown suggests this accused sought an opportunity to get rid of the person who would possibly broadcast her deceit.

Coyle's use of the words 'something like a motive' indicated to those who listened carefully that the suggested motive was somewhat deficient in explaining the subsequent murder. If Harry was motivated to murder Annie to prevent her from disclosing his sexual deceit, why did he wait eight months after she had discovered his true identity? Indeed, why would Annie suddenly threaten to reveal his identity so long after discovering it? If Harry 'sought an opportunity' to get rid of Annie when that deceit was discovered, why did he not use the many other opportunities that he must have had during the intervening months?

With this opening address, which in some respects was quite detailed but in others deliberately deficient, Coyle explained to the members of the jury what they were about to hear in the evidence. Upon him resuming his seat, many members of the press quickly left their box and the courtroom to race over to the eastern side of the building and up the steep wooden stairs to the press room, where there was a bank of five telephones they could use to inform their offices of what had just happened in the court-room. Those who got upstairs first were able to get in their copy first. The others had to impatiently wait their turn for the telephones, hoping that their editors would not find out that other journalists had made their calls before them – not that it really mattered, because the newspapers did not get printed until about 6 pm each evening and they all came out at around the same time early the next morning.

For the third time that morning, Chief Justice Cullen said the words, 'Yes, Mr Crown,' and with that the evidence in the Crown case began.

CHAPTER 18

FAMILY WITNESSES

Bill Coyle thought long and hard about the order in which he would call his witnesses. His normal practice was to call them in chronological order, as this was the easiest for the jury to follow. However, in this unusual case he decided that it would be desirable that his first few witnesses establish some sort of empathy for the deceased, Annie Birkett. He therefore chose to start his case with Annie's sister, Lily Nugent, and to follow with Annie's son, Harry Bell Birkett. Both Lily and Harry Jnr represented a live connection with the deceased Annie, and Coyle considered that they would readily elicit the sympathy of the jury.

Lily Nugent adopted quite a belligerent attitude – clearly directed at the accused – and from time to time, she would look across at Eugenia in the dock with disdain. After some background evidence about Annie and her child Harry Jnr, her marriage to Harry Crawford, and her confectionery and soft drink business in Balmain, Coyle moved to the important part of Lily's evidence: her identification of the jewellery that had been found on the body in the Lane Cove River Park in 1917, but not identified until 1920. It went like this:

> Coyle KC: Would you have a look at this item of jewellery (kidney-shaped stone shown to witness)?
> Lily Nugent: That belonged to my sister. It was attached to a pin. I saw her wearing that. (Above stone tendered and marked exhibit C).
> Coyle KC: Would you have a look at this chain and heart-shaped pendant?
> Lily Nugent: I've seen my sister wearing that. I recognise that as my sister's. (Above chain and pendant tendered and marked exhibit D).
> Coyle KC: In the year 1917, how often did you see your sister?
> Lily Nugent: During the year 1917, I did not see my sister frequently. I saw her twice. My sister wrote to me and she wanted to tell me something. The accused came with her. Just shortly before my sister went, she told

*me something. The accused was not present when she told me. That
was about January 1917.*

Coyle deliberately did not ask the next obvious question: what was
it that Annie told you that was so important? That was because the law
considered the answer to be inadmissible hearsay, because only Annie could
give evidence of what she knew, and she wasn't around to say.[1] However,
the jury already inevitably knew the answer to this unasked question – that
Annie had told Lily she had found out that Harry was not a man – because
at least some of them would have read it when it was published in every
newspaper[2] during the committal proceedings in the Police Court just
two months earlier.

Lily Nugent continued her evidence and got quite tied up in knots over
the appropriate personal pronoun to use when referring to Harry/Eugenia:
'I never saw him again after I knew that he was a man. I mean, I never saw
her after I knew she was a woman.'

This highlighted a technical problem that Coyle had never met before
and was unlikely to meet again, and he had no real way of dealing with
it: should he refer to the accused as 'he' or 'she'? He decided that the best
way to deal with it was for him to choose the personal pronoun according to whichever identity the accused had adopted at any particular time.
When the accused was Harry Crawford, Coyle would use 'he', and when
the accused was Eugenia Falleni, Coyle would use 'she'. However, Coyle
was well aware that the witnesses in the case would have constant difficulty
with the appropriate pronoun, and in fact they did. Some of the time they
referred to the accused as 'he', sometimes as 'she', and sometimes both in
the same sentence. On one occasion, a witness referred to the accused as 'it'.

During McDonell's cross-examination of Lily Nugent her antagonism
rose to a heightened level – one that was almost unacceptable for a solemn
hearing in the Supreme Court. The first question referred her to the
evidence she had given in the committal proceedings at the Police Court.
It went like this:

McDonell: *At the Police Court, when you were examined by Mr Kidston,
you said, 'The question of the defendant's sex never came up.' Is that
a fact?*
Lily Nugent: *I made no mention at the Police Court of having discovered that
she was a woman. I said nothing about it at the Police Court. I further
said [at the Police Court] 'The defendant never admitted anything
to me about her sex.' Neither did she. She never admitted anything. I*

never saw her after I knew it. I never saw Falleni after I knew she was a woman.'

In this answer, Archie McDonell elicited Lily's evidence at the committal proceedings that she had not known *anything* about Harry's true gender, which was quite contrary to what she was now asserting. She attempted to squirm out of this discrepancy by saying that what she meant in her evidence at the committal was that she had not been told anything *by the accused*. This was a disingenuous answer, and McDonell should have probed this line further, but he chose to leave her answer as it was, thereby allowing her to escape with her credibility relatively unscathed.

A defence cross-examiner should never ask a question that allows a prosecution witness free rein to denigrate the accused. That was exactly what McDonell did in this next open-ended question:

McDonell: *Did you see any signs that the relations between your sister and the accused were not good?*
Lily Nugent: *With regard to the relations between my sister and the accused, I do not know who appeared to be more attached to the other partner. I did not notice anything. You may take it that the accused was more anxious to continue the company of my sister than my sister was.*

Again, there were further questions that McDonell could have asked to mitigate this answer, but again he chose not to.

Archie McDonell asked not a single question of Lily Nugent about her identification of the two items of jewellery that had been found on or near the body in the Park. His failure to question her on this topic sent a very clear message to Bill Coyle and the rest of the courtroom that the defence was not challenging the fact that it was Annie Birkett's body that had been found in the Park. There was a very strict rule of procedure in the criminal courts, one that had existed since time immemorial and still exists today, that if the defence were going to submit to the jury that the evidence of a prosecution witness was mistaken, the defence counsel, in fairness, had to put the allegation to the witness to give them an opportunity to refute it and to explain why. This is the reason why McDonell's failure to challenge the identification of the jewellery signalled to Coyle that there was no challenge by the defence to the identification of the body.

Coyle was hardly surprised that the defence was not challenging the identification of the body. As he had said in his opening address, there was an abundance of evidence to prove that it was Annie's. There were a number of other significant issues in the Crown case which were on much shakier ground, and Coyle was convinced that the defence would focus on these, rather than on the identification of the body, on which the Crown case was overwhelming.

The next to give evidence was Harry Bell Birkett, Annie's son. After providing background details about his mother, he gave evidence about how she had met Harry Crawford at Dr Clarke's at Wahroonga:

> Coyle KC: Tell us about the time when the accused was courting your mother?
> Harry Birkett: I was 11 or 12 years old then. The accused was always hanging around there and bothering my mother, coming there every day and evening, and eventually she was forced to marry him. Then the accused came to live with my mother as her husband. We lived in that shop in Balmain for about six months after that. Then my mother sold the business.

He gave evidence about the state of their marriage in 1917:

> Coyle KC: What was the relationship like between your mother and the accused before your mother disappeared?
> Harry Birkett: During 1917 there were always rows. A week never went by without a row. The accused was always grumbling about something and always swearing. He could not speak more than two or three words without swearing. He used to call my mother all sorts of things. He made use of the filthiest language you could think of to my mother.

These answers exhibited an understandable hostility by a young son whose widowed mother had taken on a new partner. Harry Jnr gave evidence that the last time he had seen his mother was on the morning of Friday 28 September, prior to the Eight-Hour Day weekend. When he came home that night at about 10 pm, he did not see anybody awake and he assumed that his mother and the accused were asleep in their bedroom.[3] The following morning, Saturday, he again didn't see anyone before he went to work. When he came home on the Saturday evening, he again saw nobody and thought nothing of it. He then went with the Bone family to Collaroy for the long weekend. This is the account that he gave about his return home from Collaroy on the evening of Monday, 1 October, at about 8.30 pm:

Coyle KC: When you got home, what did you see?

Harry Birkett: The front door was open and I walked in, out into the kitchen, and the accused was sitting on a chair there, and a bottle of Johnnie Walker whisky was there and a small glass. The first thing I said to the accused was 'Where is my mother?' He replied, 'I do not know.' I asked him again and he said, 'She has gone to North Sydney with Mrs Murray and her daughter.'

Coyle KC: When you got up the next morning, what did you see?

Harry Birkett: The accused was still in the kitchen and looked as though he had not gone to bed. I saw the whisky. On the night before it was just on three-quarters full, and there was only about a quarter of it left then.

The evidence of Harry's enebriated state was equally consistent with the Crown version that he had just murdered Annie as it was with the defence version that Annie had just left him for another man. It was therefore implacably neutral as evidence in support of the prosecution case. The false explanation given to Harry Jnr on the Monday night was possibly explicable as an attempt to soften what was a terrible blow for a young boy of his age, in which case it would have been equally consistent with the prosecution case and the defence case. Harry Jnr testified that he went back to work for Mr and Mrs Bone on Tuesday 2 October, and that night again returned home. Coyle asked him:

Coyle KC: What happened that night?

Harry Birkett: I had my tea and not long after that, he told me to go to bed early, as he wanted me to get up early the next morning, so I went to bed. That was Tuesday.

Coyle KC: What happened next morning?

Harry Birkett: On the next morning I woke up about 6.30 am and I was getting dressed when the accused came through, he passed through the dining room and the kitchen. Not long after that the accused told me to go with him. He took me up to the tram into the city, got off at the railway and walked about the streets and eventually got to Circular Quay. We went to the Watson's Bay ferry and went and bought two single tickets, he saying that we would come back by tram. We went to Watson's Bay. We were some time at Watson's Bay. We went up the hill towards The Gap, round the cliffs. After that, the accused went outside the fence—

(Evidence objected to. Evidence not pressed by the Crown.)

Coyle knew that Harry Jnr was going to go on to describe what had happened at The Gap. McDonell quite rightly objected to this evidence, as it had no bearing on the alleged murder of Annie and was highly prejudicial to the accused. Coyle probably considered that the evidence about The Gap was so ambiguous that he decided not to rely upon it. In any event, evidence about this event had been given in the Police Court and been extensively reported in the press,[4] so the jury would undoubtedly have been aware of it. The fact that Harry Crawford had bought two single tickets on the ferry seemed to suggest that his plan involved neither of them returning to the city. If the accused was intending to commit suicide, this may support the proposition that Annie's death had been a terrible accident, rather than a planned crime. In his distress at losing Annie, Crawford may have misguidedly thought that it was in the boy's best interests, having lost both his father and his mother, to end the boy's life as well as his own. Ultimately, a suicide and mercy killing at The Gap was equally consistent with an accidental death of Annie as it was with a deliberate murder. Coyle clearly decided that the permutations and combinations were just so complex, variable and uncertain that it was not worthwhile pursuing this line of evidence. The other problem with this material was that the jury might disbelieve it and think that it was just the ravings of a guilt-ridden son who had failed to act when his mother suspiciously disappeared.

It was guileful of Coyle to ask any questions at all about The Gap if he was not intending to press the point in the event that an objection was raised by the defence. On McDonell's part, he left it much too late to voice his objection. He must have known what was about to be said concerning the events of that night, so he should have raised his objection at the very first question. By waiting until after there had been mention of Watson's Bay and The Gap, he allowed Coyle to subtly remind the jury of the press coverage about those topics during the committal proceedings. From a tactical point of view, Coyle had effectively reminded the jury of that evidence without a single word being said about what had actually happened at The Gap. He was able to convey the impression of an intention to commit a desperate act of violence against the unsuspecting boy without the jury hearing the evidence, warts and all, and without the defence being able to cross-examine on it.

For the same reason that Coyle did not lead evidence from Harry Birkett about what had happened at The Gap, he did not adduce evidence about what had occurred several nights later when the accused took the boy to the sandhills at Woollahra. Surprisingly, Coyle did elicit from Mrs Schieblich what happened at her home before and after the trip to Woollahra, including the threats that had been made by Crawford to kill the boy. If both the trip to The Gap and to Woollahra were irrelevant, and hence inadmissible, Coyle ought not to have elicited the other material from Mrs Schieblich and McDonell should have objected to it.

Harry Birkett's extraordinary account of what happened at The Gap and at Woollahra in the week after his mother's death almost defies belief. He was the only source of information about these events, and he only disclosed it for the first time nearly three years later when, at the instigation of his aunt, Lily Nugent, he finally provided a statement to the police on 13 June 1920. He did not mention anything about these events to the kindly Mrs Schieblich, with whom he was lodging at the time, and he did not mention anything about them to Lily Nugent when he finally made contact with her in May 1920. On the other hand, Mrs Schieblich was able to confirm what had happened at her home before and after the Woollahra incident.

One wonders whether Harry Birkett's perception of these events was distorted by his youth, or whether his subconscious mind constructed some or all of the drama of this tale because of the deep guilt that he felt at his failure to report his mother as a missing person in 1917.

Despite these events, Harry Jnr continued to live for several weeks in the same house, indeed in the same bedroom, as his stepfather, thereby displaying that he held no great fear of the older man. One would have thought that if these events had really occurred as he related them to the police, he would have been far too fearful to have spent any further time alone with Crawford. Rather, he lived at lodging houses with his stepfather and allowed the older man to help him find work. It was only when he moved to Sans Souci in mid-1918 that Harry Birkett lost contact with Harry Crawford until early 1920 when he happened to come across him working at a hotel. Again, if the events that he described to the police had really happened, one would have expected Harry Birkett to want nothing more to do with his stepfather when he unexpectedly met him again. Instead, he seems to have been quite pleased to see him after several years of no contact. For all these reasons, the account by Harry Birkett must be treated with caution and scepticism.

If his account of events was accurate, what on earth was Crawford planning to do at The Gap and at Woollahra? Clearly, by purchasing two single tickets to go by ferry to Watson's Bay, Crawford was intending that neither he nor the boy were going to return. Was this planned as a murder-suicide? So far as the incident in the scrub at Woollahra was concerned, if Crawford seriously intended killing the boy, by all accounts he had every opportunity to do so, but chose not to.

If Crawford planned to kill the boy and himself, this was just as consistent with Annie having died an accidental death as it was of a deliberate murder. In each instance, Crawford's actions could be seen as a desperate plan to relieve his own pain and to achieve what he delusionally considered to be in the boy's best interests. For these reasons, what happened at The Gap and Woollahra does not help us decide what had happened several days earlier in the Lane Cove River Park when Annie Birkett died.

Coyle then took this witness to the items found in the park. Harry Jnr was able to identify the pair of shoes that had been found on the body in 1917 as being similar to those that had belonged to his mother:

> Coyle KC: Would you have a look at this newspaper from 1917. Do you see that there is a photograph of a pair of shoes? What do you say about those shoes?
> Harry Birkett: I remember my mother's shoes. My mother had a pair of shoes with patches on the side. The accused patched them. (Pair of shoes handed to the witness.) He put similar patches on to those, and just roughed them. I say these shoes are similar to those my mother had. I remember the patching.

Coyle then showed him the enamel cup that had been found in the clearing near the body:

> Coyle KC: Would you have a look at this enamelled cup. What do you say about that?
> Harry Birkett: We had that in our house at Drummoyne. That was in the house. The accused used to take it to work at first, and then it was left home afterwards. I recognise it by those marks on the bottom. (Cup tendered and marked exhibit G.)

Harry Jnr then identified the same items of jewellery that had been identified by Lily Nugent. He also identified some other items of jewellery that had been found on the body: a diamond ring and a brooch. He claimed that a piece of gabardine material that had survived the fire was similar in appearance to an overcoat worn by his mother, and also recognised an item of her underwear. He finally identified the picnic basket that had been found near the body as having belonged to his mother, as he recognised some torn paper lining inside the lid that he himself had put there.

Harry Birkett's identification of all these items as being either similar or identical to what his mother had owned must have been very convincing evidence for the jury that the body found in 1917 was indeed Annie Birkett's. In cross-examination of Harry Birkett, Archie McDonell again did not dispute the identification of any of these items that had been found at the scene. It would have been open to McDonell to draw attention to the fact that Harry Jnr had failed to recognise the photograph of the same shoes when it had been published in the newspaper within a fortnight of his mother's disappearance, on the occasion that he was asked by his step-father to read the newspaper article. McDonell's failure to take such a point was interpreted as signifying that the defence raised no challenge that the body was that of Annie Birkett.

McDonell was careful not to antagonise the jury by cross-examining too severely this young man who had suffered so much. He merely asked him some fairly mundane questions about the relationship between his mother and Harry Crawford. Everyone in the courtroom must have wondered why he bothered to ask questions about topics such as how much each of them had contributed financially to the relationship, and who had bought the furniture. The only conclusion that one could come to was that McDonell was engaging in 'filler' questions – asking them just for the sake of saying something. All in all, it was an ineffective cross-examination of an important witness that provided the young man with several opportunities to denigrate his late mother's spouse.

Archie McDonell failed to ask Harry Birkett a single question about why it had taken him so long to report his mother missing. He could have embarked on an effective cross-examination along these lines:

Q: *You loved your mother very much?*

Q: *She was a very good mother to you, wasn't she?*

Q: *You were unhappy when she remarried after your father's death, weren't you?*

Q: *From your point of view, when you were a young boy it appeared to you that she had been forced to marry Harry, didn't it?*

Q: *Looking at it now from the point of view as an adult, isn't it likely that she chose to marry Harry because she was in love with him?*

Q: *When your mother disappeared after the Eight-Hour Day long weekend, was that the first time that anything like that had ever happened?*

Q: Were you surprised that she had gone without telling you, or without saying goodbye, or without leaving you any information about how to contact her?

Q: You were told that she had gone off with some friends?

Q: You would have been delighted to have been reunited with her at any time during the three years of her disappearance?

Q: Is it true you did not report her as a missing person to the police for nearly three years?

Q: There was nothing stopping you from reporting her to the police as a missing person during those three years, was there?

Q: If you had thought that something terrible had happened to her, you would have reported it to the police?

Q: You didn't report her as a missing person, because you didn't think that anything bad had happened to her, did you?

Q: You accepted that she had gone off and was leading her life somewhere else, didn't you?

Q: You were so convinced that she was still alive and living somewhere else with other people, that you did not report her missing to anyone for nearly three years?

Questions like these, and the likely answers, would have provided at least a slim basis for the defence to suggest that Annie Birkett had in fact gone to live elsewhere in 1917, and may still be there. After all, if her beloved only son had been so convinced that she was living elsewhere, how could the jury be convinced beyond a reasonable doubt that she was not?

It appeared that everyone in the courtroom accepted that Lily Nugent and Harry Jnr's evidence conclusively proved that the body that had been found in the Lane Cove River Park was Annie Birkett's. But, what would the defence case be? Which of the numerous issues that potentially arose in the evidence would McDonell select to mount his challenge to the Crown case? At this early stage of the trial, he had given nothing away and Coyle was still anxious to know where to focus his prodigious talents as an advocate.

CHAPTER 19

SIGHTING WITNESSES

A sighting or identification witness is a witness who claims to have seen the accused either at or near the scene of a crime or at some other relevant location that links the accused to the crime. Often, a sighting witness has only had an opportunity to make a very brief observation, and generally the person observed was not previously known to the witness. The experience of the courts is the same as one's everyday experience: it is easy to make a mistake when one is identifying another person, especially someone who was not previously known, and especially if the identification is based on a fleeting glimpse. The reliability of this kind of evidence depends upon a number of factors, including: the opportunity for observing the person; the length of time that the person is observed; the distance of the observer from the person seen; the quality of the observer's eyesight; the reasons for making the observation; the distinctiveness of the person observed; the qualities of memory of the observer; the length of time between the observation and the first time the observer has reason to recall it; any trauma the observer is suffering at the time of the observation; and the general observation powers of the individual observer. When sighting evidence is given for the Crown in a criminal trial, these are all fertile grounds for cross-examination by the defence counsel. Because of all these variable factors, sighting or identification evidence is inherently unreliable and must be treated with extreme care. The experience of the courts over many years is that this type of evidence, given by witnesses who are honest but mistaken, is capable of resulting in miscarriages of justice. For that reason, the law today requires this category of evidence to be treated with great scrutiny and care and it is subject to very strict rules of admissibility. It has not always been so.

One of the ways that the law strives to avoid miscarriages of justice with this type of evidence is to insist on certain procedures for the identification of suspects in police custody. A witness should not be asked whether they can identify a single suspect or a photograph of a single suspect, because it is too easy for the witness to assume that the police must have found the right person, so that the witness just goes along and identifies that individual. The very worst form of identification is what is known as a 'dock identification', in which the witness identifies the accused for the first time in court, and where it is quite obvious who is the person on trial. For this reason, the law now insists that a witness must be provided with a selection of a sufficiently large group of people to choose from, either during an identification parade or alternatively in what is called a photographic array (a folder of photographs containing a sufficient number of persons to chose from). Dock identifications are strictly prohibited. These precautions make it less likely that a witness will just pick out a single suspect whom they assume is the subject of a police enquiry or the person on trial in court. It has not always been so.

Where a witness has seen an image (like a newspaper photograph or an image on television) of the suspect between the original sighting and the subsequent identification, the image can subconsciously displace the witness's memory of the original observation. This is called the 'displacement effect'. The experience of the courts is that a witness is likely to be genuinely unable to distinguish between the original memory of the observation and the image seen in the interim. A sighting or identification witness is unlikely to be aware of the displacement effect when making a subsequent identification of a suspect. For that reason, where a witness has seen an image of the suspect between the observation and the identification, the courts today will generally not allow the witness to give evidence of the identification because of the dangers inherent in the displacement effect. It has not always been so.

The media have a special responsibility in this regard. Recognising the dangers of the displacement effect, where the identification of the perpetrator of a crime is an issue, the media today generally do not publish or broadcast an image of the person who has been arrested and charged. That is why the faces of such people are often pixelated in news reports. In this way, any subsequent identification process will not be tainted by the displacement effect. It has not always been so.

These safeguards do not prevent the media today from publishing photographs of people who have disappeared and are presumed dead. This can raise difficulties for prosecutors where there has been extensive media publicity about a missing person prior to the arrest and charging of someone for the murder of that person. The author has experienced a number of cases in which well-meaning members of the public have seen media reports of missing people and have become genuinely, but mistakenly, convinced that they have seen the missing person, and have provided the police with what they thought was valuable information about the missing person. In fact, such information can be a major distraction during the course of a trial.

By way of example, in the case of Ivan Milat, who was convicted of the murder of seven hitchhiking backpackers whose bodies were found in the Belanglo State Forest in 1992, a large number of concerned members of the public contacted the police after seeing news reports about the disappearances of the backpackers, claiming to have seen them alive and well in various parts of Australia after the date they had disappeared. Many of their accounts were particularly convincing, but were later proven to be quite wrong. Some members of the public even claimed to have seen the missing backpackers alive and well after their bodies had been found in the Belanglo Forest. Such is the power of suggestion where images of missing people are published in the media, eliciting well-meaning but erroneous sighting evidence from the public! We are aware of this danger today, and take precautions to identify and deal with it. It has not always been so.

The reliability of an identification or sighting witness depends very much upon the circumstances in which the observation was made and the length of time between the observation and the subsequent identification. If a witness were to pass a person in the street when there was no special reason to notice that person, you would not expect the witness to be able to identify that person accurately even a day later. On the other hand, if the observed person were engaged in viciously bashing someone in the street, so that there was a special reason to notice him or her, you would not be surprised if a witness claimed to be able to identify the attacker a week, a month, or even a year later.

Another important factor in the reliability of sighting witnesses is the length of time between the original observation and the subsequent identification. If a witness was to observe somebody viciously bashing another person in the street, and the witness was only asked to identify that person three years later, it may be difficult to accept that the witness could accurately recall the appearance of the attacker after such a long time. If, in the meantime, the witness has seen a photograph in the media of a person who has been arrested and charged with that bashing, the natural tendency would be for the witness's mind to displace the memory of the person seen during the attack with the image in the media. The witness may be completely unaware of this displacement effect, making their testimony in court potentially unreliable. The longer the time since the original observation, the greater is the risk of the displacement effect surreptitiously exerting an influence. We are aware of the dangers of such disruptions of memory today, and take steps to address them. It has not always been so.

These modern-day precautionary measures are predicated on the basis that the observation is of a person who was not previously known to the witness. If the person observed was somebody who was previously known to the witness, then that is a somewhat different situation. Today, such evidence is called recognition evidence. It is a category of sighting or identification evidence that has its own dangers, which are by nature less acute than the identification of a stranger. We all have had the experience of incorrectly identifying a person we thought we knew, only to realise the mistake some seconds later. If we do not correct ourselves, we are capable of being devastatingly convincing about a mistaken identification of someone we thought we knew. Again, the main danger of a miscarriage of justice arises when you have a recognition witness who is honest, but mistaken. Today we are aware of the dangers of this kind of evidence. It has not always been so.

Crown Prosecutor Bill Coyle KC called a number of witnesses who claimed to have seen Harry Crawford at various times and in various places between the Friday and the Monday of the Eight-Hour Day weekend in 1917. Three of those witnesses claimed to have seen him in the vicinity of the Cumberland Paper Mills in the Lane Cove River Park near to where the body of Annie Birkett was found several days later. Those witnesses were:

- Mrs Irene Carroll – a passer-by, who was visiting the Cumberland Paper Mills. She claimed that at about 3 pm on the Friday before Eight-Hour Day, she had seen a man sitting on a rock near the mills with his head buried in his hands. As she passed him, she startled him, and he dropped his hands from his face and looked up at her. About half an hour later, as she left the area having done her business at the mills, she saw the same man walking on some rock in the direction of where the body was later found. Nearly three years later, she attended the Central Criminal Court where about twenty men were lined up. She identified the accused as the man from the mills. In cross-examination she admitted to Archie McDonell that she had seen the accused's photograph in the paper before the line-up, but she claimed that she did not read the article and did not know what it was all about.

- Mr James Hicks – an employee at the Cumberland Paper Mills. Mr Hicks gave evidence that on the Sunday morning before Eight-Hour

Day, between 5.30 am and 7 am, he saw a man who was acting strangely walking up the canal from the Lane Cove River towards the paper mills. He saw the man looking up towards the spot where the body was later found. On 22 July 1920, nearly three years later, Mr Hicks identified the accused during a line-up of between fifteen and twenty men at the Central Police Court as being the person that he had seen at the mills on that Sunday morning in September 1917. Later on the same day, Detective Sergeant Robson and two other police took the accused (in custody) with Mr Hicks to the scene of where the body had been found. About twenty yards in a westerly direction from the paper mills, Mr Hicks pointed to a spot near the mills and said to the accused, 'That is where I saw you on that morning,' to which the accused made no reply. The accused was then asked by Detective Robson whether he knew the locality, and he said, 'I have never been here in my life.' A little while later, the accused admitted that he had worked at the nearby Chicago Flour Mills for one week many years earlier. In cross-examination, Mr Hicks admitted that before the identification process he had seen a picture of the accused in *The Sun* newspaper. He gave evidence that, 'It was after I had a good look at the picture in *The Sun* that I identified the accused.'

• Mr James Woodbury – a watchman and labourer at the Cumberland Paper Mills. Mr Woodbury gave evidence that was very similar to that of Mr Hicks: that at about 7 am on Sunday 30 September 1917 he had seen a man who excited his suspicions walking past the mills and this man had looked up at the area where the body had later been found. Mr Woodbury did a 'dock identification' of Eugenia, identifying her for the first time in court as the person he had seen three years earlier near the mills. McDonell elicited in cross-examination that despite working that day as a watchmen, and despite hearing about the finding of the body a day or two later, Mr Woodbury had not come forward to tell his employer or the police about the man he had seen, even though the police had come to the mills making enquiries about a body. McDonell completed his cross-examination with a question that was really in the form of a submission to the jury:

> McDonell: And you still say that although you had seen this suspicious
> man acting in a peculiar manner, you had taken so much trouble
> to identify him, and that you were so certain of the identity and
> are so certain of it now, and yet when you knew that there was an
> enquiry being made as to the cause of this body being found on

> the mountainside, you never spoke a word to the police or to your
> employer about it?
> James Woodbury: I did not wish to be drawn into anything in the
> matter.'

As well as these three sighting witnesses from the mills, there should
have been a fourth witness from the vicinity of the Lane Cove River Park:
Miss Hewitt, who lived on the edge of the park and whom Coyle had
mentioned to the jury during his opening address. Although she was not,
strictly speaking, a sighting witness, her evidence was particularly important to establish the time of Annie's death. Coyle had told the jury that
on Monday 1 October, Miss Hewitt had been at home and had seen a fire
burning in the Lane Cove River Park in the location where Annie Birkett's
body was later found. However, for tactical reasons Coyle decided that he
would not call Miss Hewitt to give evidence, even though he had told the
jury about her evidence during his opening address. Neither did Coyle at
any time tell the jury that another witness, a watchman employed at the
Cumberland Paper Mills, had also noticed smoke coming from the bush a
couple of hundred yards away from the mills at about four o'clock on the
Monday afternoon. These omissions were highly unorthodox.

If Harry and Annie went for the picnic on Friday 28 September,
how was Coyle to explain to the jury the two sighting witnesses who
claimed to have seen the accused in the vicinity of the mills on Sunday
the 30th? Even more problematically, how could he account for the fire
that had been seen by Miss Hewitt and the watchman at the Paper Mills
on Monday 1 October, Eight-Hour Day? If Annie was burned alive, then
what happened to her between the Friday when she went for the picnic
and Monday when the fire was seen burning? This was why, after a lot
of thought, Coyle took the tactical decision not call Miss Hewitt and the
watchman from the mills to give evidence, preferring not to confuse
the jury even further with their evidence, despite having mentioned
Miss Hewitt's evidence during his opening address. The risk that Coyle
ran by omitting these witnesses was that Archie McDonell might severely
criticise the Crown in his closing address for failing to call them. But that
was a risk that Coyle was prepared to take, rather than confusing the jury
even further with their evidence.

There were four sighting witnesses who were called who lived near to
Harry and Annie Crawford in Drummoyne and who gave evidence of
sightings at Drummoyne. Those witnesses were:

- Mrs Jane Wigg – who lived at 7 The Avenue, Drummoyne. Mrs Wigg gave evidence that on the Friday before Eight-Hour Day, in the morning, she saw her neighbours, Mr and Mrs Crawford, walking up The Avenue towards the tram in Lyons Road. One of them was carrying a small suitcase. Mrs Crawford was wearing a gabardine coat.

- Mr George Smith – a neighbour living in nearby Bush Street, Drummoyne. As previously noted, Mr Smith gave evidence that on one of the Friday evenings before Eight-Hour Day (he could not remember which one) he went to the Crawfords' home between 7 pm and 8 pm to ask whether Mrs Crawford could come and do some housework in his home, as his wife was ill. The accused told him, 'Oh, you are too late. She has cleared out with a plumber over in Balmain.' Mr Smith noticed that everything inside the accused's house was packed up as if they were ready to go away.

- Mrs Lydia Parnell – a resident of Drummoyne. She gave evidence that she saw the accused on the Monday of Eight-Hour Day between 7.15 pm and 7.45 pm walking from the tram terminus towards his home. She also gave evidence that she used to see the Crawfords on a Saturday morning when they were out shopping together, and they would often be arm-in-arm. She said that to all outward appearances they seemed most affectionate towards each other.

- Mrs Edith Hoyes – a resident who lived at 3 The Avenue, Drummoyne next door to the Crawfords. She gave evidence that she saw the accused approaching his home in a somewhat agitated state between 7 pm and 8 pm on the Monday of Eight-Hour Day. In cross-examination, she gave evidence that the accused always seemed a very decent and respectable man, that he and Annie Crawford always seemed agreeable when they were out, and that the accused seemed genuinely fond of her.

Coyle must have appreciated that there were real difficulties associated with all of these sighting witnesses. For a start, two of the three witnesses who claimed to have seen a man acting suspiciously in the vicinity of the Cumberland Paper Mills had come forward and identified the accused (dressed as a male) only after seeing his photograph in the paper and after a request for information by the police had been published in the newspapers. This had the effect of making a subsequent identification parade a complete sham. The displacement effect would have rendered any identification completely unreliable and such evidence would never be admitted in a criminal trial today. How could there be any validity in a witness selecting a person in a line-up when an image of the same person charged with the very crime had previously been widely published in the newspapers and seen by these witnesses? Not one of these witnesses had come forward when the body had been found in 1917, despite publicity in the press at the time.

If ever there was a complete and utter farce, it was the charade orchestrated by the police in taking the accused and Mr James Hicks to the vicinity of the Cumberland Paper Mills so that Mr Hicks could identify exactly where he had made the observation back in 1917. This was after he had already identified Eugenia (dressed as a male) in a line-up. If the purpose was to identify the spot, he could have done that without Eugenia being present. If the purpose was to prompt some sort of confession from Eugenia, it failed dismally.[1]

However, the worst example of dangerously unreliable sighting evidence was the 'dock identification' of Eugenia by Mr James Woodbury. Three years after a transitory sighting of a man walking past him, with no particular reason to note him at the time, Mr Woodbury claimed to be able to identify the accused in the dock as the person he had seen, despite the fact that she was now a different gender. All the shortcomings of a dock identification were highlighted and exemplified by his evidence. He had a choice of one person, knowing that that individual was then facing trial for the crime of murder, and, unsurprisingly, he identified that person. There does not seem to have been any exploration by McDonell of whether or not Mr Woodbury had seen photographs of the accused prior to the trial. The fact that Woodbury had not reported his sighting of this man to the police after the body had been found just went to demonstrate that there had been no particular reason for him to notice the man at the time.

The next difficulty with the three sighting witnesses from the mills was that they claimed to be able to perform the extraordinary feat of remembering the precise day and time that they had seen this man, who was a perfect stranger to them at the time, even though nearly three years had passed before they were asked to recall their observation. Such an extraordinary feat of memory defied common sense and Coyle must have known that the jury would have difficulty accepting the accuracy of their timing.

The sighting witnesses from Drummoyne were in a somewhat stronger position, because they at least were able to say that they already knew the accused and his wife from the area and were therefore in a position to easily identify him. This was really recognition evidence. Once again, it was difficult to justify their precise recollections of the exact day and time after such a long period. There must have been numerous occasions before the long weekend in 1917 when these neighbours had seen Mr and Mrs Crawford walking in the vicinity of their home and one wonders how they were able to isolate any particular occasion nearly three years later.

The other difficulty with the sighting witnesses from Drummoyne was that their evidence in no way correlated with the sighting witnesses from the mills. If one tried to create a timeline of all the sighting evidence, from both the mills and Drummoyne, the only conclusion that one could draw was that Harry Crawford had gone straight home after killing Annie and in the space of a couple of hours packed up all his and Annie's worldly possessions, only to go back to the scene of his crime several times over the next three days. Why on earth would he do that, and what would possess him to act in such an obviously suspicious way – looking in a distressed fashion towards the area where the body was later located – in front of the witnesses at the mills? The only conclusion that one could come to was that the sighting witnesses were hopelessly inaccurate in their observations and in their recollections of dates and times. With his wealth of experience, Bill Coyle must have been aware of this.

Although Coyle knew that the jury could well reject the accuracy of the sighting witnesses from the mills, he thought that they would probably accept the evidence of Mr George Smith that when he visited the Craw-fords' house that weekend, Harry had already packed up all of his and his wife's worldly possessions. However, Coyle was less sure that the jury would accept the evidence of the timing of Mr Smith's visit to the accused's home. Mr Smith was adamant that it had been on a Friday night, which must surely have been Friday 28 September, the very day of the picnic. It is highly unlikely that Harry would have had sufficient time after returning to Drummoyne to pack up all of their worldly possessions by 7 or 8 pm. The jury may have concluded that it could well have been on the Saturday or even the Sunday night that Mr Smith came and spoke to Harry.

One can only conclude that the sighting evidence in this trial was replete with inconsistencies and unreliability. Most of it would not be admissible in a criminal trial today. Did Eugenia's jury appreciate the inadequacies of this evidence? There was certainly plenty of scope for Archie McDonell to tear this evidence to shreds in cross-examination, but for some inexplicable reason he chose not to do so. He asked some of these witnesses whether they had seen mention of the matter or a photograph in the papers before going to the police, or whether they had discussed the case with their families, and focused most of his energies on eliciting evidence from them of the relationship between Harry and Annie. He did not suggest to a single one of them that their identification of the accused was wrong. This misleadingly transmitted to Coyle and the rest of the court that the defence were not challenging Harry Crawford's presence in the Lane Cove River Park on that long weekend in 1917. McDonell may have thought that he could still point out the weaknesses in the testimony of these witnesses during his closing address. But would he?

Coyle planned to deal with the shortcomings of the sighting witnesses in his closing address by submitting to the jury that they should look past the inconsistencies between the different witnesses and accept that their differences were what you would expect from people doing their best to recollect events that had occurred some years previously. He planned to tell the jury in his closing address that they did not need to rely upon the accuracy of the sighting witnesses, because they could come to several other important conclusions that would justify the conviction of the accused, namely:

- that Harry and Annie Crawford had set off together on the Friday morning to go for a picnic in the Lane Cove River Park;
- that Annie had died an unnatural death during that picnic;
- that Annie had been burned alive;
- that the accused was the only person with her when she died;
- that the accused had returned home that night and shortly afterwards packed up all their worldly possessions for sale; and
- that the accused had a very clear motive to kill Annie Birkett in order to prevent disclosure of the sexual deception.

Coyle believed that if the jury came to these conclusions, they would have no difficulty convicting Eugenia Falleni of the murder of Annie Birkett, even if they rejected the accuracy of the sighting witnesses.

CHAPTER 20

EXPERT WITNESSES

With one exception, the law requires witnesses to give evidence of facts and not opinions. The exception is the expert witness. In order for the opinions of expert witnesses to be admissible, it is necessary for them to establish that they have sufficient professional knowledge, expertise and experience in a field of specialised knowledge that is accepted as reliable by the community of their professional peers. Generally, their knowledge and expertise will derive from tertiary education followed by professional practice. Occasionally, an expert will be permitted to give evidence based only on knowledge and experience that has been gained through practice alone. The evidence of an expert witness must be limited to their area of specialisation. The courts are careful to prevent expert witnesses from venturing outside their field of knowledge. Expert witnesses are meant to be impartial, however those who have spent many years in the courts will tell you that some expert witnesses who make a living from giving evidence are renowned for favouring one side or the other.

There are as many types of expert witnesses as there are areas of specialised knowledge and practice. They include experts in every speciality of medicine, science, engineering, traffic-accident analysis, fire analysis, handwriting, fingerprints, psychology and a myriad of other specialist areas. Prosecutors have a particular responsibility to ensure that the expert witnesses they call are proficient, accurate and reliable. That is because of what is sometimes called the 'white coat' effect. Jurors, who are not experts, tend to be overly impressed by the weight of authority that expert witnesses bring to their evidence in court. They can easily be overwhelmed by the titles, university degrees, conference papers, published books and articles, and official positions that are listed in the curricula vitae of experts. It is therefore incumbent on a Crown Prosecutor to ensure that the opinions of those experts who are called in the prosecution case are solidly based in an area of expertise that is recognised by the expert's professional peers, so that if necessary, those opinions can be verified.

Two expert witnesses were called by the Crown in the trial of Eugenia Falleni. They were Dr Arthur Palmer and Dr Stratford Sheldon. Both of them were highly experienced, professional forensic pathologists who had previously conducted numerous autopsies at the Sydney Morgue situated in the basement under the Coroner's Court at 102–104 George Street, The Rocks. Both of them had previously given evidence in numerous trials. Both of them were readily accepted by the court as experts in their field of forensic pathology. Both of them had been present at the first autopsy conducted on the body of Annie Birkett in 1917 and at the second one nearly three years later after her body was exhumed.

For all intents and purposes, the evidence-in-chief of the two forensic pathologists was almost identical. They both agreed that at the first autopsy, conducted very shortly after the finding of Annie Birkett's body, they had found no evidence of any violence to her. Both of them acknowledged that when they next saw the body in July 1920, it had deteriorated considerably. Despite this, on re-examining the skull after X-rays had been taken, both doctors were of the view that one of the seven cracks found in her skull could have been caused by violence. Dr Palmer, who was the more senior of the two pathologists and the first to give evidence, said this:

> We especially examined the bone of the skull by X-ray. We found a number of fissures or cracks or breaks, as we call them, in the skull. There were at least seven of them – at least six, and one special one that I put aside. Those six fractures were all due to the heat, and they are what you would expect to find.
>
> 'There was a linear crack at the back of the skull, through a thick portion of the skull, on the right side of the back of the skull. It is about two and a half inches, I think. We both saw it at about the same time. We thought it was undoubtedly due to violence. At the time, my impression was that this crack was undoubtedly due to violence. It is just a linear crack which is hardly visible.

At this point, Dr Palmer reached down towards his bag on the floor in the witness box next to him and offered to produce Annie Birkett's skull to the court, so as to explain what he was talking about. The judge permitted him to do this and to indicate the relevant crack to the jury. The impact on everyone in the courtroom of producing the skull of the deceased to demonstrate her injuries would have been enormous. Nobody seems to have held any concerns about this procedure.[1]

After producing the skull, Dr Palmer said:

This is the skull cap that we remove first. (Witness shows the fissures to the jury.) The fissures caused by the fire are such as this in the front. That is a crack caused by fire, undoubtedly, and that is another one. (Witness continues demonstrating the skull to the jury.) I say at the time I formed the impression with regard to that particular lesion, our opinion at the time was that that was caused by violence.

The skull was admitted into evidence as exhibit T and, together with all the other exhibits, would have been available for inspection by the jury during their deliberations in the jury room at the end stage of the trial.

Both doctors were firmly of the view that death had been caused by the heat of the fire. The basis for this opinion was, in Dr Palmer's words:

At the junction of the charred portions with the portions unburned there was a good deal of blistering; large blisters being formed with thick fluid in them, and the blisters were surrounded by a red margin, the skin being red. On opening the blisters, the bottom of the blisters was red also.

I formed the opinion that the burning took place during life – probably. That was entirely from the description I have given you really of the blistering – redness and so on. From that, I could not say whether she would be conscious or unconscious.

In effect, Drs Palmer and Sheldon were relying upon two findings to conclude that Annie Birkett had been burned to death: the blistering at the margins of the burns and one of the cracks in the skull. The clear implication was that Annie had been struck on the head, thereby rendering her unconscious or senseless, which enabled the accused to place her body on the fire, resulting in her death.

The prosecution case was that Eugenia Falleni, as Harry Crawford, had burned his wife while she was still alive. The effect of this evidence on the jury can hardly be overemphasised. Once the jury accepted the accuracy of these expert opinions, they would inevitably have come to the conclusion that whoever did such an evil deed must have intended to kill. Dr Arthur Palmer, as the first of the two experts to give evidence and the more senior, was the more influential of them. In a very meaningful way, the testimony of Dr Palmer was the defining evidence in the trial. If the jury accepted his evidence, a conviction was almost inevitable. Archibald McDonell fully realised the importance of his evidence and, for that reason, he devoted more time and effort to the cross-examination of Dr Palmer than to any other witness in the trial.

Before asking Dr Palmer specific questions about his findings or opinions, in a demonstration of good advocacy, McDonell put Dr Palmer in his place through the following interchange which successfully demeaned the expert:

> *Mr McDonell: Is it not a fact, Doctor, that a bone taken freshly from the human body contains 50% water?*
> *Dr Palmer: I doubt that very much.*
> *Mr McDonell: May I approach the witness, your Honour?*
> *His Honour: Yes, of course.*
> *Mr McDonell: I show you Halliburton's Physiology, 1904 edition.*[2] *Do you acknowledge this as an authority?*
> *Dr Palmer: It is an authentic work.*
> *Mr McDonell: Do you see this paragraph? Do you now agree with my proposition? (laughter at the back of the court)*
> *Dr Palmer: Yes, you are right.*

McDonell next skilfully elicited from Dr Palmer his earlier view, held with great firmness after the first autopsy, that there were no marks of violence on the body. He then cross-examined the doctor about his evidence that the blisters indicated that burning had occurred while the victim was still alive. The doctor's evidence in answer to McDonell's questions was this:

> *I noticed signs of reaction at the edges of the burning, that there were many blisters, and the blisters had thick serum. There was also the red line of demarcation between the burning and burning [sic]. Most authorities believe that that could only occur during life – that if the burning or scorching took place after death, if there were any blisters at all, they would only contain air or gas, or occasionally a thin fluid if done immediately after death, I think. You would not get the reaction, the red line. I feel no doubt that these were caused during life. I am quite satisfied about that. It is an opinion, of course, and I have consulted many authorities, and after studying the authorities, and from my own experience, I think that is correct.*

McDonell also obtained these important concessions from Dr Palmer's about his lack of expertise concerning the effects of fire:

I am not an authority on the effect of heat in these things. I admit I have had very much more experience in violence than I have in fires. As a rule, where a person is burned, no post-mortem is required by the Coroner, because it is usually caused under circumstances that are obvious. Violence is a different matter.

McDonell had elicited some hesitation and reservation in the doctor's view about the significance of the blisters. If *most authorities* believed that the blistering could only occur during life, that suggested that there were others who thought differently. When the doctor said, 'It is an opinion, of course,' he was really acknowledging that the views of others may vary. In a case such as this, the law insists on proof beyond a reasonable doubt about a fact as critical as the cause of death. So, this part of Dr Palmer's evidence was clearly capable of being utilised by McDonell during his closing address to argue to the jury that the Crown had not proven this fact to that high degree of proof. But would he do so?

More importantly, McDonell had exposed the fact that, while Dr Palmer was a highly skilled forensic pathologist, he was not an expert on the effects of fire on a body. This opened up a fabulous opportunity for him to call a witness in the defence case who *was* an expert on the effects of fire to give evidence supporting the proposition that all of the cracks in the skull could have been caused by the heat of the fire. But would he do so?

McDonell then began a lengthy cross-examination of Dr Palmer about the single fracture to the skull that he had said could have been caused by violence. The cross-examination on this point was extensive, technical and went into great detail about topics such as the composition of bone, the thickness of the skull and the effect of heat on bone. McDonell frequently took Dr Palmer back to the concessions in the committal proceedings that had been obtained from him by Maddocks Cohen. At the conclusion of this part of the cross-examination, Dr Palmer had to concede that the seventh crack could well have been caused, like all the others, by the heat of the fire. His final position was:

Taking the nature and extent of that fracture, it would be just as likely to be caused by intense heat as by violence. I admit that as far as I know, heat may cause a fracture like that. I admit that, but I am not prepared to admit that it is more likely to do it than violence. Of course, it depends entirely on the violence.

Archibald McDonell, in what was a proficient cross-examination of a critical prosecution witness, had skilfully disposed of any definite conclusions about either the blisters or the cracks in the skull. He was now in a position to demolish the Crown case in his closing address to the jury by explaining that the fire had not been proven to be the cause of Annie's death, so that Annie may well have already been deceased when her body was burned. That left the Crown with no evidence to prove beyond a reasonable doubt what had caused Annie Birkett's death. In the absence of any such proof, how could the jury be satisfied that she had been deliberately murdered by the accused? But, would McDonell advance these arguments in his closing address, and would he call evidence in the defence case from his own fire expert?

Up until this point in time, Archie McDonell had done an exemplary job of cross-examining Dr Palmer, the main prosecution expert witness. However, his questioning of Dr Palmer then took a very strange and unexpected turn. McDonell began asking the Crown's pathologist questions about 'sexual inversion'.

Sexual inversion was a concept that had been formulated by Havelock Ellis (1859–1939), British sexologist, physician, psychologist and social reformer.[3] By the time of the Falleni trial, Ellis was considered the foremost sexologist in the world. In 1897, Ellis had published *Sexual Inversion*, the first of his six-volume *Studies in the Psychology of Sex*, and the first medical textbook in English on homosexuality. It had been published the year before in German, then considered as the language of science. The year after its English publication, a stockist of the book in England was prosecuted for having 'sold and uttered a certain lewd, wicked, bawdy, scandalous and obscene libel in the form of a book entitled *Studies in the Psychology of Sex: Sexual Inversion*.' It should be remembered that just a few years earlier, Oscar Wilde had been condemned and sentenced for having sexual relations with another man.

Ellis's book contained the first objective study of homosexuality. He disliked the term 'homosexual', which he considered as 'a barbarously hybrid word' because it contained a mixture of Greek and Latin roots. Unusually for his day, Ellis did not characterise sexual inversion as a disease, or immoral, or a crime. He defined sexual inversion as 'sexual instinct turned by inborn constitutional abnormality towards persons of the same sex'. He believed it to be an innate reversal of the normal gender traits, so that male inverts were, to some degree, inclined to traditionally female pursuits and dress, and vice versa. With its emphasis on gender role reversal, the theory of sexual inversion incorporated some concepts of transgender sexuality. There was no separate concept of transsexualism.[4]

By the time of the Falleni trial, Sigmund Freud had written important articles on sexual inversion: in 1905 ('Three Essays on the Theory of Sexuality') and 1920 ('Three Contributions to the Theory of Sex'). Freud frequently called homosexuality an 'inversion', by which he meant something that was distinct from pathological perversions. Freud believed that all humans were innately bisexual, by which he meant that everyone incorporated aspects of both sexes. In his view, this was true both anatomically and psychologically. He believed that heterosexuality and homosexuality both developed from this original bisexual disposition. Freud also considered that one of the causes of homosexuality was a previous distressing heterosexual experience. He wrote: 'Those cases are of particular interest in which the libido changes over to an inverted sexual object after a distressing experience with a normal one.'

Archibald McDonell's extensive personal library included many volumes on the topic of sexual inversion. It was an area in which he had a great personal interest and had read extensively.

McDonell's cross-examination of Dr Palmer on the topic of sexual inversion was seemingly based on the premise that, being a medical practitioner, the doctor would know of such matters. However, knowledge of such topics and being an expert qualified to give evidence in a criminal trial were two entirely different propositions. Coyle objected to the line of questioning and the following interchange occurred:

> Coyle KC: I object! This is not an area of expertise, but rather common knowledge.
> Dr Palmer: Sexual inversion is not a matter of common knowledge with me. I have read considerably. In the last few years, a very large quantity of literature has cropped up.
> His Honour: Mr McDonell, what is your purpose in this line of questioning?
> Mr McDonell: I am endeavouring to clear up the matter of the sex fraud which has been conveyed to the jury [by the prosecution], and showing that there is such a thing as true sexual inversion.
> His Honour: Are you setting up insanity, or not?

Mr McDonell: Oh, certainly not.

(The judge permitted the questioning to continue.)

Mr McDonell: (to the witness) Is it not a fact that when the hands are extended normally in front of the body, palms upwards, the elbows of a woman are closer together than those of a man?

His Honour: That might have some bearing on the case if you were setting up insanity, but as you say you are not, I cannot see what it is leading to.

Mr McDonell: I want to show, your Honour, that the accused has a masculine angle of arms.

(The judge again permitted the questioning to continue.)

Chief Justice Cullen was quite right to question McDonell on the purpose of these questions. It was not at all clear what counsel's aim was in venturing into this labyrinth. The trial judge believed that he might be trying to establish that his client was insane, which, if successful, would have resulted in a special verdict of not guilty on the grounds of mental illness. In order to successfully raise the defence of insanity, an accused must establish (on the balance of probabilities) that at the time of the crime he was suffering from a defect of reason, due to a disease of the mind, so that he did not know the nature and quality of his act or that his actions were morally wrong.[5] However, McDonell was not seeking to prove his client was insane. His stated objective, according to what he told the judge, was to deal with the Crown's allegation that the accused had engaged in a sexual fraud against Annie Birkett by proving that his client was a 'true sexual invert'. This requires some analysis.

In some cases, it can be beneficial for the defence counsel to attempt to elicit sympathy for his or her client. This is particularly so in cases where the jury may identify with the accused in their predicament and apply the aphorism: 'There, but for the grace of God, go I.' For example, where an accused is charged with dangerous driving causing death, it will often be advantageous to create some sympathy for the accused, because most jurors are also drivers. However, in the case of Eugenia Falleni, there was no possibility that any of the jurors would identify with her or with what she had done in changing gender, marrying someone of the same sex and engaging in sexual intercourse by means of a secreted dildo. They were highly unlikely to overlook the sexual deception that the accused had perpetrated upon both wives.

It appears that Archibald McDonell believed that if he could show that his client was a 'true sexual invert', the jury might accept that she had some inborn physical and psychological traits that biologically made her a type of male, so that what she had done to Annie Birkett and Lizzie Allison was less of a sexual fraud than it would otherwise have been. If she possessed some of the physical traits of a male, reasoned McDonell, and if she was psychologically a sort of male, that would mean that she had not truly engaged in sexual fraud, because she had been holding herself out to be someone or something that, in a sense, she really was. McDonell must have thought that by doing this, he would dissipate some of the jury's antipathy towards Eugenia for the sexual duplicity that she had engaged in with both wives. This was an utterly academic approach that showed a remarkable lack of understanding for the thinking of ordinary men at that time. Even today, most jurors would be unmoved by such an argument. It would appear that McDonell's extensive self-education in the privacy of his bedroom in his brother's home had blinded himself to current community opinions. By venturing down the track of attempting to prove that she was an innate 'sexual invert', he was much more likely to convince the jurors that his client was a freak of nature and a menace to the moral fabric of society.

McDonell handed Dr Palmer a copy of the book *Degeneracy: its Causes, Signs, and Results* by American physician, Eugene Talbot,[6] which contained plates of people of ambiguous gender, and asked him if he could assign the correct gender to each of the plates, but Dr Palmer would not be drawn on this and wisely answered:

> *I am not prepared to say whether [each of these pictures] is the figure of a male or female. I would have a good deal of doubt about laying down anything from the physical formation, any more than the old idea of diagnosing criminals from their appearance.[7] Conduct must be the test.*

After asking the doctor a series of questions in the field of embryology, concerning intrauterine life in which the rudiments of both sexual organs appear, McDonell put a series of disjointed, unintelligible, open-ended questions to the doctor that were really a vain attempt to state his position about his client's sexual identity:

> *Mr McDonell: Consequently, we have men who are more or less feminine and women who are more or less masculine. There is no doubt about that, I suppose. And this implantation of the sexual impulse may vary in degree one to the other, from all those tendencies, to have the impulse of the opposite sex to almost only one per cent or something of that kind?*
> *Dr Palmer: That is so, I believe.*

Mr McDonell: When we find a person who was said to have an inverted impulse in that direction, is it not a fact that usually the organs of that sex are complete? For instance, a man may be apparently a well-developed man, and yet have a hankering after his own sex instead of the opposite sex?

Dr Palmer: Well, I have not seen many. In some I have seen that. In one instance, the testicles of the male were dried up. In many cases, I am inclined to think if they were thoroughly examined you would find some changes. There would be some other change. I do not say that that is invariable. I cannot say that it is invariably so.'

If McDonell thought that this interchange would swing the jury in his client's favour, he was seriously misguided.

Finally, McDonell referred Dr Palmer to the physical examination the doctor had conducted of Eugenia at the Central police station on the day of her arrest, when her female gender had been confirmed. McDonell asked him how long it had taken to ascertain her sex, and the doctor replied, 'I suppose it took half a second.'

Following McDonell's cross-examination, Coyle KC had the right of re-examining Dr Palmer. Coyle saw this as an ideal opportunity to address some of the discrepancies in the Crown case that have already been mentioned. Coyle's solution was an ingenuous attempt to massage the evidence to fit with the Crown theory. His questioning went like this:

Coyle KC: (referring to the single lesion to the back of the head) Had that lesion been caused by violence, that would have rendered her unconscious?

Dr Palmer: Well, probably. I would not say for certain. I think probably it would.

Coyle KC: How long would that unconsciousness last?

Dr Palmer: Once a person is unconscious, I cannot say how long the state of unconsciousness may last. It may last for a short while, or it may last for days. With a blow like that, if it caused unconsciousness, she may have been unconscious for two or three days.

Coyle KC: While unconscious, would she have had any power of movement? While unconscious, if she were burned unconscious, she would have no power of moving?

Dr Palmer: Probably she would not move, except locally, with regard to the expansion of the muscle and so on.

Coyle was attempting to get some support from this witness for the proposition that Annie Birkett could have been rendered unconscious on the Friday and remained in that state until the Monday, when her body was burned, thereby causing her death. As if a murderously inclined Harry Crawford would render Annie unconscious on the Friday, leave her in that condition in the bush, wait three days, and then return on the Monday to finish her off by burning her to death! The bizarreness of this proposition demonstrated how weak the Crown case really was on this critical point and how desperate Coyle still remained to reconcile the various conflicting Crown witnesses.

CHAPTER 21

LIES

Part of the prosecution case against Eugenia Falleni consisted of the lies that, as Harry Crawford, she had told to various people. They included the different accounts that Harry had given to a large number of people about where and with whom Annie Birkett had supposedly gone after leaving their marital home at Drummoyne. It also included Eugenia's assertion to the police when they took her to the vicinity of the Cumberland Paper Mills several days after her arrest, and she initially claimed not to have any familiarity with the area, but subsequently admitted that many years earlier she had worked for a week at the nearby Chicago Flour Mills. Most importantly, this category of evidence included the typewritten statement that had been signed by Harry Crawford at the Criminal Investigation Branch offices in Sydney on the day of his arrest, shortly prior to the revelation of his true identity. The statement was based on answers provided by Eugenia in response to questions from Detective Sergeant Robson and had been typewritten by an official police typist. Robson had handed it to Crawford, who appeared to read it, and then signed it. Despite the fact that Crawford could not read, there was no challenge during the trial to the veracity of this statement and there was no objection by the defence to its admission into evidence.

The statement read:

My correct name is Harry Crawford, and I am 44 years of age. I am a Scotchman and was born at Edinburgh on July 25, 1875. My father's name was Henry Crawford and he was a dealer by occupation. My mother's name was Lizzy Crawford. About 18 months after I was born I was taken to New Zealand by my parents and lived first at Torrie Street, Wellington, with them. I left my parents' home at Torrie Street, Wellington, when about 18 years of age, and worked my passage on a vessel – I think it was the steamship Australia – direct to New South Wales and landed at Sydney.

The statement went on to detail the various workplaces where Crawford had been employed and the boarding houses where he had lived. It then continued:

I now reside at 47 Durham Street, Stanmore, with my wife, whose maiden name was Lizzie Allison. I was married at the Canterbury registry office in September, 1919. Up to that time I was a single man. My wife is the only personal friend I have had since arriving in Australia, either male or female.

The statement contained a number of lies – the most incriminating one being the assertion that he had not previously been married. Shortly after the creation of this statement, the interchange took place that has previously been related which led to Harry Crawford being revealed as a female. As already described, Detective Sergeant Robson then brought Harry Birkett into the interview room, and he identified the accused as his stepfather. After Birkett had left the room, Sergeant Robson read Birkett's statement to the accused, followed by the exchange about why she had not mentioned the first wife before. Robson then asked her some further questions:

Robson: When was the last time you saw your wife?
Falleni: On the Friday before Eight-Hour Day.
Robson: In what year?
Falleni: 1917. She then sold up the furniture and cleared out.
Robson: Have you seen her since?
Falleni: Yes, when she came back on the Wednesday.
Robson: Who did she sell the furniture to?
Falleni: Someone in Lyons Road.
Robson: What was the last time you actually saw your wife?
Falleni: On the Wednesday night when she came back to get half the money for the furniture
Robson: But you just told me she sold the furniture.
Falleni: No, that is wrong. It was I that sold the furniture and she came back for half the money.
Robson: Was that on the Wednesday night immediately after Eight-Hour Day?
Falleni: Yes.

Implicit in these answers was the assertion that, as Harry Crawford, the accused had not gone on a picnic with Annie to the Lane Cove River Park on the weekend that Annie died.

The treatment of lies in a criminal trial today is very strictly confined. According to the modern-day approach, there are two different types of lies. The first and more serious kind are lies that are so closely connected to the crime itself that, upon proof of their falsity, the telling of them amounts to a tacit or implied admission of guilt, because the lies have been told by the accused out of a realisation that the truth would implicate him or her in the commission of the offence. Lawyers call these 'consciousness of guilt lies'. The second kind of lies, which are more frequently encountered, are those which are more remote from the immediate circumstances of the crime and are called 'credibility lies' because they can only be used to attack the general credibility or reliability of the accused and not to infer guilt. In order for a lie of either sort to be admissible, there must be a body of evidence to prove the deliberate untruthfulness of it. It is not sufficient for an accused to be shown to have made an accidental error. The law also requires that proof of the lie must not depend upon a finding of guilt on the charge that the accused is facing, because that would involve circuitous reasoning.

There are many reasons why suspects might tell a lie, quite apart from a deliberate attempt to hide the fact that they have committed a crime. Lies are told out of embarrassment, or a fear of being unjustifiably accused of a crime, or because another less serious crime has been committed which the suspect is trying to hide. In order for a lie to be probative of guilt on a particular charge, a jury must be able to exclude other possible reasons for that lie. To use an example completely removed from the facts of the Falleni case: if an accused were charged with a bank robbery in a stolen getaway car, and the Crown can prove that the accused has told a lie about not being in the vicinity of where the car was stolen, the lie is perfectly explicable as an attempt by the accused to hide the theft of the car. It, therefore, cannot be said that the lie is evidence of his guilt for the bank robbery. Today, all of these considerations about the legitimate use that can be made of lies are the subject of careful directions from the trial judge to the jury during the summing up just before they retire to consider their verdict.

When Eugenia Falleni went to trial in 1920, the directions from the trial judge were nowhere near as extensive as they would be today. The only warning that was given to the jury by Chief Justice Cullen was that they should not necessarily infer that the telling of a lie *of itself* proves the guilt of the accused. If one looks at the different types of lies that were relied upon by the Crown Prosecutor in this trial, it becomes apparent that most, if not all of them, were explicable by other reasons. On the assumption that Harry Crawford was present in the Lane Cove River Park at the time that Annie died, and that he burned her body to prevent identification of it, the telling of the lies about how Annie had left their marriage and his denial that he was anywhere near the park are explicable on a number of other bases. Harry may have told the lies because he realised that he had committed a crime in burning the body and he wished to hide the commission of that offence. Harry may well have thought, quite correctly as it turned out, that if the body was identified, he would immediately be blamed for the death. Above all else, the telling of the lies was explicable as a desperate attempt by Harry to prevent any investigation by the police that might have the additional consequence of revealing his true identity as a female and exposing his sexual deception of both wives.

These alternative explanations, and possibly others, ought to have made it very difficult, or even impermissible, for the jury to use Eugenia's lies as evidence of her guilt. Even Harry's lie about not having been married before meeting Lizzie Allison was explicable on the basis that he had not told Lizzie about his previous marriage or his daughter, so he was hardly likely to admit these facts to the police. These considerations did not make the lies inadmissible as evidence against Eugenia, but they ought to have made them relevant only to her credibility and not evidence of her guilt. They raised a number of avenues for McDonell to make powerful submissions to the jury in his closing address about how they were explicable for reasons other than guilt. But would he?

CHAPTER 22

POLICE WITNESSES

It is invariably a difficult decision for a prosecutor to decide which witness to call last before closing the Crown case. Most prosecutors like to complete their case with some dramatic evidence that will remain reverberating in the jurors' minds long after counsel have sat down. William Coyle KC did not need to give a lot of thought to the question of how to finish his case in a memorable way. His last witness was Detective Sergeant Stewart Robson, the officer-in-charge of the police investigation and the one who had charged Eugenia Falleni with the murder of Annie Birkett.

As has already been mentioned, Detective Robson and his offsider, Detective Watkins, took Harry Crawford from the Empire Hotel at Annandale to the detectives' office at the Criminal Investigation Branch in Sydney without notifying him whether or not he was under arrest. By saying to him, 'I am going to take you to the Central Court or the Detectives' Office to make further investigations,' Sergeant Robson was clearly intimating that Crawford had no choice but to come with them, without formally arresting him. The law placed an obligation on a police officer who placed a suspect under arrest to bring them before a magistrate 'without unreasonable delay' and by the most reasonably direct route.[1] Because the police did not say to Harry Crawford the magic words, 'You are under arrest,' they possibly thought they could later claim that their suspect had chosen of his own accord to come with them. If they thought that this relieved them of their obligation to bring him before a magistrate, they were wrong. However this was a very common tactic by the police to avoid the rigours of the law in this area.

The detectives arrived at the Empire Hotel at about 11.30 am, giving them plenty of time to take Harry Crawford to the Central Police Court in Liverpool Street, if that had been their intention. In fact, it was never their intention. Their real plan was to take him to the Criminal Investigation Branch in order to question him there. Failure to comply with the rules potentially rendered any later admission or statement by the suspect inadmissible in a trial. At no stage did Archibald McDonell raise any of these issues or object to any of his client's conversations with the police after being taken to the police station. McDonell asked not a single question of the police about these sly tactics.

Once at the Criminal Investigation Branch, Crawford was introduced to Superintendent Bannan, the officer in charge of the branch, who informed Crawford that he would be questioned, and that his participation in this questioning should be 'absolutely voluntary', with which Crawford agreed. What Superintendent Bannan had done was to advise Crawford of his right to silence by issuing what is known as a police caution.

The right to silence has been a fundamental entitlement of all suspects and accused persons throughout the British common law world for many hundreds of years. It was inherited by all of the Australian Colonial States from the very earliest days of European settlement. The right to silence has a number of different aspects to it. The best-known one is the right of a suspect not to answer questions from the police. Almost as well known is the rule that an accused person cannot be obliged to give evidence at a trial. What most non-lawyers do *not* know is that, because of this right, the silence of an accused person at any time, either during the investigation or during legal proceedings, cannot be used against them in any way, either to infer guilt or even to cast doubts upon the credibility of the accused's case at a trial. This means that if a suspect declines an opportunity to provide an explanation during the police investigation and only advances it for the first time at the trial, the Crown is prevented from making the otherwise obvious and logical comment that the accused's failure to provide the explanation at an earlier time makes it less likely that it is true.

The duty of police to issue a caution to a suspect before questioning has existed throughout the British common law world for many hundreds of years. This is to ensure that the suspect knows of his or her right to silence and is aware of the fact that anything said after the caution can be used in evidence at a subsequent trial. The caution has two parts: advising the suspect of their right to remain silent and advising the suspect that any answers given may be used in evidence against them. For some reason, Superintendent Bannan only gave Harry Crawford the first part of the traditional caution. Normally, one would expect that this would be the subject of an application by the defence counsel to exclude any subsequent conversations or statements. Once again, Archibald McDonell raised no objection on this ground and once again he asked not a single question of any of the police about their failure to issue the complete caution.

Detective Sergeant Robson then gave evidence of the circumstances in which Harry Crawford had come to disclose that he was a woman (which has been related earlier), and then explained to the court how one of the sighting witnesses had come to identify the accused dressed as a man (also related earlier).

The last piece of evidence-in-chief given by Detective Sergeant Robson, and indeed the last piece of evidence elicited by the prosecutor in the Crown case, was about the search conducted at Harry Crawford's home at 47 Durham Street, Stanmore. Detective Robson gave evidence that he went there with Detective Truskett. As already described, Harry's wife Lizzie was at their home, crying, and Harry begged the police not to let Lizzie see what was in the cloth bag inside the portmanteau. Detective Robson's evidence went like this:

> I opened the bag. I got the article from it and asked the accused "What's that?" – meaning the article I found in the bag. "Did your first wife know that you were using anything like this?" The accused said, "No, not till about the latter part of our marriage, not till about the latter stages of our married life. I think somebody had been talking." I opened a portmanteau and in it I found a fully loaded revolver and also an exhibit. (Revolver shown to witness.) This is the revolver and also the exhibit. I said to the accused, "Is this what you referred to as having used on your wife?" And the accused said, "Yes." (Article in question shown to witness.) That is what I found.

At this point, the Chief Justice seems to have got quite annoyed at Sergeant Robson for referring to the dildo as 'the exhibit'. Perhaps his annoyance was because he had not yet allowed the object to be admitted into evidence as an official court exhibit. Whatever the reason, Robson corrected himself and said: 'By "exhibit", I mean an article.' The judge then noisily used his pen to scratch out the word *exhibit* in his notebook and wrote underneath it the word *article* – and then promptly admitted the article as an exhibit! Within a few minutes, Sergeant Robson had finished his evidence-in-chief and Coyle KC sat down, content in the knowledge that his case was complete.

Coyle's final piece of evidence had involved producing the article itself, an object that the jurors had probably been eagerly waiting to see for the duration of the Crown case. He had skilfully ensured that the prosecution case ended in a most dramatic and memorable way.

While the admission into evidence of the dildo was perfectly legitimate, because it was relevant to prove the sexual fraud perpetrated on Annie

Birkett and the alleged motive for the murder, no such justification could possibly be found for the mention of the revolver. Evidence of unrelated criminal conduct, like the possession of an unlicenced revolver, was only rarely admitted into evidence in a criminal trial – and then only when it was strikingly similar to the events in question.[2] That could not be said about this revolver. There was no allegation that Annie Birkett had been shot, so the revolver had no possible relevance to the murder charge. In this case, the revolver had no probative value whatsoever. By introducing evidence about the finding of the revolver and the cartridges and producing them to the court, Coyle created an enormous amount of unfair prejudice against the accused – not only because it disclosed that she had had possession of an illegal firearm, but also because two of the cartridges had been fired, which suggested that at some time in the past she had used it. This potentially created the impression that the accused might have been involved in firing the gun during some violent criminal activity. Coyle KC should never have led this highly damaging and irrelevant evidence and McDonell should have protested to the fullest possible extent before it was given.

In the event of such evidence being unexpectedly introduced without any warning, the remedy that is available to the defence is for the judge to bring the trial to an end, discharge the jurors without a verdict, and order a new trial to begin before another jury that has not heard the prejudicial material.[3] The introduction of evidence about the revolver was so damaging and so utterly irrelevant that such a remedy would have been appropriate in this instance. Yet, Archibald McDonell did not ask for a discharge of the jury. He did not even object to the evidence when it was led. In fact, in his cross-examination of Detective Sergeant Robson, he asked quite a few questions himself about the revolver and the cartridges. McDonell then compounded his errors by requesting that the revolver and the cartridges be admitted as exhibits in the trial and marked exhibit H1. This prompted Chief Justice Cullen to say to him:

> This [the finding of the gun and cartridges] was three years after the occurrence at Lane Cove. It would not have any bearing [on the case]. I never took it as having any bearing.

In a subtle way, without alerting the jury, the Chief Justice was letting McDonell know that he had made an egregious error by allowing some irrelevant and prejudicial evidence to be led by the Crown Prosecutor.[4] As if this was not bad enough, McDonell then elicited from Detective Robson that the accused had told him that the gun had been obtained from the manager of the Coogee Beach Hotel. This allowed the detective to reply that he had interviewed the manager of the hotel who had denied that any such thing had ever occurred. This conveyed to the jury even further irrelevant and suspicious innuendoes about how Eugenia had come to be in possession of the gun.

McDonell's penultimate line of cross-examination of Detective Sergeant Robson involved asking him questions about the dangers of identification evidence. McDonell's questions were so loose, open-ended and expansive that the detective was able to give this evidence:

'It is the fact that the police have to be particularly careful in securing identification. They must be very careful. If they are not very careful, there is liable to be trouble on both sides. I would not say exactly that that would be through the unconscious readiness to identify [a suspect] on the part of some people. But it is very often that people that can identify a person are so nervous that they fail. I have never met a case myself of others failing through being too eager to identify, but I have heard that such cases have existed. I have never met one. I will admit that mistakes are very frequently made and honestly made in identification, in every walk of life. They are made everywhere – courts and everywhere else.'

In effect, Sergeant Robson was making the astounding assertion that the only mistaken identification cases that he had ever come across involved witnesses *failing* to identify suspects when they should have, and that he had never experienced a witness who had incorrectly made a positive identification of a suspect. This, of course, was complete nonsense and defied common sense. The courts have always recognised that the main danger of identification evidence lies with witnesses mistakenly identifying suspects.

McDonell's final question of Detective Sergeant Robson was again extraordinary for its looseness and open-endedness. It was also an impermissible question, because it called for the expression of an opinion. The answer would not have assisted the jury one jot in deciding whether Eugenia was guilty or not guilty. The question was this:

Being largely engaged in the investigation of crime, would you be able to express an opinion on whether the majority, or any definite proportion, of murderers are finally run down?

Coyle could have objected to this question on a number of bases, but he chose not to, probably because he realised that he had nothing to lose from the answer. It is difficult to know what McDonell hoped to gain from it. If the answer had been that most murderers are brought to justice, it is difficult to see how that would have assisted his client's case. Similarly, if the answer had been that most murderers successfully evade justice, it is difficult to ascertain how it would have benefited his client. In his answer, Robson sat on the fence, probably because he could not see where McDonell was heading:

There are many untraced, and many traced – both ways.

With that bland and unhelpful answer, McDonell sat down – ending his cross-examination with a whimper rather than a bang. Coyle decided not to ask any questions in re-examination, as he was in as good a position as any prosecutor could hope to be, and he wasn't going to run the risk of spoiling it with 'one question too many' – a trap so often fallen into by less-experienced barristers. Detective Sergeant Robson was excused from the witness box. Coyle KC stood up at the Bar table and slowly but purposely announced, 'If your Honour pleases, that is the case for the Crown,' formally signifying the end of the prosecution case.

CHAPTER 23

DEFENCE CASE AND CASE IN REPLY

The commencement of the defence case, immediately after the Crown case has concluded, always requires one particularly important decision to be made: whether or not the accused will give evidence. In 1920, there was a third choice available, which was somewhat of a middle ground between giving evidence and not giving evidence. That was the option of making an unsworn 'statement from the dock'.[1] A statement from the dock consisted of the accused standing up in the dock, where he or she had been during the trial, and making an unprompted, unsworn oral statement to the jury.

The main advantage of a dock statement was that the Crown Prosecutor did not get an opportunity to cross-examine the accused. There were very few restrictions on what an accused could say in a dock statement, and it was therefore a good opportunity for an accused to present their version of the facts to the jury without the risk of being demolished in cross-examination. It was also an opportunity, where the accused had no prior criminal convictions, to place some positive, personal material about their character before the jury. For that reason, in the vast majority of criminal trials, defence counsel would advise their clients to make a dock statement rather than going into the witness box and giving sworn evidence which would be tested through rigorous cross-examination by the Crown Prosecutor.

There were three drawbacks to the option of a dock statement. The first was that if the accused was going to make a dock statement, the defence counsel would not also be permitted to give an opening address. The second drawback was that the accused had to make the statement entirely on their own, rather than in response to questions from their counsel. There was the possibility, however, if an accused forgot to mention a distinct topic, for the judge to give defence counsel permission to stand up at the end of the statement and say, 'Would the accused like to say anything about the topic of X?' However, it was undesirable to do this in front of the jury more than once. The third drawback was that during the judge's summing up, the jury would be told that the dock statement was 'unsworn' and was not subject to cross-examination, and that they should treat it like any other account that the accused had given out of court. Jurors generally knew about the three options, and so by making a dock statement the accused ran the risk of the jury thinking that they had been unwilling to withstand cross-examination like all the other witnesses in the trial. It was, however, generally better than saying nothing at all.

In most cases, defence counsel would help their client prepare a dock statement. Often counsel would actually write out the dock statement in full and get the accused to memorise it, and there was nothing to stop counsel listening to a practice run and making suggestions to improve it.

Any sensible defence counsel would have a serious discussion with their client about the three options that were available for the accused in the defence case. If the decision was made without proper consultation with the client and the client was subsequently convicted, they may well blame the barrister and complain: 'If only I had given evidence/not given evidence/made a dock statement, I would have gotten off.' For that reason, it was always advisable for defence counsel to inform the client about the advantages and disadvantages of each option, but to leave the ultimate decision to the accused. The defence solicitor would then make a written record of the decision on their file and get the client to 'sign up'.

One can only assume that Archibald McDonell had such a discussion with Eugenia Falleni and that she wisely decided to make a dock statement. It would have been a very foolish accused who thought that they could hold their own during cross-examination by 'the Bulldog'. One can only think that McDonell discussed with Eugenia the topics she should cover in her dock statement. Based upon the case that was put to the jury, the topics should have included: a denial of the murder, a denial of being in the park on the Eight-Hour Day weekend, an assertion that Annie had left their home and their marriage, a denial of the correctness of the sighting witnesses, an explanation for selling the furniture, a denial of any plan to murder Harry Jnr and, for good measure, an expression of concern for Annie Birkett wherever she may be. In light of all of these possible topics, when one looks at what she actually said, one can only be dumbstruck.

The defence case began with McDonell standing up and saying to the assembled court, 'The accused will make a statement to the jury.' As he promptly sat down, all eyes and ears were firmly fixed on Eugenia as she slowly stood up and for the first time looked the jurors firmly in the face. For almost everyone in the courtroom – jurors, journalists, court staff, members of the public – this was the first time that they had actually heard her speak, apart from her almost inaudible plea of not guilty at the beginning of the trial, and they were enthralled at finally hearing something directly from the 'man-woman'. Her entire dock statement consisted of these few words:

> *Your Honour and Gentlemen of the Jury. I have been three months in Long Bay Gaol, and with this terrible charge hanging over my head, and I am real nervous.*

At this point the court reporter was having great difficulty hearing her, which prompted the judge to ask her to speak up. She began again:

> *Your Honour and Gentlemen of the Jury. I have been three months in Long Bay Gaol. I am a real nervous breakdown. I would like to make a statement, but my constitution will not allow me. I do not know anything at all about this charge. I am perfectly innocent. I do not know what made the woman leave her home. We never had any serious rows, only just a few words, but nothing to speak of. So, therefore, I am absolutely innocent of this charge that is over me.*

To say that this dock statement was woefully inadequate is an understatement. It would have been viewed by the jury as such a pathetic effort at responding to the Crown case that it was tantamount to an admission of guilt. It may have been better for her to have said nothing. It is quite inconceivable that McDonell would have allowed his client to make such a statement if he knew that she was going to perform so poorly. If McDonell had no warning of how deficient the dock statement was going to be, he should at least have taken the opportunity to remind his client about some of the topics that should have been included in it. It was a most ignominious beginning to the defence case.

Following her dock statement, Archibald McDonell called one witness, Mr David Love, who was the manager of the Chicago Flour Mills. He gave evidence of seeing a mad, derelict woman a number of times in the area of the mills. On one particular occasion, he had seen her only a couple of hundred yards away from where the body was later found. He said that she had been hanging around that bush locality for about a week or so and she would be there every evening at about 5.30pm when he was going home from the mills. He got the impression that she was a half-witted lunatic who was camping in the bush. The last time he had seen her was on the Thursday night prior to the Eight-Hour Day weekend, and he had not seen her since then. He had been shown some cloth material in the Coroner's Court which was similar to the dress that this woman had worn.

The evidence-in-chief of this witness was clearly designed to suggest that the burned body found in the park could have been this unidentified woman. This was the very first warning Coyle KC had been given that the defence were challenging the identification of the body as Annie Birkett's. None of the witnesses who had identified her jewellery, gabardine clothing material, shoes, dental plates and picnic basket had been the subject of any challenge by the defence. To suddenly turn around at the very end of the trial and, for the first time, challenge the identity of the body was tactically disastrous. In cross-examination of Mr Love, Coyle KC elicited from him that after the first Inquest he had been told by the police that the derelict woman had in fact been located alive. This effectively demolished any slight advantage that the defence may have obtained from Mr Love.

Having led this feeble and unimpressive evidence, Archibald McDonell stood up and announced to the court that the defence case was complete. He did not call a single expert witness to assist the court on some critical issues that had arisen during the trial, such as: the cracks in the skull being caused by the heat of the fire rather than by violence; that the blisters found on Annie Birkett's body did not indicate that she had been burned alive; or some medical evidence that her death could have been the result of an accident, such as a fall.

It is very rare for a trial judge to allow the Crown to call a case in reply after the defence case has closed, because the Crown has an obligation to call all of its evidence prior to the defence case. The only circumstance in which the Crown will be permitted to call a case in reply after the defence case has been completed is where the defence have raised an issue or called some evidence that could not have been anticipated by the Crown during its own case. Such was the situation here. The Crown could not have anticipated that there would be any challenge to the identification of the body, so Coyle was permitted to call an additional witness in a Crown case in reply.

Coyle KC called Inspector John Maze who, in 1917, had been the sergeant-in-charge of the Chatswood police station. He gave evidence about making enquiries concerning a demented woman who had been seen near the Chicago Paper Mills. He informed the court that, as far as he could recollect, the matter had been satisfactorily cleared up and the woman had been located living somewhere in North Sydney. Tactically, this witness was devastating for the defence. The very last witness in the case had effectively demolished the one and only witness called on behalf of the accused. The jury would have been left with the firm impression that the only line pursued in the defence case had failed dismally. The jury would also have been completely unimpressed with the belated attempt by the defence to challenge the Crown evidence on the identification of the body. It is a complete enigma why McDonell chose to call only that one witness, and to attack the strongest part of the Crown case, and why he left it so late to do so. Incomprehensibly, the defence did *not* raise the very live issue of whether Annie might have died accidentally. In fact, at no time during the trial did McDonell offer any alternative explanation of how Annie may have died.

This marked the end of the evidence in the trial of Eugenia Falleni. What still remained were the closing addresses by counsel, the summing up by the trial judge and the deliberations of the jury.

CHAPTER 24

CLOSING ADDRESSES

The last stage of a criminal trial involves a closing address from each counsel and the summing up by the judge. The closing addresses are a particularly important part of a trial because they give each of the opposing barristers an opportunity to analyse the evidence and advance arguments why the jury should view it in a way that supports their case. Often, each counsel will attempt to construct a different picture from the very same pieces of evidence.

In 1920, as had been the practice in British common law countries for many centuries, the defence closing address was presented first, followed by that of the Crown.[1] It was universal wisdom that the counsel who gave the last address had a distinct advantage, because it was the last thing that the jury heard from either barrister before retiring to consider their verdict.

The defence closing address is sometimes a rather rambling affair in which counsel roams over the whole of the Crown case, pointing out faults and deficiencies here and there. It is a basic rule of good defence advocacy that the most concerted attack must be directed at the weakest part or parts of the prosecution case. Where an aspect of the Crown case is particularly strong, it is generally best to ignore it, or at least gloss over it, in the defence closing address. Whether one is a Crown Prosecutor or a defence counsel, it is critically important to maintain one's credibility with the jury. The surest way to destroy one's credibility is to direct one's most vehement attack on a part of the opposition's case that is irrefutable or unassailable. That is precisely what Archie McDonell attempted to do in his closing address on behalf of Eugenia Falleni.

The strongest part of the Crown case against Eugenia Falleni was the identification of the body that had been found in the Lane Cove River Park as being the remains of Annie Birkett. Not only had her jewellery and clothing been identified by her son, Harry Jnr, and her sister, Lily, but two dentists had given evidence identifying her top and bottom sets of false teeth as being their handiwork. There was also the fact that she had not been heard of since the Eight-Hour Day weekend in 1917 and the association of that date with the finding of the body in the park. To say that the evidence on this point was overwhelming is not an exaggeration. And yet, Archie McDonell chose as his principal argument in his closing address to submit to the jury that they could not be satisfied that the body in the park was that of Annie Birkett. His address, which went for a little over an hour, was reported in *The Truth* on 10 October 1920:

> *In his address to the jury, Mr McDonell, after traversing the evidence given and arguing that the identification of the dead body was far from satisfactory, made the suggestion that it was not only possible, but probable that Mrs Birkett was still living, and hiding her identity at the present time.*
>
> *[McDonell submitted that] 'she was in no way at fault, but look at the matter from this point of view. If a man commits a murder, he can live again, and in time become respectable, but if he commits a sexual crime, can he lift his head and ever assume respectability? And if a man would be so ostracised, what would happen to a woman when her mistake became public?'*

What McDonell was trying to say in this last paragraph, albeit in a clumsy way, was that Annie Birkett had every reason for disappearing after discovering that her husband was a woman. The jury must have heard the submission by McDonell about the identity of the body and thought, You must be kidding. *That* is your strongest point? The judge in his summing up to the jury confirmed that 'the question chiefly discussed in the case set up by the defence arises on the identity of the charred body that was found, [compared] with that of Mrs Birkett'.

The next most convincing part of the Crown case was that Harry Crawford was in the park with Annie when she died. Even if one dismissed the sighting witnesses from the vicinity of the Cumberland Paper Mills, there were neighbours who had seen Harry and Annie leaving Drummoyne together on the Friday morning and Harry arriving back on his own that night. Harry's actions, almost immediately on his return, of packing up their goods, selling their furniture and giving away some of Annie's jewellery and other possessions, proved that he knew that Annie would never be coming back. If Annie had merely left him for another man, there was the very real probability that she would return for her possessions. His actions clearly revealed that he knew she was dead, and he could only have known that if he had been with her when she died. There was, therefore, a very powerful case for the Crown that Harry had been with Annie at the clearing in the park when she died. And yet, this also was subjected to a major challenge in the defence address.

There were other far more convincing arguments available to McDonell on which he could have addressed the jury. Assuming that the body was Annie Birkett's and that Harry had been with her when she died, the evidence from the forensic scientists who had conducted both post-mortems was full of holes. Neither of the two doctors, Dr Palmer and Dr Sheldon, was prepared to categorically state that the crack could only have been occasioned by a blow, as opposed to being caused by the heat of the fire, like all the other cracks in the skull. Both doctors were of the opinion that the deceased had *probably* been burned while still alive. Neither doctor was prepared to categorically state that Annie Birkett *must* have been alive when her body was burned. To put it another way, neither doctor was prepared to deny the *reasonable possibility* that she had been burned after death.

The criminal law does not deal in absolute certainties, as nothing can be proved to that degree, but the law does insist on the prosecution proving essential facts beyond a reasonable doubt. The accused is entitled to claim the benefit of anything less than that. Undoubtedly Annie had died, and undoubtedly her death had occurred at the clearing in the park. However, the Crown had not proven beyond a reasonable doubt how Annie Birkett had died. The defence was therefore entitled to the version that was the most favourable to the accused. The absence of proof of the precise cause of death should have been the main issue raised by the defence during this trial and the principal focus of the defence address should have been whether Annie had died by accident. However, Archie McDonell completely overlooked this point in his address and the trial judge did not raise it for the jury's consideration. In fact, in his summing up, the judge said:

There is no evidence placed before you that would indicate the probability of her having met her death by accident.

The fact that the Crown is not able to prove the exact cause of death is not fatal to a prosecution for murder. In fact, there have been a number of cases in Australia and other similar jurisdictions where a murder conviction has been obtained and upheld without the body ever having been found.[2] However, the absence of evidence to prove the cause of death can make it more difficult for the Crown to identify the circumstances in which the deceased came to die and therefore to prove the involvement of the accused and his or her intention at the time of the death. For a murder conviction, the Crown must prove that the accused had the intention to kill or to cause grievous bodily harm (really serious bodily injury). Where there is a real question of whether the deceased died by the deliberate infliction of violence or arising out of an accident, the absence of evidence to prove the cause of death can be critical.

McDonell faced an ethical and a tactical problem in that his client had categorically denied being in the park with Annie on that fateful day of her death. In those circumstances, is it proper and ethical for a defence counsel to advance arguments that are contrary to his client's instructions? Was McDonell in a position to argue that, even if the body was Annie's and his client was in the park when she died, the death might have been a terrible accident? There is nothing ethically improper in a defence counsel pointing out to the jury where there are gaps or weaknesses in the prosecution case, even if that is inconsistent with their instructions. Even a defence counsel who has received a confession from the client is entitled to point out deficiencies in the prosecution case. Sometimes, it is tactically necessary for a defence counsel to argue hypothetical positions that are contrary to the defence case. By way of example, if a male is charged with sexual intercourse of a female without her consent, and the instructions of the accused to his barrister are that the alleged victim is mistaken about the identity of her assailant, there is nothing to stop the defence barrister pointing out to the jury that the alleged victim may have consented to sexual intercourse. This is because one of the essential ingredients for the Crown to prove beyond a reasonable doubt is the victim's lack of consent to sexual intercourse. Similarly, there were no ethical constraints that prevented McDonell glossing over the identity of the body and his client's denial of having been in the park, and submitting to the jury that Annie's death could have been accidental.

There were abundant arguments available to Archie McDonell to support a submission that Annie Birkett may have died in a tragic accident. The arguments available to refute a premeditated murder were as follows:

- If Harry had planned beforehand to murder Annie, why would he take her to a place in the park which was almost within view and hearing of the Cumberland Paper Mills and why would he take her to a place where at any moment a picnicker or bushwalker may come past?
- If Harry had planned beforehand to murder Annie, why would he take her to a place where it was impossible to bury the body or otherwise dispose of it without trace?

- If Harry had planned beforehand to murder Annie, why would he have been so careless when removing her personal item from the scene? Surely the fact that he overlooked the three items of jewellery and her shoes shows that he was in a panic and not thinking rationally.

The jury could only conclude that Harry had not committed a premeditated murder. What about an unpremeditated murder in a fit of rage at the scene? McDonell could have submitted:

- If Harry had killed Annie in a fit of rage at the scene, isn't it likely that there would have been some indications of a struggle and unequivocal signs of violence on the body, even though it was burned?

However, the strongest argument of all was this:

- The evidence led at the trial was equally supportive of an accidental death as it was of Harry killing Annie in a sudden fit of rage. The accused was therefore entitled to the benefit of the most favourable version of the facts, namely that it was a tragic accident. Putting it another way, the Crown had failed to exclude the reasonable possibility that Annie had died by accident. There were any number of scenarios in which Annie could have come to accidentally hit her head on something hard like a rock or a tree root, thereby causing a cerebral haemorrhage which led to her death. Then, in a panic, Harry did something very foolish by rendering her remains unidentifiable.

McDonell could also have submitted these arguments:

- Harry's actions in burning her body were equally consistent with a fear of exposure as a female and a fear that he would unjustifiably be blamed for her death as they were with feelings of guilt for her murder.
- Likewise, Harry's actions in telling repeated lies after her death to a whole host of people about how Annie had left him, and with whom, and where she had gone, were equally consistent with both accident and murder.
- Ultimately, because the evidence was equally consistent with accident and murder, the Crown had failed to prove its case beyond a reasonable doubt.
- Even if the jury concluded that Harry had deliberately struck Annie on the head, the injury to her skull was not sufficiently grave to enable the

jury to conclude from that alone that Harry intended to kill her or to do her grievous bodily harm. If the jury concluded that there remained a reasonable possibility that he had intended to do her some harm falling short of grievous bodily harm, this would constitute manslaughter rather than murder.

At Eugenia's trial, her counsel would have done much better accepting that the body was Annie's, glossing over his client's denial of being in the Park, and focusing instead on the real issues, which were that the prosecution had failed to prove:

- the cause of death;
- that her death was not an accident; and
- any intention on Harry's part to cause death or grievous bodily harm.

Had these arguments been advanced by her counsel, Eugenia's chances of an acquittal, or a conviction for manslaughter rather than murder, would have been immeasurably increased.

Another argument advanced by McDonell during his closing address to the jury was that the Crown had not adequately proven that Eugenia Falleni, as Harry Crawford, had had any motive to kill Annie Birkett. Once again, this argument was foolish and counter-productive. Right from the beginning of the trial, Coyle KC had identified the sexual deception practised so skilfully by Crawford on his wife, and the threat of exposing that, as a sufficient motive for the murder. McDonell highlighted the fact that the couple appeared to have lived together in relative harmony for eight months after Harry's true identity had been revealed, and that nothing out of the ordinary had happened in the days prior to the death, so that it was inexplicable that his client would then suddenly perpetrate such a dreadful deed. However, the lack of a reason to kill Annie at *that* particular time did not mean that there was no motive to kill her *at all*. The real problem with this argument was that if the jury accepted that the body was Annie's, that Harry was with her in the park when she died, and that her death had been a violent one, it did not matter whether or not there had been any particular event in the previous few days to warrant a sudden act of fury. The fear of denunciation and prosecution for sexual deception was reason enough on its own as a motive to kill, and to argue to the contrary was futile, and indeed counterproductive.

By advancing the unconvincing argument that the Crown had proven no motive, McDonell handed Coyle KC – 'Bulldog' and 'sly fox' rolled into one – a gift on a plate – one which Coyle received with glee and took full advantage of in his own address! Coyle's response was discretely reported by an anonymous journalist who wrote a popular column in *Smith's Weekly* called 'The Man in The Mask'. After attending both closing addresses, he (as it surely was a male) reported on 16 October 1920:

> *I saw her [Eugenia] stand beneath the hundred-eyed gaze of curiosity, and listen to an incisive, dynamic voice declaiming against her. I saw the owner of that voice [Coyle], with practised dramatic gesture and well-ordered disgust, cast before the eyes of her judges [the jury] the grotesque symbol of her distorted longings.*

The 'grotesque symbol of her distorted longings' was 'the article', which Coyle ostentatiously brandished in front of the jury during his closing address. The jurors would have been absolutely mesmerised as the prosecutor waved in front of them what had been the object of so much speculation and wonderment – like a snake charmer hypnotising a cobra. This emotive tactic would have been remarkably effective in completely negating the defence argument that there had been no motive proven for the murder. In the jury room a few hours later, while deliberating on their verdict, all that the jurors would have remembered would have been 'the article', dangled in front of them during the course of a very powerful address by the Senior Crown Prosecutor. As a tactic, it was like a precision guided missile which totally disintegrated its target, leaving the enemy completely blinded by the dust of the explosion.

Coyle KC then calmly and methodically went over the evidence that implicated Eugenia Falleni in the commission of the murder. He divided his address into three different parts. The first part was an analysis of the evidence that proved that the body found in the park was that of Annie Birkett. The second part was an examination of the evidence that proved that Annie Birkett had died a violent death at someone's hands. The third part was a consideration of the evidence that proved that her death had been at the hands of Harry Crawford. There were no submissions at all about what Harry's intention had been at the time of the death. It was just assumed by everyone in the courtroom that if it was his act that had caused her death, it must have been done with the intention of killing her.

The jurors could not have failed to observe the differences between the two addresses.

CHAPTER 25

THE LAW SPEAKS

The summing up by Chief Justice Sir William Cullen took only thirty-seven minutes.[1] In that time, he gave the jurors the directions of law that were required for them to come to a decision, and he briefly referred to the most important issues that had arisen during the trial. He told the jurors that they had to make a decision whether or not they were satisfied beyond a reasonable doubt about three essential facts: the identity of the body as that of Annie Birkett; whether Annie Birkett was murdered; and whether the person who committed that murder was the accused. He correctly told the jury that this was a circumstantial case, which meant that they had to be able to dispel any reasonable hypothesis consistent with her innocence before they could convict. He pointed out that, with one exception, the defence had not suggested that any of the witnesses had shown an inclination 'to exaggerate or say anything they do not believe to be true'.

The judge then referred to Eugenia's past, and remarked:

Her own record, of course, has been bad. But you are not because of the badness of a person's record, you are not because a person is of bad character, deceitful, untruthful, to come to the conclusion that that person is guilty of a particular offence charged.

There is a rule of law in the criminal courts that the general character of an accused is not relevant to the issue of guilt unless the accused raises his or her good character, in which case the prosecution is entitled to raise evidence of bad character to challenge that assertion. In this trial, neither in her dock statement nor in McDonell's cross-examination had it been suggested that Eugenia Falleni was a person of good character who was unlikely to have committed such an atrocious crime. What the Chief Justice was trying to do was to allay any prejudice against her because of the evidence that had emerged about her lies and deceitfulness within the marriage and to the police. However, in doing so, he was forced to remind the jury of the very evidence that painted her in a grim light.

Sir William then told the jury that the main issue challenged by the defence 'arises on the identity of the charred body that was found with that of Mrs Birkett'. The judge quite clearly intimated to the jury what his own personal view was on this subject when he said:

> Counsel for the Crown has put so clearly to you the facts on which the Crown case rests in that particular, that I need not say very much about it.

He reminded the jury about all of the items that had been found at the death scene that linked the body to Annie Birkett, and concluded by saying 'No one has been called to suggest that she was ever seen afterwards.' The jury would have been under no doubt whose body the judge thought it was. This dealt with the first issue that the jury had to decide.

Regarding the second issue, whether Annie Birkett had been murdered, his Honour reminded the jury of the evidence of the two doctors:

> Both of the doctors say that their own opinion, though they could not testify absolutely to it, was that one of the injuries or one of the fissures on the skull was caused by violence, but they also say that a person might be stunned without a fracture of the skull.

This was an oversimplification of the evidence, and it glossed over the shortcomings of the expert evidence. He continued:

> There is no evidence placed before you that would indicate the probability of her having met her death by accident. The doctors, in the first instance, not knowing who the woman was, not knowing anything at all about the previous history of this unknown woman whose charred body was found in the bush, thought it a reasonable idea that she might have tumbled into a fire. That was an opinion expressed by them. That was three years ago, when this body was found. But there is no evidence – none whatever – to help in dealing with the question whether that was an accidental occurrence or not.

In this passage, having reminded the jury of the doctors' original view that the deceased may have 'tumbled into a fire' – a scenario that involved an accidental death – the Chief Justice then said that there was no evidence whatsoever to suggest an accidental death. The jurors would have been excused for thinking that the Chief Justice was speaking in riddles. Surely, the original opinion of both doctors, based upon their first autopsy, provided some support for an accidental death.

Regarding the relationship between Harry and Annie, the judge remarked that the evidence showed that there had been 'an unhappy condition of things existing between them' and suggested that:

> It would almost seem incredible that two people could live together for three years without Mrs Birkett discovering that an imposition had been practised.'

By 'imposition', the Chief Justice meant the surreptitious use of 'the article.

The judge then briefly summarised the evidence of the sighting witnesses, making no real attempt to analyse their shortcomings and leaving it to the jury to decide whether or not they were reliable. Regarding the evidence of the different versions that Harry had given about Annie's disappearance, his Honour said:

> The testimony of these witnesses who refer to expressions used by the accused with reference to the occasion when Mrs Birkett ceased to be an occupant of his house, no doubt will be taken into consideration by you. There is the evidence that these versions were given of his wife's disappearance and her belongings being appropriated. If you are satisfied that the accused was in that place [in the park] on that day with the woman Mrs Birkett, then the different statements made by him in regard to her disappearance are matters which touch the reasonableness of the theory set up by the Crown.

This was the judge's entire direction on how the jury should treat the lies that had been told by Harry Crawford about his wife's disappearance. There was no attempt made to analyse what other reasons may have prompted the telling of these lies – probably because defence counsel had not made any submissions on that topic, and it was not the judge's role to advance arguments on the accused's behalf. In accordance with the practice of the day, there was no suggestion to the jury that they might use this as evidence of her lack of credibility rather than as evidence pointing to her guilt.

After telling the jurors that they could come back into court and ask to be reminded of any evidence, Chief Justice Cullen invited them to retire to the jury room to consider their verdict. It was 6.15 pm on the second day of the trial when the jurors began what was, and continues to be, a sacred duty of deliberating on the fate of the accused.

Trial by jury has been a feature of English law for nearly 1000 years. One of the central clauses of Magna Carta in 1215 enshrined this right:

> *No free man shall be imprisoned, nor will we proceed against him by force or by arms, except by the lawful judgment of his peers.*

Many centuries ago, English juries in criminal trials were sometimes compelled to deliberate 'without food, water or fire' and in certain rare cases even without a chamber pot.[2] This had the practical benefit of discouraging protracted discussions and disagreements amongst the twelve jurors, but it also tended to unduly press individual jurors to compromise their views. In New South Wales in 1920, juries were provided with the necessities of life, but in capital cases, such as murder, the law compelled the judge to keep them locked up until they had completed their deliberations, either by a verdict or, in the event of intractable disagreement, by the judge discharging them. If their deliberations were not completed on the day that they began, they were locked up overnight in segregated dormitories.[3] At the Darlinghurst courthouse, the dormitories had been constructed in the 1880s, and they were quite Spartan. Jurors, understandably, had a preference to reach a verdict without having to stay overnight at the courthouse. By sending the Falleni jury out at 6.15 pm, the Chief Justice placed them under a lot of pressure. This may well have been a deliberate tactic to encourage them to reach agreement that night. Sure enough, after deliberating for just under two hours, the jury returned to court at 8.07 pm with their verdict.

The whole court reassembled and, unusually for that time of night, the public gallery was overcrowded. There was a most sombre atmosphere in the courtroom. After the Chief Justice had come onto the Bench, he ordered that the accused be brought up from the cell below. Eugenia was desperately weary after the ordeal of her two-day trial and she looked deathly pale. Sir William then directed the court officer to bring the jury into their box in the courtroom. While everyone waited for the jurors, there was complete and utter silence, as everyone appreciated that a particularly poignant part of the trial was about to occur. As the jurors filed into the courtroom, not one of them looked up at the accused. Both prosecutor and defence counsel knew that this was an ominous, telltale sign. After the jurors had taken their seats in the jury box, the judge's associate asked first the accused and then the foreman to stand. The associate then read out the murder charge from the indictment:

The accused stands charged that on or about 1 October 1917 at Lane Cove in the State of New South Wales she did feloniously and maliciously murder Annie Crawford, also known as Annie Birkett. [Turning to look at the foreman] How say you: is she guilty or not guilty?

The foreman of the jury paused, briefly turned to face Eugenia, then turned back to the judge and said in a loud and clear voice, 'Guilty, your Honour.'

There were numerous audible gasps in the public gallery and the press box, not because of any surprise at the verdict, but because of the enormity of the moment. Eugenia felt completely crushed by the events of the previous two days and the verdict was just one more assault on her psyche. To the objective observer, she showed no signs of emotion, however inside she felt a sense of unbridled panic as she realised that the case had gone against her and that her nightmare was not going to end soon.

The judge then looked sharply at Eugenia and said to her the time-honoured words: 'Do you have anything to say why this court should not pass sentence of death upon you according to law?'[4] Most prisoners would say nothing, or at most, 'No, your Honour.' Surprisingly, Eugenia felt a sudden jolt of outrage and, in her hopeless predicament, a sense of entitlement, and so she responded to the judge's invitation by saying:

I am not guilty, your Honour. The jury found me guilty on false evidence. I know nothing about this charge.

The judge completely ignored her reply, then gave an almost imperceptible nod to the sheriff's officer who was waiting in the body of the court, and who knew exactly what the gesture meant. He walked to the front of the court, mounted the stairs to the bench, walked around the back of the judge to the two, large, hinged curtain rods that were normally flush on the wall behind the bench, each rod carrying a black velvet curtain, and swung them forward to a position on either side of the judge. By ancient tradition, this signalled that a death sentence was about to be handed down. This quaint practice symbolically isolated the judge from all side distractions and influences and focussed his attention on the prisoner directly in front of him, so as to assist him in discharging the distasteful task at hand.

The Chief Justice then delivered the court's sentence:

Eugenia Falleni, you have been found guilty by the jury on the charge of murder. In accordance with the law, I have no choice but to order that you be taken to the place from whence you have come, and there to be hanged by the neck until your body be dead. May the Lord have mercy upon your soul.

The judge then swiftly adjourned the court and rushed off the bench into the sanctuary of his adjoining judicial chambers, leaving the discharged jurors to slowly file out through a separate side door. The members of the press also hurried out of the courtroom to file their reports. Not that there was any real need for haste, because at this hour of the night it was way past the deadline for the next morning's papers.

As Eugenia slumped to her seat in the dock, her body went into involuntary tremors. She felt in a totally dissociative state, as though she were floating above the courtroom observing everything and everyone, including herself. Archibald McDonell came up to her and whispered a few words of comfort, but she probably did not hear him. Those who remained in the public gallery pretended to be slowly leaving, but out of the corners of their eyes they were avidly observing as two female gaol officers gingerly assisted Eugenia to the narrow, steep steps that led down into the cell complex below. Only after she had gone did the silence in the public gallery erupt into a raucous clattering of voices, and the court officers had to stridently urge people to leave the courtroom and talk outside.

William Coyle KC left the Central Criminal Court with his instructing solicitor, Mr John Gonsalves, in tow. After taking off his professional robes in the Crown's chambers, he left the court complex through the main gate on Taylor Square, where numerous reporters, cameramen and members of the public congregated to congratulate him on the fabulous result. Archibald McDonell and Maddocks Cohen left the complex through a side-gate on Oxford Street. Nobody was there to say anything to them.

Eugenia was quickly whisked to the secure laneway at the back of the court complex where the prison van was waiting for her. Being now late at night, she was the only prisoner in the van, and the prison officers were anxious to get underway. The vehicle drove out of the driveway at the back of the court and into Forbes Street, where there was a throng of people on the pavement waiting for her. Many of the newspaper cameramen held their cameras high above their heads in a vain attempt to get a photograph of her inside the van. As the van drove past, several members of the public screamed abuse at her, using words like 'freak' and 'pervert' interspersed with predictions of her fate to rot in hell. Eugenia's life as a sentenced prisoner had begun.

The next morning, the newspapers reported the verdict in a matter-of-fact way. The *Daily Telegraph* stated:

> *Eugene Falleni, described as the 'man-woman' who is 45 years of age, was yesterday found guilty of the murder of Annie Crawford, formerly Birkett, at Lane Cove on September 28, 1917, and sentence of death was passed.*

The legal proceedings and press attention, as well as her incarceration and the loss of contact with Lizzie, had all taken an enormous toll on Eugenia, and a photograph of her at the gaol on 21 October, just a fortnight after her trial, showed how much she had deteriorated physically and psychologically in a little more than three months since her photograph had been taken by the police on the day of her arrest.

Between 1900 and 1920, only seventeen people were executed in New South Wales, all of whom were men. All of the other prisoners who had received the death penalty had had their sentences commuted by the government to life imprisonment. The last woman to be executed was Louisa Collins, who was hanged in 1889. Due to the fact that she had poisoned both of her husbands for their life insurance monies, Collins was dubbed by the press as 'the Lucretia Borgia of Botany'. Her execution aroused an enormous outcry, not only because was she a woman, but also because she was a mother. In addition, her execution at Darlinghurst Gaol was botched when the trapdoor pin jammed, requiring a warder to hit the pin four or five times with a mallet. Many expressed the view at the time that, as women were barred from voting and sitting on juries, they should not be held accountable to the law in the same way as men. In any event, Eugenia Falleni in 1920 was hardly at risk of losing her life to the hangman, and this was one of the reassurances that Archie McDonell had whispered to her in court immediately after her sentence had been pronounced.

Just six weeks later, on 12 November 1920, Eugenia Falleni appealed against her conviction and sentence to the New South Wales Court of Criminal Appeal. As was the usual practice, the appeal was heard by three Supreme Court judges, in this case Justices Pring, Ferguson and Wade. William Coyle KC again appeared for the Crown. Archibald McDonell, instructed by Maddocks Cohen, again represented Eugenia Falleni – now the appellant. McDonell by this time must have realised some of the points that he should have taken at the trial, and he belatedly tried to raise them at the appeal. He argued that the jury's verdict was against the evidence and that the Crown case had been weak and merely circumstantial. He suggested that the Crown's theory about the death had been destroyed by its own medical witnesses, resulting in a failure to prove how Annie Birkett had died. He even submitted that the identification evidence had been found quite unsatisfactory. He informed the court that 'owing to nervous prostration at the trial' his client had been physically unable to make the proper dock statement that would have answered the circumstantial evidence adduced against her. Having said nothing about this at the time to Sir William Cullen, this last argument was particularly unpersuasive.

The three judges were unmoved by the accused's trial counsel advancing cogent arguments on an appeal that he had failed to put forward at the trial. Mr Justice Pring, delivering the short judgement of the court, stated their view that the evidence had been sufficient to prove all the essential ingredients of the crime. They held that it was not necessary for the Crown to prove the exact mode of death, so long as it had been brought about by the appellant. The appeal was dismissed and the conviction and sentence confirmed.

Less than a month later, at a State Cabinet meeting on 6 December 1920, one of the topics for discussion was whether or not to commute Eugenia Falleni's sentence of death to penal servitude for life. The Attorney-General expressed the view that the electorate would not like the idea of a woman being hanged. The Premier was doubtful whether the electorate would, in fact, view her as a woman, but eventually the whole Cabinet agreed that, the execution of females having been in a state of abeyance for many years, this was not an appropriate case to revive the practice. On the same day, an announcement was made to the press that the New South Wales Cabinet, exercising its prerogative of mercy, had resolved to commute to life imprisonment the death sentence that had been passed on Eugenia Falleni.

The last word should go to the man behind 'The Man in the Mask' in *Smith's Weekly*. When the verdict was delivered, he wrote on 16 October:

The foreman of the jury spoke one word instead of the expected two, and changed the whole setting in an instant. I saw the other notes required to complete the bizarre chord. They were: the unseemly scarlet robes of a judge, whose voice was broken as he spoke sentence of death; the slack jaw of a yawning juryman; the portly figure of the female witness who, refer-ring to the accused, had said volubly: 'Yes, I know her, and she knows me,' as though inviting the doomed half-human to a quarrel over the front fence of the dock; the dynamic imperturbability of the Crown counsel, who had placed another shining horsehair in his legal halo; and, above all, the tragic calmness of the central figure – the keynote that bound these bizarre contradictions into a harmonious whole. At that word 'guilty' those different notes had lept instantly to their places, and the effect was a mighty chord of pain – a wall of tragedy.

Eugenia now faced the prospect of the remainder of her life, or at least a substantial part of it, in the Women's Reformatory at Long Bay Gaol.

PART III

INCARCERATION AND RELEASE

CHAPTER 26

PRISONER

The Long Bay prison complex at Malabar, on the coastline about eight miles south of the city of Sydney, was the first in Australia to be planned with separate sections for men and women. This was largely due to the actions of Frederick Neitenstein, a former British mercantile marine captain and forward-thinking juvenile delinquent reformer who was the Comptroller-General of New South Wales prisons from 1895 to 1909. The construction of the new prison complex at Long Bay provided an enlightened and modern replacement for the Darlinghurst Gaol, which had been Sydney's main prison since 1840.[1] Construction of the State Reformatory for Women at Long Bay began in 1901 and it opened in 1909, the year that Neitenstein retired. It was regarded as a model prison and highly praised as one of the few purpose-designed women's prisons in the world. Its Federation Gothic entrance block and octagonal radial design were highly admired at the time. The average daily occupancy in the female prison in the year that it opened was 124, growing to 199 by 1916, but numbers then declined. The male penitentiary opened in 1914. By 1920, the whole Long Bay prison complex housed over 70 per cent of all New South Wales prisoners, including remand inmates, and was seriously overcrowded.

For a person who had spent most of her working life in a wide variety of manual jobs, many of them outdoors, Eugenia Falleni found it difficult as a sentenced prisoner in the Long Bay Women's Reformatory to adjust to being restricted to a cell for nearly twelve hours a day. What she found at Long Bay was a realm that had its own rules and social conventions. Within a few months of beginning her sentence in October 1920, she realised that she was one of many unorthodox inmates who would be described as misfits in ordinary society but who were accepted as part of the normal spectrum in this cloistered community within a community. No one inside batted an eyelid at her male proclivities and, although they were required to wear women's prison uniforms, there was latitude in terms of how they could be adapted to make them appropriate for the more intensive jobs, such as sweeping and cleaning.

Incarceration at Long Bay had one similarity to life at sea, and that was that nobody judged you on what you had done before or where you had come from – so long as you had not hurt any children. To batter your spouse to death was almost considered a badge of honour, because most women who had been sentenced for murdering their husbands had themselves been victims of violence for many years. As a prisoner who had been convicted of killing her wife, Eugenia was viewed as being merely a variant of the norm. Almost all new prisoners protested their innocence, so few took any special note of the grave injustices that their fellow prisoners claimed had been perpetrated on them by the court system. These were the conditions that enabled Eugenia to adjust fairly rapidly to the strict conditions of the newest and largest prison in New South Wales. While Eugenia had initially been very fearful of violence, within a few months she learned that if one played by the unique rules and conventions of the place, violence was very infrequent. There were, in fact, two sets of rules: one for dealing with the prison warders and one for dealing with fellow prisoners. Despite the reforms that had been introduced when Long Bay was opened, there was still a gaping divide between the warders and the prisoners. One heard rumours that new arrivals at the men's prison would be forced to run a gauntlet of prison officers wielding batons against them as they ran from the van that had transported them from court into the reception area where they received their prison uniforms. The warders viewed this as an important step to set the stage for who was in control. No such introduction welcomed the inmates of the Women's Reformatory.

The other surprise that was in store for Eugenia was that there were some exceedingly stable and loving relationships that formed in the harsh prison environment. While a sexual relationship between two women in ordinary society was an anathema, in prison it was considered an entitlement. Not one of the prison warders attempted to prevent or thwart such liaisons. In fact, they welcomed them, because it made the task of administering the prisoners easier. A harmonious and satisfying relationship did much for the morale of the prisoners concerned and also those around them. Occasionally, especially when relationships broke up, there would be terrible, acrimonious accusations and fights. Generally, the warders would allow the prisoners to sort these out for themselves, knowing that to intervene would achieve nothing. Occasionally, when two prisoners were fighting over the affections of a third, they would resolve it by agreeing to constitute a 'family' of three. Relationships often lasted for lengthy periods of time. When it came time for a prisoner to be released, if she had been in a long-term relationship with another prisoner who was not due to be freed for a long time, there would be much anguish and pathos, and when the fateful day came, copious tears would flow with protestations of enduring fidelity on both sides. However, once on the outside, the released prisoner would rarely come to visit and the relationship would gradually fade into history as new ones formed. In fact, hardly any of the relationships inside the prison continued once both parties were released.

Eugenia found that her ability to converse and amuse was just as useful inside the prison as it had been in everyday life outside. This made her exceedingly popular with her fellow prisoners. Her fondness for manual labour made her well liked by the warders and she quickly came to be viewed by them as a model prisoner. The reward for being a model prisoner was to be left alone. While alcohol and tobacco were not plentiful, they were available at a price. Newspapers and books were readily available, but, due to Eugenia's illiteracy, this was of no use to her. Some basic educational programs had recently been introduced, including teaching prisoners to read and write, but Eugenia was uninterested. The main problem for all prisoners was the ineffable boredom inherent in the daily routine of prison life.

In early 1922, Eugenia changed her first name, both formally in the prison records and informally by usage, to 'Jean'. This may well have been an attempt to avert some of the prejudice against her because of her Italian origins. Prison life brought out the most extreme tribal instincts in the inmates and these institutions were, and still are, hotbeds for irrational racial and ethnic prejudices.

Within several months of Jean's trial, in early 1921, she came into contact with a prisoner who was to completely change her life. That prisoner was Dorothy Mort. Dorothy Mort was an educated, well-groomed, affluent member of Sydney's high society who was married to Harold Sutcliffe Mort.[2] Together with their two young children, they lived at 'Inglebrae' in Howard Street, Lindfield. Just a couple of miles away at a house called 'Shireen' in Boundary Road, Roseville, lived Dr Claude Tozer, a tall, handsome and dashing general medical practitioner with a very successful practice, who was also an accomplished test cricketer. Claude Tozer had qualified in medicine at Sydney University in 1914 at the young age of twenty-four, having represented the university in first-grade cricket. In the same year, he enlisted in the Australian Army Medical Corps and was given the rank of captain. He served with gallantry as a battlefield doctor at Gallipoli, Egypt and on the Western Front, was badly wounded, then promoted to major, and eventually awarded the Distinguished Service Order (DSO). Back in Australia, he played first grade for the Gordon cricket club, where his performance was so exceptional that he was chosen to captain the New South Wales team in 1920, and was fully expected to make the Australian test side for the forthcoming summer.

Dr Claude Tozer was treating Dorothy Mort for long-standing depression and, unwisely, he was also in a sexual relationship with her. In December 1920, he was due to captain the New South Wales cricket team in a match against Queensland on New Year's Day 1921. On 21 December 1920, Dr Tozer came to Dorothy Mort's home to tell her that their relationship was over because he was engaged to marry another woman. She would not accept his announcement and, as he sat on a couch in her living room, she shot him with a pistol in the back of the head, the temple and the chest, killing him instantly. Mort then unsuccessfully attempted to kill herself by taking an overdose of laudanum[3] and shooting herself in the breast with the pistol. When the police arrived many hours later, she was still alive, so they took her to the Royal North Shore Hospital, where she was treated for some weeks and brought back to health. The killing of Dr Tozer caused an enormous outpouring of grief in New South Wales and it attracted a great deal of publicity.

Dorothy Mort went to trial in March 1921 charged with the murder of Dr Tozer. The trial was presided over by Chief Justice Sir William Cullen. The defence tactics at her trial were singularly more effective than those at the trial of Eugenia Falleni. The *Argus* (Melbourne) reported on 8 April 1921:

Mrs Mort (heavily veiled, her features being unrecognisable behind a dense black gossamer) was brought into court and partly assisted into the prisoner's dock at seven minutes past 10 o'clock. The Chief Justice had taken his seat on the bench five minutes before, and a grim silence prevailed while preparations were being made for swearing in the jury. Mr Mack KC, who had been retained for the defence, and entered the court a minute in advance of Mrs Mort, inserted his hand between the bars of the dock and shook hands with the frail, dejected woman in black, who sat motionless and seemingly spellbound, with her eyes fixed on the ground. A woman warder entered and sat beside Mrs Mort. The jury having been sworn in, Mr Mack asked the Chief Justice to permit Mrs Mort to leave the dock and sit on the floor of the court. The request was acceded, and Mrs Mort was provided with a chair at the barristers' table opposite her counsel. The woman warder sat at her side.

Dorothy Mort had everything going for her that Eugenia Falleni did not: she was of Anglo background; she was a heterosexual; she was a member of an affluent, well-connected, upper-class North-Shore family; her barrister's fees were paid privately by the Mort family; her senior counsel, Sidney Mack KC, was an astute criminal trial tactician who from the beginning had a game plan that he stuck to and carried out with great aplomb; the trial judge was generous in his directions to the jury; and the press took a far more benevolent attitude to her case. The whole tone of her trial was starkly different to Eugenia Falleni's ordeal. Dorothy Mort played her assigned part, and sat for most of the trial with her head resting on the shoulder of a prison warder sitting next to her in the dock.

The defence was one of insanity. Dr Arthur Palmer was again the principal expert witness, this time on the completely different topic of the accused's state of mind.[4] He gave evidence that when he interviewed Mrs Mort three days after the shooting, she had declared to him that she had had sexual relations with Dr Tozer on the day of his death from which she had become pregnant. When Dr Palmer replied that it was impossible for her to know that she was pregnant so soon after having intercourse, Mrs Mort expressed a desire that another medical practitioner, a Dr Murray, should examine her and that he would be able to determine that she was indeed pregnant. Dr Palmer gave evidence that Mrs Mort talked about these things as though she was talking about the weather. His conclusion, which he confidently testified to at her trial, was that at the time of the murder Mrs Mort was certifiably insane. The result was inevitable. The jury duly found Dorothy Mort not guilty of murder on the grounds of mental illness. As the law required, she was directed to be incarcerated 'at the Governor's pleasure'. This should have entailed a lengthy period of confinement in a locked ward of a mental asylum, but at that time such facilities for women were almost non-existent and, in default, she took up residence in a cell at the Women's Reformatory at Long Bay. It was at this time that she came into contact with Jean Falleni.

Dorothy Mort was educated, clever, charming, witty, sophisticated and had an enormous store of general knowledge, which made her different from most of the other prisoners. Jean found her presence quite intoxicating and Dorothy Mort became the third great influence in Jean's adult life.[5] They had a deep friendship behind the prison walls for the eight years that they were together at Long Bay. It was this that enabled Jean to mentally survive the rigours of a life sentence and it was this, more than anything, that caused Jean to mellow and accept herself for the person she really was. Over many years, she gained an understanding of the torments that had plagued her for most of her life and, as a result, became more tolerant and aware of the needs of others. She became determined that, if ever she were to be released, she would lead a life of integrity that would earn the respect of others and, more importantly, develop her self respect.

At the time of Eugenia's arrest, her daughter Josephine still harboured deep and abiding resentments against her mother for the many years of distress that she had put her and Granny De Angelis through. She was severely traumatised by the media attention that her evidence at the committal proceedings had generated. At that time, she had little sympathy for her mother's plight and deliberately tried to distance herself from the evolving calamity of her mother's legal ordeals. During the time that Eugenia was in custody awaiting her trial, on 18 August 1920, Josephine, now twenty-two, married her long-time partner, Arthur Whitby, who by this time was a twenty-four-year-old seaman with the Royal Australian Navy. The wedding took place at the Anglican Church in St Peter's. Naturally, Eugenia was unable to attend. Josephine and her husband took up residence at 54 Darlington Road, Darlington. Only a few months later, Josephine fell pregnant with her second child. She immediately became very concerned about the health of this baby, due to the unfortunate death of her first child six years earlier. On 20 November 1921, Josephine gave birth to a baby girl, Rita Josephine Whitby. When Jean was informed about Rita's birth, she was seized with a love and concern for this granddaughter that she had never felt when her own daughter was a child.

For most prisoners at the Women's Reformatory at Long Bay, the main event of each week was the two hours on Sunday when visitors were permitted to come into the gaol. This was of little solace to Jean because, with one possible exception, not a single family member or friend came to visit her. That possible exception was her daughter, Josephine. There are no longer records in existence of visitors at Long Bay at this time, so one cannot know whether or not there was personal contact between Jean and Josephine after the trial. It is known that Jean was particularly isolated from contact with the outside world, although she was informed of the birth of her granddaughter. It is quite possible that Josephine decided to make a clean break and to keep her new family well away from the parent who had abandoned her soon after birth and who had been the source of so much trauma as she was growing up. However, there is nothing like a baby to make a woman desire contact with her own mother, and one can imagine that this most recent pregnancy may have caused Josephine to soften her stance towards Jean and maybe even given Josephine the maturity to have a rudimentary understanding of why her mother had been so different from everyone else's. By this time, Jean was more emotionally accessible than she had ever been before, due to the fact that, for the first time, she was not living a life of deceit. As far as Jean's attitude towards Josephine was concerned, for the first time since she had given birth to her, she was not at risk of her daughter accidentally disclosing her true identity.

After several years of incarceration, a visitor did come twice to see Jean. His name was Dr Herbert Moran and he was a friend of William Coyle KC, the prosecutor who had done such a good job of convicting Jean. Dr Moran was a prominent Sydney surgeon who had been appointed as the Honorary Surgeon at St Vincent's Hospital in 1916 at the age of thirty-one. Moran was also a keen Italophile, with a good knowledge of the Italian language, who was inspired by 'the art, letters and antiquities of Italy and the majestic history of Rome and the Renaissance'. Coyle was probably motivated by an ethical and possibly a religious concern for the rehabilitation and psychological welfare of his erstwhile defendant when he prevailed upon this friend, with his good language skills, to visit Jean and to bring her some succour in her native tongue. Coyle, in fact, had a reputation for showing kindness and generosity towards his former accused prisoners. He managed to get permission for Moran's visit from none other than William McKell MLA, then the State Minister for Justice.

One can imagine the hullabaloo in the gaol from both warders and prisoners when it became known that Jean was to receive a visit from a doctor at the instigation of the Senior Crown Prosecutor and on the invitation of the Minister for Justice. These unusual visits to the gaol, like the arrival of police seeking information from prisoners, spread like wildfire through the whole prison population. To cooperate with the police was an anathema among the prisoners and liable to lead to complete ostracism if the prisoner was perceived to have assisted. Jean was mystified when she heard about her visitor and immediately suspected that there was some nefarious purpose to it. Perhaps the doctor had been sent to assess her as a mad woman or possibly to extract some post-conviction confession from her. Whatever the reason, Jean was convinced that no good could come of it. She resolved to be totally uncooperative with him and to be constantly on her guard.

Dr Moran, on the other hand, was totally oblivious of the impact of his visit on the prison population. When he arrived at the gaol, he was surprised at how dejected everyone looked – both staff and inmates. He had no idea that the former saw him as a spy for the Minister and the latter as a representative of the establishment that was responsible for their incarceration. He later wrote about the visit:

> *The dejection of the prisoners, their hangdog looks, their earthy complexions in spite of the exposure to sunlight, the dull eyes of those who were obviously practising the solitary vice, the slow footsteps which had lost all alertness – all these things appalled me. Merriment seemed gone forever from their lives. In its place was a sort of brooding hopelessness. The horizon of these men was a wall! And yet there was an ocean outside and beyond. The turnkeys all seemed to have hard iron eyes. Their faces bore the mark of alcoholic bouts. Were they seeking thus to exorcise the phantoms which pursued them? They must surely have always around them the spectre of these murdered lives. What a place to live in! Existence itself had a growth of green mould upon it. These gaolers could not afford to show sympathy. To yield once meant a complete surrender. So, with the years, the tough hide of an artificial indifference had become a carapace which outsiders mistook for brutality.*

Prior to arriving at the gaol, Moran had gone to a lot of trouble to find out as much as he could about Jean and her crime. Much of his information had come from his friend, William Coyle. Of course, he was well aware of the publicity that had been generated at the time of her trial. Moran came to the visit with many preconceptions about Jean's sexuality and her crime. He classified her as being a 'homosexualist'. Like many people of his day, he had little understanding of the differences between transsexualism and homosexuality. He viewed her in this way:

> *She was born with a twisted outlook, a so-called psychical hermaphrodite, with a man's sexuality in a normal woman's body.*
>
> *If the horror I feel for male inversion remains intense, I feel strangely tolerant towards women given to homosexuality and can bring to the subject a detached, even a sympathetic, attitude.*

Moran waited for Jean in the reception room, which was where all the visitors normally arrived on Sundays, but that day, being a weekday, he was the only visitor in the room. A female member of staff was seated with him. Being accustomed to hospitals and completely ignorant of prison life, he saw her as a 'benevolent matron', whereas in reality she was one of the senior prison warders. While they were waiting, the matron told him that Jean had a female friend, another murderess, with whom she shared a cell and to whom she was deeply attached.

When Jean came into the room, he noticed that she did so 'shyly and suspiciously', completely failing to appreciate the vast battleground that lay between his world and hers. He described her physical appearance thus:

The stature was short and the gait slouching. She still seemed to be deliberately exaggerating the stride of a man. The grey eyes were restless and afraid; the face olive-tinted, lined, hairless. Such a head would easily pass for a man's. Her hair indeed was still short. It was brushed straight back and there were patches of grey. The nose was thick and undistinguished. She was flat in the bust. The voice was low-pitched and raucous, the manner subservient but distrustful. Obviously her intellect was fixed permanently in low gear. Her hands were large and spade-like, suggesting those of the manual labourer.

Dr Moran and Jean had a relatively short conversation. He spoke to her in rather simple, but grammatically correct Italian, with a strong Australian accent. She replied to him in English. He remained seated and she remained standing. He spoke to her about his beloved Florence, thinking that she had been born there. She just listened and did not feel the need to correct him that she had been born in Livorno. He told her that his mission was to help her in any way he could. She looked blankly at him and did not reply. He told her that he may be able to take some steps to get her returned to her native country, Italy – completely ignoring the fact that she had left that country at the age of two, spent the rest of her formative years in New Zealand and the last quarter century in Australia. She told him that her immediate family was here, and that she had no interest in being sent to Italy. He asked her how her life was in this unfortunate place. She replied cautiously and complained that the main difficulty was the monotony. He made some brief allusion to her trial, and she responded that it had all been based on suspicion rather than proof, which caused Moran to look at her quizzically. Clearly, he thought, she was deceiving herself about reality. All the time she was guardedly watching him. The conversation was over in less than twenty minutes. As soon as it was finished, a prison officer came to take her away and the doctor was escorted by the 'matron' to the main gate.

Moran completely misinterpreted his interchange with Jean. His conclusion was this:

Obviously this was a woman with the mental capacity of some lower animal. She had none of the brilliant attainments of so many perverts.

Nor was she aggressively masculine. There was nothing of the bearded woman about her. She had no religious sentiments of any kind, and not the slightest evidence of any spirituality. She was just a half-wild creature who felt herself apart and different, who had grown cunning and furtive, hiding her secret and satisfying her needs. She must have long since learned how the common people hated the habit she practised. She must have gone always harassed with fear. It is only by the light of that ever-present fear we can hope to understand her problem and her crime.

Dr Moran visited Jean at the gaol on one other occasion, with a very similar result. He did not know that he would see her on two further occasions many years later in the course of his medical practice, when she was no longer in custody.

Dr Moran later used this unique opportunity he had been given to visit one of the State's most prominent prisoners to advance theories about the nature of the subconscious:

I am not competent in the modern researches which have made so great a contribution to our knowledge of psychical phenomena, but even now we know so little of the subconscious. It appears at times like an enlightened dungeon from which comes scurrying forth the famished rodents of our senses. I cannot say then if Falleni's perversion was or was not a perturbation of the Oedipus complex. I do not know if in hiding herself from the realities of her environment she was seeking refuge under the maternal skirts and near a mother's breast. This, at least, seems clear. Falleni was not of that group which seeks fresh novelties of sensation in the lucky dips of a sexual bazaar. Hers was not a jaded palate asking for violent stimulation. Nor was she of that over sophisticated class of artists and litterateurs who are bewildered by beauty or crazed by a longing to create something new. Still less had she kinship with those whose dammed-up normal desires seek new vents and hollow out new channels. She was condemned even from her birth and her abnormality derived from the very nature of her being. The temperamental outbursts, the vulgar debauches, the filthy speech, were but minor manifestations of her interior disorder.

William Coyle, in a further act of generosity and concern, later sent his wife, Margaret, to visit Jean in gaol, armed with culinary delicacies as well as books and magazines that Jean was unable to read.

In late 1923, Jean's daughter, Josephine Whitby, contracted pulmonary tuberculosis, a common disease in those days. Josephine died suddenly on 19 December 1924. She was only twenty-seven years old. Her death left her husband, Arthur, now retired from the navy and working as a postal officer, to care for their three-year-old daughter, Rita. Josephine was buried in the Roman Catholic section of Rookwood cemetery. Naturally, her mother was unable to attend the funeral. As a result of her daughter's death, Jean Falleni lost her principal connection with the outside world and she was seized by a terrible depression that crushed her into virtual catatonia for many months. During that time, she had many physical illnesses, which were no doubt due to her poor psychological state. Were it not for the support of other prisoners, particularly Dorothy Mort, she would undoubtedly have died.

Arthur Whitby, now a widower, felt incapable of raising his three-year-old daughter, Rita, on his own, and so he sent her to his sister, Jean Goodwin, and her husband in Bellingen on the north coast of New South Wales. In 1926, for reasons that have faded into the mists of time, Rita was placed in a Catholic institution in Macksville, not far from her aunt's home in Bellingen. From the time that Rita was sent north, her father abrogated all responsibility for his young daughter and had no contact with her. When Jean Falleni discovered that her granddaughter had been placed in an institution, she was seized by an intense bitterness towards Rita's paternal relatives and frustration that she could do nothing to alleviate the child's abandonment. Jean now became consumed by an overwhelming desire to one day be released so that she could care for her neglected granddaughter.

CHAPTER 27

RELEASE

In 1929, a concerted movement began to secure the release of both Dorothy Mort and Jean Falleni. At that time, Jean had served nine years of a life sentence.[1] Her health had gradually deteriorated while she had been in custody and by all accounts she had been a model prisoner. On 7 July 1929, in an extensive article under the heading 'Is Eugene Falleni innocent?' *The Sunday News* called for an enquiry into her conviction. For the first time, the article publicly identified the real issues that should have been raised at the time of her trial. The author of the article also drew attention to the disparity with Dorothy Mort's trial:

> *Her guilt is much in doubt. There are many hypotheses open. Even assuming that the dead woman were Annie Birkett, she may have died a lonely death in the bush from natural causes, or from poison self-administered.*
>
> *The fractured skull could have been caused by her falling heavily upon the rock on which she was found or by the wilful act of some person other than Falleni, but there is absolutely no evidence that Falleni took the woman's life.*
>
> *Of the two women in Long Bay Gaol who each stood trial for wilful murder, one has many friends ceaselessly working for release. The other is a piece of human flotsam, convicted upon evidence entirely circumstantial, quite unconvincing and as slender as evidence could possibly be. She is without hope, utterly friendless, and by the world forgot.*

In October 1929, after eight years of incarceration, Dorothy Mort was released. This caused great distress to Jean, not only because she was torn away from her closest friend, but also because she felt there was such a sharp and unjustifiable difference between the way that she and Dorothy had been treated. Jean was quite convinced that her friend had been dealt with much more leniently because of her upper-class origins and social contacts, and that she herself had been treated more harshly because of her Italian background and, of course, her former identity as a man. However, Dorothy Mort's release eventually proved to be Jean Falleni's salvation, as Dorothy played a major role in the fight to secure Jean's freedom.

Following the freeing of Dorothy Mort, a group of Sydney women under her leadership, many of them from prominent families, rallied together to lobby the New South Wales Government for the release of Jean Falleni on merciful grounds. This group of women also advanced the view that Jean Falleni's treatment had been unfair and discriminatory when compared with that of Dorothy Mort. By this time, Jean was the only female life-sentence prisoner at Long Bay. *Smith's Weekly* on 8 March 1930 reported about her rehabilitation as follows:

Of 'Jean', as she is known in the women's section of Long Bay Penitentiary, they speak in the highest terms. With a deep knowledge of frail human nature, these people in authority have learnt to make a sharp distinction between people as they were and people as they are. They are willing to blot out yesterday if today be fair. And they speak of Jean Falleni as a model prisoner, as a woman who carries out in exemplary fashion the jobs allotted to her, who causes no trouble, and against whose name no stone can now be cast. Jean has no enemies in Long Bay, no critics even. She is looked on only with understanding sympathy.

However, there were a number of significant people who opposed Jean's release, including Harry Birkett.

In early 1930, the editors of two competing Sydney weekly newspapers, *Smith's Weekly* and *The Truth* – the former published on Saturdays and the latter on Sundays – appropriated the battle over Jean Falleni's release, and used the controversy as a rallying point for their own battle for readership. *Smith's Weekly* came out strongly in favour of Jean's release, while *The Truth* vehemently opposed it. On 8 March 1930, under a front-page pencil sketch of Jean's head and shoulders behind metal bars and the heading 'Frail prisoner is pathetic figure in gaol', *Smith's Weekly* reported:

Falleni, who says she will be 60 years of age on July 24,[2] is a frail little woman, to all appearances a bundle of femininity – nothing strident or raucous about her. She is quiet, and with the discipline of 10 years ingrained in her, intensely obedient.

She reads a little, but her real hobby is gardening; and when there are any jobs, such as painting to be done, she does them willingly when she is well.

Jean Falleni feels acutely what she regards as unfair discrimination. If Mrs Mort can get her freedom, why can't she get hers? 'Nearly 10 years ago I was convicted on circumstantial evidence,' she said. 'I did not have a chance. I had no education. I was what other people made me. Mrs Mort had advantages that I never had. They said she was insane, but she was no more insane than I was.'

Meanwhile, Jean out at Long Bay loses count of the days, weeks, months, even years. Life there is always the same. She has a cough and so is in hospital at present. The doctor wants her to get all the fresh air she can. She frets. All she has in the world is a little grandchild at a Sydney orphanage – her daughter died in 1924 – and she longs to see the child.'

The following weekend, on Sunday, 16 March 1930, *The Truth* responded with a scathing attack on Jean Falleni, purporting to present facts that had never before been made public. The front-page heading made quite clear what position *The Truth* was taking: 'Fiendish Man Woman, Murderess – Should Be No Misplaced Sympathy for Despicable Human Monster'. The article was full of misstatements and inaccuracies about her life history and her crime. It informed the public that Harry Birkett, now happily married himself, was against the attempt to gain liberty for Falleni. The article stated:

Telling her story in pleading terms and in phrases that indicate a crushed and broken spirit in a martyred woman, Falleni shows a different side of her character to that known ten years ago.

Yes, Falleni has evidently changed her choice of vocabulary, even though she reveals sufficient ugliness smouldering in her nature to vilify the name of Annie Birkett, whom she 'married', savagely murdered, and burnt.

Since the attempt has been made to appeal to public sympathy on behalf of Eugene Falleni, Truth states in the interests of justice that Falleni has no right whatever to be again allowed loose among society.'

The newspaper then proceeded to assert a number of egregious misstatements about her, including:

Falleni had already looked over the ground [the death scene in Lane Cove River Park] *and chosen the spot with the murder in her mind, and her plans were complete to the last detail.*

Purchasing a bottle of a well-known brand of whiskey, she took Mrs Birkett to the spot and drugged her with whiskey. Having succeeded in placing the woman in a stupor, Falleni smashed in the skull of Mrs Birkett with a large stone. Next she saturated her victim's clothing with kerosene and set alight to the body.

Falleni, still using the name of Harry Crawford, married again, this time to a Scotchwoman, who disappeared during the Falleni trial, and has never been heard of since.[3]

'Marriage' [to Lizzie] did not cause Falleni to cease attempts on the boy's life, and shortly afterwards he nearly died of poisoning.

The article concluded with a final word of caution:

The murderous instincts of this woman should be a warning to the public against misplacing its sympathy in such an undeserving quarter. The son of the murdered woman and her other relatives have every reason for being appalled and shocked by such an attempt to free the cruel and murderous Eugene Falleni.

In the meantime, on Saturday 15 March 1930, *Smith's Weekly* had reported that extraordinary interest had been aroused by the publication of their article in the previous weekend's edition. An unnamed Macquarie Street specialist, who had made a special study of the Falleni case from a medical point of view, had informed the paper of his carefully considered conclusions about her:

That Eugene Falleni was physically a woman with the psychology of a man. It was possible that any hereditary influences had been aggravated by the brutal treatment meted out to her as a girl by a man with whom she had come in contact. She had then revolted against the dominancy of the masculine over the feminine, and carried her revolt to the extent which everybody knows.

It was reasonable to suppose, said the specialist, that Eugene Falleni, having approached old-age, would now be calmer in body and spirit than when, tortured by the entanglements of sex, she committed the deeds which made her name a byword. He was definitely of the opinion that, if she were subject to some sort of supervision, her release would not be harmful to the community or herself.'

The following week, in a short and unsubtle salvo against the opposition, *The Truth* referred to Falleni as 'a fiendish human monster, murderess,

sexual pervert, liar, hypocrite, and filthy tongued "man-woman"." Jean
Falleni had been caught in the vicious crossfire between these two major
public institutions – so much so, that now the battle for her freedom
became politicised.

The final decision on whether a prisoner should be released on licence
lay, at that time, with the Minister for Justice. The Minister for Justice in
1929 and until October in 1930 was Mr John (Jack) Robert Lee, a member
of the Nationalist Party, who was indifferent to the calls for Jean's release. In
response to the agitation for her to be freed, Mr Lee promised an enquiry,
but nothing formal eventuated. *Smith's Weekly* on 15 March 1930 reported
that Mr Lee had carefully gone through the depositions[4] of the case himself
and had decided that 'having regard to the circumstances and the enormity
of her offence, Eugene Falleni should remain in gaol'.

However, on 25 October 1930 there was a State election in New South
Wales. The previous Nationalist-Country Party government was soundly
defeated and in its place was elected a Labor government under Premier
Jack Lang, which held a comfortable majority of twenty seats. Australia
at that time was sunk in the midst of the worst of the Great Depression.
Unemployment was sky-high, exports were low and creditor countries such
as Britain and the United States were requiring debtor countries such as
Australia to repay loans to alleviate the Depression in their own economies.
New South Wales had the highest level of public expenditure of any government in Australia. Jack Lang, who had revolutionised welfare services
during his first term as Premier between 1925 and 1927, now found that
these services were accounting for a large proportion of the State's finances.
The Government's budget fell well short of its interest repayments – in
fact by a bigger margin than those of all the other States of Australia put
together. In addition to this, over twenty per cent of adult males in New
South Wales were unemployed. His second term in office was not going to
be an easy time for Premier Jack Lang.

Following the election, in November 1930, Mr Joseph (Joe) Lamaro
became Minister for Justice. Joe Lamaro was the son of Sicilian immigrants
and, understandably, he was much more sympathetic to Jean Falleni's
cause than his predecessor had been. In February 1931, renewed repre-
sentations were made by Jean's supporters and prison reform workers to
the new Justice Minister. Lamaro sought the opinions of the governor
of the Long Bay Gaol, the gaol doctor and the Under-Secretary of Justice.
All of them recommended her release on compassionate grounds due to
her age, her ill health and her good behaviour as a prisoner. That sort of
information is impossible to keep confidential in a gaol environment, so

inevitably Jean found out about these recommendations and her band of supporters became very excited at the prospect of her imminent release. However, Minister Lamaro decided that he wanted to personally interview Jean Falleni before making a final decision.

Joe Lamaro decided to pay Jean Falleni a surprise visit at the Women's Reformatory at Long Bay. This sort of personal attendance by a Minister of the Crown on a serving prisoner was, and still is, unprecedented. When the Minister arrived at Long Bay, it caused great consternation among the staff. The first that Jean knew about it was when a prison warden came to her as she was working and told her that the Minister for Justice had arrived at the gaol and wanted to speak to her. Jean became very excited, thinking that he would only come to see her if he had good news and that there was a possibility of her immediate release then and there. She was ushered into a room and introduced to the Minister. He began talking to her in the Italian of his parents, but she was unable to understand his Sicilian dialect. They quickly reverted to English. She felt terribly overwhelmed by the power this man held over her future and incredibly excited at what she thought he was going to say. He asked a few questions about her health and her incarceration and what plans she had for her future if she were to be released, but she was too dumbstruck by the enormity of the occasion and said very little. At the end of the interview, the Minister got up, shook her hand and walked out, leaving Jean devastated that he had not conveyed the good news she was expecting. Had her inability to answer his questions meant that she had lost any prospect of release? Mr Lamaro came away from the interview none the wiser about her future plans, but still determined to release her. He reported his visit as follows:

She could scarcely speak. I asked her a few questions, but she could not answer. She seemed a dear old lady, very, very ill. One could never believe to look at her that she had led the life of a man.

The result was that, about a week later, on 19 February 1931, Jean Falleni was released on licence under section 463 of the *Crimes Act*. This section permitted an offender to be released into the community, subject to certain conditions that the prisoner had to agree to abide by. Release under this section did not revoke or reduce the prisoner's sentence, but simply enabled the prisoner to serve the remainder of it in the community rather than in gaol.[5] For that reason, the sentence continued to hang over the offender's head, even after release. Jean Falleni readily signed the release papers, thereby accepting the conditions of her freedom. One of those conditions was an undertaking by her 'to be of good behaviour and to keep the peace' for the duration of her sentence. Jean was under no illusion what 'to be of good behaviour' meant. In the context of her life history and her conviction, it meant that she was effectively prohibited from adopting an identity as a male or even dressing as a male. As she had been sentenced to imprisonment for life, Jean knew that this undertaking would hang over her for the rest of her natural life. If she were ever to infringe it, she knew that she could immediately be returned to her former custody. So strong was her desire for freedom, however, that Jean was prepared to sign this undertaking.

As was only to be expected, *The Truth* immediately published a strong criticism of the Minister's decision on the first page of the edition on 22 February 1931. The paper ensured that there was a strong political sting in the article by contrasting the release of Jean Falleni to the predicament of unemployed husbands in the midst of the Depression who had been gaoled for defaulting on their maintenance and alimony payments. This was an undisguised personal attack on Minister Lamaro. The article stated:

While Minister for Justice Lamaro is opening the gaol gates to long-term prisoners convicted of major and often ghastly crimes, the same big clattering sheets of iron are clanging ceaselessly upon men who are guilty of no crime at all – save that they cannot find work. Truth has again to point to the number of men who, because Depression has snatched their employment, are being gaoled for arrears of maintenance and alimony. Lawyers, judges, publicists, and politicians have often riled at the cruel immutability of this law. But the evil continues unabated; often as have amendments of the law been promised, so have they been forgotten. Long Bay Gaol seems now to be a veritable debtors' prison.

The law demands rigorous punishment for ghastly crimes. Courts impose sentences. Public confidence is maintained when wrongdoers get their due. Whilst mercy should be exercised in certain cases, there are many more deserving cases in gaol than that of Falleni, whose crime, which brought to light all her monstrous sex perversion, revealed her as a menace to the community.

According to the *Evening News,* upon her release Jean had been 'given into the care of friends and taken away into the country for peaceful seclusion for the declining years of a strangely warped and tragic existence'. The *Daily Telegraph* reported that her destination was a closely kept secret. According to *The Truth,* she had:

gone to a home of luxury. A wealthy woman living at Lindfield, who has on previous occasions interested herself in well-known prisoners, has given the queer old woman shelter. When she is well enough she may wander in a spacious garden; every comfort and care is at her disposal.

When Jean Falleni was released from gaol, she had a tearful reunion with Dorothy Mort. However, by this time, Dorothy was already well on the way to re-establishing herself as a member of Sydney's high society, and it quickly became apparent that they now had little in common. While the class differences had meant nothing when they were living in the same prison, those differences now assumed gargantuan proportions. At their first meeting, both of them were immediately aware of their divergent backgrounds. Within a matter of weeks, they had drifted apart and they were never to have contact again. Dorothy Mort had, however, played a most significant part in Jean's life. Apart from being her principal companion in the Women's Reformatory and having played a significant role in securing her release, Dorothy had given her the confidence and self-knowledge to ensure that her post-release existence would be quite different from her life before her incarceration.

Jean left the Women's Reformatory with mixed feelings about her future. On the one hand, she possessed a determination to make something of herself and to create a new life that she could be proud of. The first task that she had set herself was to search for her granddaughter, Rita, who by this time would have been ten years old.[6] On the other hand, Jean was unsure how she would deal with the restrictions imposed upon her by the terms of her release. Would she be irrepressibly driven, as she had been in the years before her imprisonment, to live life as a man and to dress as a man? Even at the age of fifty-six, how would she dissipate the considerable emotional and sexual energy that still resided within her? Would she inexorably be attracted to closeness with another woman? Would she ever fall in love again? Would the press continually hound her, or would she be able to sink into anonymous obscurity in suburban Sydney? Would she be able to hide her identity from the people around her in her new life or would she inevitably be recognised and branded as the 'man-woman murderer'?

CHAPTER 28

JEAN FORD

When Jean Falleni was granted her freedom by the Minister for Justice in 1931, she was plunged right into the middle of the Great Depression, the worst financial recession that the modern world had ever seen. Australia suffered one of the highest unemployment rates of the developed world, rising as high as 32 per cent in mid-1932. Many hundreds of thousands of Australians faced humiliating unemployment and poverty. With the exception of those involved in the construction of the Sydney Harbour Bridge, which opened in March 1932, most businesses and government organisations were laying people off rather than taking on new employees. Soup kitchens run by charitable organisations sprouted up everywhere to feed those who were destitute and starving. Some of those who were unemployed were former soldiers that had fought in the First World War, who were now in their mid-thirties, many of whom still suffered from the trauma of their wartime experiences. In Sydney, a large number of men and women slept outdoors covered in newspapers – particularly in the Domain. The Salvation Army, the Benevolent Society and the Sydney City Mission were inundated with requests for help from desperate families seeking food and shelter. Makeshift dwellings without any heating or sanitation sprouted up all over the city and suburbs. The only form of government social welfare available were sustenance payments, colloquially known as 'the Susso', provided only to the truly destitute where the breadwinner had been unemployed for a lengthy period and had no assets or savings whatsoever. At a time when the basic wage for a man was £2/11/8d,[1] the Susso was three shillings, or 4/6d for a man with a wife and children.

Many men could not afford the cost of a newspaper to look for work and would walk for miles in search of employment. A large number of city men who could not find work went 'on track', which involved travelling and walking around the countryside in the hope of picking up some odd jobs on farms. Many of these men would 'jump the rattler', catching lifts on freight trains without paying a fare. This sometimes involved jumping on or off fast-moving trains, and it was not unusual for men to receive serious injuries or even be killed while doing this. At the wharves in Sydney, so many men would turn up seeking work for the day that a system was introduced whereby tickets would be thrown up into the air and those who were lucky enough to catch a ticket would receive one shift of work. Even for those who had work, their standard of living was not necessarily much better. At the height of the Great Depression, nearly twenty per cent of people earned less than £2 per week. Those who had work often had to support relatives who did not. For most Australians, life was a daily struggle.

Jean Falleni was aware of the intense public controversy that had raged for nearly two years prior to her release in February 1931. When she came out of gaol, she was fêted as a victim of the male-dominated justice system by the group of women who had supported her, however she knew that a substantial portion of the community had opposed her release. To some extent, she had become a *cause célèbre*, especially among prison reformers and anarchists, and she even received some invitations to speak at parlour talks in private homes, which she politely declined. Whenever she was asked to provide her name, whether at the local laundry or to claim the Susso, as soon as she mentioned 'Falleni', people would stare at her and whisper behind her back. There had been one occasion when a woman dragged her children out of a shop when she heard Jean mention her name to the assistant. All Jean wanted was to settle back into a normal, anonymous suburban existence in which she could begin to build some financial security for herself and regain her self-respect. Jean therefore decided that the only option was to change her surname.

Aware of the undertaking that she had signed when she was released from the Women's Reformatory 'to be of good behaviour and keep the peace', Jean approached her parole officer before taking the formal steps to change her name. Her parole officer was very understanding and had no objection to this step, so long as Jean kept him informed of her new name and her whereabouts. Jean therefore made an appointment for a formal interview at the Registrar General's head office at Prince Albert Road in the City, next to Queen Square. She was required to explain to the officer why she wished to change her name, and he wrote out what Jean told him and then asked her to sign an affidavit. Jean, still being illiterate, signed her name with a cross. When she walked out of the Registrar General's Office, her new legal name was Jean Ford.

By 1934, Jean Ford had made some steady progress in developing her new identity. She was working as a housekeeper for an Italian woman who suffered from advanced breast cancer. Jean was quite convinced that this Italian woman and her family knew nothing of her past. On Jean's recommendation, the woman went to see Dr Herbert Moran to see if he could help her, and Jean accompanied her to the doctor's surgery. In the consultation room, Jean gestured behind the Italian woman's back to indicate to Dr Moran that he should say nothing about her past. Dr Moran was not able to help the Italian woman, because her cancer was too far progressed for any treatment. It turned out that the Italian woman and her family had pretended not to know of Jean's past and had taken her into their home as an act of kindness, wanting to give her a job, a place to stay and some security.

Several weeks later, Jean Ford came to see Dr Herbert Moran on her own behalf. The reason was to seek the doctor's assistance to obtain the invalid pension. An application for such a pension required a detailed certificate from a medical practitioner setting out the grounds of invalidity. Following that, the applicant would appear before a government medical officer, who would make the final determination whether or not the person was sufficiently incapacitated to receive the benefit. Dr Moran provided Jean with the necessary certificate, referring to her age and ill health, however, this proved to be insufficient and her application for the invalid pension was rejected.

Jean Ford held a number of jobs, including working as a domestic in boarding houses of the kind that, as Harry Crawford, she had lived in for many years prior to her incarceration. She was always aware of the need to wear women's clothing, so as not to breach her licence conditions. Jean found it hard to repress her desire to wear men's clothes and to engage in hard manual labour. However, she knew only too well what the consequences would be if she reverted back to a male identity, so there was no question of what she needed to do. When out, she dressed in clothes that were nominally female, in that they had been bought in a women's clothing shop, but they were loose-fitting, formless garments that did nothing to accentuate any female attributes, and they were generally covered by an androgynous overcoat. In the privacy of her own home she would quickly change out of her day clothes and into a long-sleeved dressing gown made from a heavy fabric with a button front, shawl collar and cuffs, in a style derived from men's robes. Her hair was always cut short. Jean repressed all her desires for personal intimacy, including any attraction she felt for other women, and threw herself into building her financial security. Thankfully, her change of name had the desired effect, and hardly anyone made the connection to her previous life. The press, too, were mercifully absent.

Over time, Jean Ford accumulated a reasonable sum of money, so that by 1934 she had enough to pay 'key money'[2] on a small residence which she took over as head tenant. She then established her own boarding house in this residence. Over a period of months, she cleaned and painted the premises, bought some good quality, second-hand furniture and then let out individual bedrooms to lodgers, both male and female. She managed this boarding house quite strictly and exceedingly efficiently. She provided meals and washing services for some of the male lodgers, which supplemented her income. Most of the residents were very impressed with her firm but fair management style. Those who were not satisfied were generally the rowdy ones or the late-payers, whom she quickly evicted. Jean developed a reputation as a manager of a good quality, reasonably priced lodging. Over time, she found that more and more single women were attracted to her residence, and she encouraged this. Her success as a boarding house proprietor gave her self-confidence and a sense of security that she had never known before, which in some measure made up for the personal price she continued to pay for her freedom. In order to keep any temptations at bay, Jean kept herself apart from others and, although there were many people with whom she conducted business who liked and respected her, she had very few friends.

After Jean had operated her first boarding house for about a year, she sold it and made a handsome profit. Within a month she had purchased a second one in which she used the same successful formula. Over a number of years, Jean Ford bought and sold many boarding houses, all of them converted by her into good quality, clean and efficiently run establishments. Each time, she sold them for a considerable profit. In all of these transactions, she consulted a man who was her financial confidant.[3] He was later to say about her conduct of boarding houses:

> She came to me whenever she conducted any business. She could neither read nor write, and used to sign the documents with a mark. She told me a lot about her past life, but never mentioned the 'man-woman' matter. In business dealings she was scrupulously honest. She was thin, very active and weighed about 6st. 7lbs.[4]

One of her lodgers, who was later interviewed by Harry Cox, a reporter from the *Sunday Sun*, described Jean Ford as 'a fine woman'.

In early 1938, Jean Ford purchased another boarding house situated at 27 Glenmore Road, Paddington, not far from the main shopping venue in Oxford Street. During the Great Depression, Paddington was still a working-class suburb and its inhabitants suffered very greatly from the privations of the period. The site of several slums, the suburb was considered to be polluted, dirty and overcrowded.[5] By 1938, this situation had been somewhat alleviated as the Depression lifted, but it was still very much a working-class suburb. Yet again, Jean Ford purchased, renovated and operated this boarding house with her own brand of efficiency. After three or four months, she was ready to sell it. She reached an agreement with a purchaser for a price of £100. In 1938, £100 was a fairly large sum of money, but not a huge amount. By way of comparison, an average factory worker in Sydney earned about £250 per year. It was therefore a bit less than half a year's income for an average male worker.

On the morning of 9 June 1938, Jean Ford attended at the office of the agent who had negotiated the sale of her Glenmore Road boarding house, and she was given the £100 in cash. Elated at her renewed financial security, she contemplated the next financial venture which she had in mind, which again involved purchasing an old and dilapidated lodging house, renovating it, replacing the poor-paying lodgers with good ones, running it efficiently for several months, and then selling it, thereby making a further profit. As she left the agent's premises, she contemplated how far she had come in just seven years since her release from the Women's Reformatory. She finally had a degree of financial security and the respect of many business contacts and tenants. It was more than she had dreamed of during the long years of her incarceration.

CHAPTER 29

TO THE BANK

As Jean Ford left the premises of the agent who had conducted the sale of her Glenmore Road boarding house, she firmly clutched her handbag, which contained the £100 that she had been paid. She was heading straight for the bank, which was situated in nearby Oxford Street, where she had held an account since owning her first boarding house about four years earlier. There was a joyous swing in her step as she weighed the advantages and disadvantages of the various properties she had recently seen advertised, one of which would become her next venture. She had calculated that if she maintained her success as a boarding house proprietor for another four or five years, she would have amassed enough money to purchase a small freehold flat in which she could retire and live a quiet, dignified life.

The value of the £100 was not just its monetary worth, but what it represented in terms of her acceptance as an astute, honest and respected businesswoman. It was some consolation for what she had had to forego in giving up any thoughts of leading life as a male. The last seven years, which she had lived ostensibly as a female, had done nothing to detract from her deep, inner sense of maleness. She had become accustomed to wearing the clothes and feigning the gestures of an alien gender. She had also come to accept that she had to be satisfied with sincere and caring, but platonic, friendships with women. Those to whom she was attracted were themselves not attracted to other women, but rather to strong, muscular, masculine men. Over time she found it easier to suppress her libido, which had, in any event, declined with age, and she found her business activities used up much of her inner vigour. The restlessness of her former existence had somewhat dissipated.

Jean arrived on the northern side of Oxford Street near William Street, looked across at her destination – the bank on the opposite side of the road – and stepped off the footpath onto the roadway between two parked cars.

That same morning, William Lamb, a carpenter who lived in Vernon Street, Bexley, was driving his car east through Paddington towards a job in another suburb. As he travelled along Oxford Street at a moderate pace, he was thinking about the various building items that he would need to purchase for the job that day. Suddenly, an elderly woman stepped from between two parked cars onto the roadway directly in front of him. He slammed on his brakes, his tyres screeched, and the woman turned her head and looked into his face with horror as the front of his car slammed into her torso.

The ambulance arrived within ten minutes and took the grievously injured and unconscious pedestrian to the nearest public casualty ward, which was at Sydney Hospital in Macquarie Street. There, she was found to have severe injuries to her head and chest. The ward sister inspected her bag and found £100 in cash, which was immediately placed into safe custody in the hospital office. Her name, Jean Ford, was ascertained from documents in her handbag. Attempts were made by hospital staff to notify relatives, but none could be located. The patient languished in a coma until the following day, 10 June 1938, when she passed away without having regained consciousness. She was sixty-three years of age. Her body was taken to the underground morgue at the hospital.

A police officer was assigned to investigate the accident and, if possible, notify relatives of the deceased. By an incredible coincidence, the police officer assigned to the case was none other than Detective Sergeant WC Watkins who, eighteen years earlier, as a Detective Constable under Detective Sergeant Robson, had investigated the death of Annie Birkett and charged Harry Crawford with her murder. When Sergeant Watkins went down to the hospital morgue the day after her death, he did not recognise the deceased woman when he gave the body a cursory glance. The name, Jean Ford, meant nothing to him. As was the protocol in such cases, he took fingerprints of the deceased woman and sent them to the fingerprint bureau of the police force. No one was more surprised than he when the result came back several days later: the victim of the fatal accident on Oxford Street was none other than Eugenia Falleni. Detective Sergeant Watkins determined that the accident was not due to any fault on the part of William Lamb and no charges were laid against him.

Not a single person came forward to claim the body of Eugenia Falleni. The only surviving relative that Eugenia had in Australia was her granddaughter, Rita Whitby, who by this time was seventeen years old.[1] Not one of her relatives in New Zealand took any steps to formally acknowledge her death. Eugenia's parents, Luigi and Isola Falleni, had never reconciled with their eldest daughter – in fact they had had no contact with her since she had left New Zealand in her early twenties. They read about Eugenia's death in the New Zealand newspapers. According to Eugenia's sister-in-law, Olga Falleni, 'When the paper came and said that Eugenia had died, she [Isola] was relieved, because before you'd never know when she would come back and cause all these problems. She was very sad, but she was also relieved, because now it was all over.'[2]

Not one of the many people with whom Eugenia had associated over the seven years of her post-gaol freedom felt strongly enough about their friendship or association to claim her body or to attend her funeral. A government contractor was therefore given the task of burying her body in the cheapest possible manner. At that time, the least expensive burial plots at the Rookwood cemetery were in the Anglican section. As a result, about a week after her death, despite the fact that she had been a Roman Catholic all her life, Eugenia Falleni was buried in an unmarked pauper's grave in the Anglican section of Rookwood cemetery.[3]

The two weekly newspapers that had played such prominent and opposing roles at the time of Eugenia's bid for release were utterly predictable and consistent in reporting her death. *Smith's Weekly* on 25 June 1938 published a sympathetic article summarising Eugenia's life and trial, and also detailing five other international examples of women who for years had surreptitiously assumed lives as men. The paper concluded:

For complete deception in the masculine role, one further subterfuge is necessary. In the case of Falleni, as in the cases of Murray Hall, de Raylan and Captain Barker, the wives were all deceived by a very simple artifice. What strange psychological warp lies behind the extraordinary deception practised by masculine women in these cases? Science now has a chemical clue which explains the problem quite simply. Because of a chemical error in the period immediately preceding her birth, such a woman starts life with the body of a woman, but the mentality of a man. Though sex is determined at the moment of conception, a chemical control takes over its maintenance in the period before birth. For a baby boy, there is one definite chemical. For a baby girl, another, differing in containing one less atom of carbon and five less of hydrogen.

This arrest of feminine development, and the appearance later of the emotions and instincts of the male, are the outstanding characteristics of men-women of the Falleni type. In recognising these amazing facts, medical science perceives a clue to future treatment or cure of sex inversion generally. Meanwhile, the unhappy victims of such sex defects demand our sympathy, rather than ridicule or disgust. They are victims of nature's cruellest practical joke, an atomic sex-change in life's most elemental stage – before ever they were born.

In sharp contrast was the article reporting her death in *The Truth* on 12 June 1938:

A life that was marked by tragedy, that brought tragedy to others, itself ended in tragedy last week. Seriously injured in a motor accident at Darlinghurst on Thursday, Eugene Falleni, 18 years ago a figure much in the public eye, and branded a murderess by a jury, died in Sydney Hospital on Friday night.

Her time up, she was released a couple of years ago. And now as she had brought tragedy to others, and robbed a son of his mother, she is dead herself.

Although Eugenia's parents, Luigi and Isola Falleni, did not officially acknowledge her death, it must have had a profound effect on them, because Luigi died in Wellington on 15 June 1938, just five days after Eugenia, and Isola died in hospital three weeks later on 3 July.

Four months later, in the Probate Jurisdiction of the Supreme Court, a judge noted that Eugenia Falleni had died intestate – that is, without having made any will. Her property consisted of a small amount of jewellery, a few personal effects, about £12 in a bank account and the £100 in cash that had been found in her handbag at the hospital. As there were no claimants on her estate, her property was forfeited to the government coffers.

To the end of her life, Eugenia proclaimed her innocence of Annie's murder.[3]

CHAPTER 30

RETROSPECTIVE

On 4 February 2005, more than a hundred people gathered in the Strangers' Dining Room at New South Wales Parliament House to celebrate the 175th anniversary of the appointment in 1830 of the first Crown Prosecutor, Frederick Garling. The guests included the Premier, the Chief Justice and the Attorney-General of New South Wales, the President of the New South Wales Bar Association, the Director of Public Prosecutions, the Solicitor -General, Judges of the New South Wales Supreme Court and District Court, three direct descendants of Frederick Garling and numerous past and present Crown Prosecutors. The gathering was addressed by a number of dignitaries. In an address in reply, the author, the 14th Senior Crown Prosecutor, said the following:

> *175 years ago, the then New South Wales Governor, Lieutenant General Ralph Darling, appointed Solicitor Frederick Garling as the first Crown Prosecutor. Since then, I estimate that there have been fewer than 300 men and women who have served this state as full-time Crown Prosecutors. Merely since the appointment of the first Director of Public Prosecutions in 1986, the Crown Prosecutors have conducted over 45,000 criminal jury trials in the District Court and over 2,000 murder trials in the Supreme Court, as well as more than 100,000 sentence proceedings. In that time, the Crown Prosecutors have also provided over 15,000 legal advices to the Director of Public Prosecutions on the continuation or termination of criminal proceedings.*
>
> *I thought it would be interesting for you if I attempted to identify the most significant trial that has been conducted by our predecessors during the last 175 years. There have been so many extraordinary, complex and bizarre trials conducted in that time that it's very difficult to single out one as the trial of all trials. Serious contenders would include: the trial of the so-called man-woman, Eugenia Falleni, in 1920 ...*

In the intervening years, I have come to consider that the trial of Eugenia Falleni in 1920 should be viewed as the single most important criminal case in those 175 years. Its prominence is not because of any lasting effect that the trial had on the law or the administration of criminal justice, but rather because of the multitude of legal and social issues that Eugenia Falleni's life and trial throw up for us to consider, so that we can use them as a yardstick to ask ourselves what we have learned and how far we have progressed since then.

While the trial of Eugenia Falleni was conducted in what was considered an appropriate manner in its day, when we look back with the benefit of hindsight we can see that she suffered a number of grave injustices and an unacceptable degree of improper prejudice at her trial, as well as an extraordinary degree of public humiliation in the national press. It is easy to look back nearly a hundred years and point out where those injustices arose, but one must hesitate before criticising any individual person or persons who participated in the investigation or trial, because every one of them was doing their best in the circumstances of their day. The trial judge, Sir William Portus Cullen, was one of the most highly regarded jurists of his day. The prosecutor at her trial, the first Senior Crown Prosecutor, William Coyle KC, was a most able, professional and highly experienced barrister. Her defence counsel, Archibald McDonell, was intent on representing her to the best of his ability, however, in my view, he was out of his depth in what was a most complex and testing Supreme Court trial. Although he handled the scientific evidence about the cause of Annie Birkett's death very creditably, he mismanaged other critical parts of the trial and failed to address what should have been the main issues: the possibility of an accidental death and the absence of sufficient evidence of intent. The Crown Prosecutor took full advantage of his opponent's weaknesses and in some instances used the disparity between them to gain an unfair advantage by introducing prejudicial material that would have made it very difficult for the jury to consider the case against Eugenia dispassionately. The evidence about the revolver that had been found with the dildo in the portmanteau was particularly detrimental. If a prosecutor led such evidence today, the trial judge would immediately stop the proceedings, discharge the jury and order a retrial in front of a new jury. Also problematical were the references in the evidence to the trips to The Gap and the Woollahra sandhills with Harry Birkett.

The police came into the investigation armed with the empowering knowledge that their suspect was probably a woman disguised as a man. They used this to toy with Harry Crawford and place him at a psychological disadvantage, so that he was more likely to comply with their desire to question him and hopefully make a confession. Sergeant Robson's early, unanswerable question to Harry: 'Have you any marks about your body that will assist in identifying you as a Scotchman and where you say you were born?' began this process. The way that Harry's 'arrest' was engineered to end up at the police station rather than at the court was quite routine for the day and, indeed, was so for almost a century.

By far the most damaging evidence against Eugenia was the scientific evidence given by the forensic pathologists, Drs Palmer and Sheldon. Modern-day science enables us to say that Dr Palmer's view, that the fluid-filled blisters on the margins of the burns meant that Annie Birkett must have been alive when her body was burned, was without any scientific basis whatsoever.[1] Blistering is caused by fluid build-up, whether the body is alive or not. The content of the blisters and its consistency is no indication of whether the burns were pre-mortem or post-mortem. The best way of determining whether someone was alive during a fire is from the presence of soot in the airways and the lungs, or from the level of carbon monoxide in the lungs. The latter was probably beyond the testing capacities of forensic pathologists in 1917, but an inspection of the airways and lungs for soot was clearly available at that time. There is nothing in the report of the first autopsy to indicate whether or not this was done. One can only assume from the absence of any such note that the airways and lungs were too burned to enable such an examination. By the time of the second autopsy, the body had, of course, disintegrated too much for this to occur.

We can also say, with the benefit of modern scientific knowledge, that Dr Palmer's final position, after thorough cross-examination, that he could not exclude the reasonable possibility that all seven cracks in the skull were caused by the heat of the fire, was scientifically correct.[2] Extensive heating of the skull causes the fluid in the brain cavity to expand. It has been described as akin to microwaving an egg. At some point, the pressure build-up inside becomes so extreme that the hard outer container around the inner fluid will crack, causing fissures and fractures as well as extrusion of the contents. In addition, the fluid within the bone marrow of the plate-shaped bones that make up the skull will also expand in a similar way, resulting in individual bones expanding. Thus, all the cracks found in Annie Birkett's skull could easily have been caused by the burning of her body.

That leads us inevitably to the conclusion that Annie Birkett's death may well have occurred shortly before the burning of her body. If so, we cannot say what brought about her death, let alone what events preceded it. If there was, indeed, a struggle in which Harry used some mild or moderate force, and if he did not intend to do her grievous bodily harm, then the appropriate verdict would have been manslaughter rather than murder. How can one say what was in Harry's mind when we do not know anything about the facts surrounding the death and cannot infer them from the mode of death? It often happens that the Crown cannot say exactly what events preceded a murder, but the jury can still infer from the cause of death that it was a deliberate act of severe violence perpetrated by the accused, so that it was necessarily performed with the intention to kill. In this case, however, where the surrounding facts and the cause of death were unknown, no such inference could reasonably have been drawn, because the possibilities of other non-incriminatory explanations could not be excluded. One does not need to go to any great lengths to postulate various scenarios in which an accidental death could have come about – through a fall or, as I have postulated in this book, during a struggle by Annie to leave the area, which was resisted by Harry with a mild or moderate degree of force.

Because of the way in which the trial was conducted, there is another distinctly possible scenario that was never canvassed. It goes like this: there was a struggle, maybe involving some mild or moderate degree of force by Harry, in which Annie was accidentally rendered unconscious. In the heat of the moment, Harry incorrectly concluded that he had killed Annie, but in reality she was still alive, though moribund. Thinking that she was dead, Harry decided to burn her body beyond recognition, but in so doing, he unknowingly caused Annie's death. In this scenario, Harry has committed the act that caused the death (burning the body) without the intention of killing her, so one of the essential ingredients of murder, intention to kill or do grievous bodily harm, is missing. If these facts were laid out before a jury, they would be compelled to acquit the accused of murder, and could instead convict of manslaughter. The basis for manslaughter is the gross criminal negligence in failing to ensure that the body was not still alive before burning it. This scenario, again, is a real possibility of what may have happened in the Lane Cove River Park when Annie Birkett. It is remarkably similar to a classic factual scenario that is presented for analysis to law students studying basic criminal law at universities around the common law world, in which the accused incorrectly thinks that he has killed the victim and so rolls his body over a cliff, thereby unintentionally killing him.

Because Eugenia Falleni's counsel did not raise the possibility of an accidental death, it was not a requirement in 1920 for the judge to explain it to the jury. If the trial were heard today, even in the absence of any submissions from the defence, the trial judge would be obliged to put this issues to the jury for their consideration.

The media interest in Eugenia's case was extreme and I have no doubt that it would be so if a similar case arose today. What would be different today is that there would be far less public commentary and conjecture about the facts, and especially about her sexuality, than there was at the time. In 1920, the press felt entitled to engage in a free-for-all up until the completion of the committal proceedings, when they became more circumspect. Today, that circumspection would commence with the arrest and charging of the suspect.

In 1920, the average Australian citizen knew appallingly little about the diverse aspects of human sexuality, including homosexuality and transsexuality. Havelock Ellis was to sexology what Charles Darwin was to the study of human evolution – an iconic pioneer in a new field of learning. In 1920, people believed that if someone was sexually attracted to others of the same sex, it was because, in some deep sense, they were genetically and biologically engineered as a member of the opposite sex. If you were a man who was attracted to other men, that was because you were, in some respects, a woman – hence the concept of the 'sexual invert'. Archibald McDonell was clearly well read in the field of sexual inversion. He unwisely thought that if he could prove that Eugenia was a 'true sexual invert' – that in some way she was really a man – he could negate the Crown case that she had perpetrated a sexual fraud when using the dildo on Annie. That was not only naïve, but also a serious misreading of the jury. A good trial counsel on either side must be able to accurately assess the impact that their arguments will have on the jury.

The law has progressed considerably in providing additional safeguards during trials that seek to prevent miscarriages of justice. As described in chapter 19, identification or sighting evidence is subject to many rules and procedures that were not part of the scene in 1920. This is because the experience of the courts has been that this is an area in which miscarriages are more likely to occur. Lies are similarly subject to many more constraints today than a hundred years ago. It is only a very small minority of lies that can be used by the prosecution today as evidence of the guilt of an accused. The caution before questioning by police is more carefully scrutinised than was the practice in 1920. Even judicial statements about the onus and standard of proof are more specifically crafted today to ensure that they do not inadvertently reverse the onus of proof and suggest that the accused has the obligation of proving something.

There was one area of evidence above all others that was the real culprit in securing Eugenia's unjustifiable conviction for murder: the expert scientific evidence by the two government forensic pathologists that formed the basis of the Crown's submission that Annie Birkett was probably burned while still alive. Science is constantly in a state of flux. What is universally accepted as self-evident at one time can become unanimously rejected as unfounded at another. Yesterday's orthodoxy is today's heresy, and vice versa. That does not mean that one cannot rely on scientific evidence in a criminal trial. Many significant advances in the investigation of crime, such as fingerprints and DNA, have been based on solid and reputable science that has stood the test of time. The real challenge is to restrict experts to what is a recognised field of learning and practice and to prevent them from encroaching into other allied areas in which they are not truly proficient. Drs Palmer and Sheldon were clearly not experts in the effects of fire on a body. The evidence about the blisters was not only wrong, but was not based on any real knowledge, experience or expertise in this area on their part. One can imagine the two government doctors, on the day before giving their evidence, avidly reading their textbooks about the effects of fire on a body. Their views about the skull fractures, which were based on early, unsophisticated X-rays, completely contradicted the opinions they had formed when they had the body in front of them during the first autopsy. It was regrettable that McDonell did not call a properly qualified expert on the effects of fire on a body to dispel the impression that the two Crown witnesses had left – that Annie had been knocked on the head, thereby rendering her unconscious, which enabled Harry to place her moribund body over the fire. Once the jury accepted this scenario, a conviction was not only justified, but inevitable.

It will not have escaped the attention of any reader that Eugenia's trial lasted only two days. In its time, a two-day murder trial was considered quite unexceptional. A trial of similar complexity today would in all probability extend for at least eight or ten weeks – more than twenty times as long as Eugenia's trial in 1920. The cost to the community of such a lengthy trial is immense. The sacrifice that jurors are required to make when serving on a long trial is verging on untenable. It is interesting to explore the reasons for the extraordinary extension in the duration of trials over the intervening one hundred years.

The first observation I would make is that most of that change has only come about in the last three decades. While trials have become more complex, especially when they involve expert scientific witnesses, that is

only a small part of the explanation. By far the largest factor in the length-
ening duration of trials has been a change in the culture of court advocacy.
For many modern defence counsel, cross-examination of the Crown's
witnesses is an opportunity for a protracted fishing expedition rather than
part of a carefully constructed and strategic campaign. It is not considered unacceptable today for a defence counsel to cross-examine a Crown
witness for several days without achieving any significant concessions. It is
not uncommon for a closing address on either side to extend over three or
four days after a month or two of evidence.

Is justice served any better for such prolixity? I doubt it – certainly
not twenty times better! In the age of the ten-second news 'grab' or the
thirty-second 'infomercial', a verbose barrister who is repetitive or unable
to focus his or her thoughts is an anathema to the ordinary juror. The
greatest sin of an advocate is to bore the audience. If advertisers, television
and movie directors, publishers and authors, visual artists, teachers, politicians and others only succeed if they can engage with their audiences,
why is it that trial counsel are permitted to drive their jurors into a state
of conscious coma? Do we need a courtroom 'worm' to electronically
monitor the depths of boredom and the heights of interest generated by
opposing counsel, or do we need to take steps to ensure that judges have
the backbone to curtail unhelpful verbosity?

The result of this trend towards lengthier, more expensive trials is that
there is a concerted push in some circles to restrict, or even abolish, jury
trials in the mistaken belief that trials by judge alone are more efficient
and less costly. How should those of us who are avid supporters of the jury
system confront these trends? In my opinion, it is only through education
– of judges, magistrates, barristers and solicitors – in techniques of good,
efficient and objective-driven advocacy that we can reverse the trend.

Eugenia Falleni was a transgender warrior at a time when there was no
understanding of her condition and no support for her cause. The author
behind the 'Man in the Mask' column in *Smith's Weekly* made a vain
attempt at understanding why Eugenia had lived as a man. He expressed
the abhorrence that members of the public (including jurors) felt for her
gender and sexual transgressions. After attending the closing addresses in
her trial, on 16 October 1920 under the heading 'The Falleni Tragedy' and
a subheading 'The Intruder' he wrote this:

> *The body it had thought to inhabit as a mansion, wherefrom to make*
> *excursions about that wide panorama – the body it had thought to rule*

– was already ruled by an intruder. For that dainty soul-thing it had become but a prison.

The body was a house divided – a misused mansion – an ugliness where nature hid its naked beauty in rags of bestiality. The dwelling that had been designed for the sacred ceremonies of motherhood became a ribald clubhouse for mock rights of masculinity. The cowering soul-thing was forced to witness those rites, even to participate in them, and instead of being able to breathe the clean ecstasy of life, had to content itself with suffocating gusts of falsehood.

So it was that a pathetic figure, longing to be a man, because it knew itself no longer woman, went nervously through the days, doubly afraid of the loneliness that all souls fear, and seeking sly means to win companionship, and to satisfy the fantastic curiosity of the ghoul that ruled it.

With these words, the 'Man in the Mask' described Eugenia as neither male nor female, but as the site of an internal struggle which he described using demonic terminology. According to this view, a 'ghoul' had invaded her and used her body to perpetrate sexual acts upon her unsuspecting female victims. In a sense, these acts were viewed at the time as Eugenia's principal crime, rather than the murder. The focus of the press was primarily upon her gender-crossing, so that the alleged murder was almost a secondary offence. By the time of her trial she had been convicted in the court of public opinion of masquerading as a male, which made it easier for the jury to find her guilty of murder. The killing of Annie Birkett was represented as a cold-blooded and deliberate act to preserve her terrible secret, rather than a crime of passion by a spurned lover. The central object at Eugenia's trial – 'the article' – was always referred to by euphemisms. In declining to refer to it by its proper name, it assumed a significance way out of proportion to what it deserved. Underlying its role as a court exhibit, what it represented was a challenge to society's rigid boundaries between male and female. The 'article' was the offensive weapon that had been used by the accused in the perpetration of an offence far worse than murder. She had challenged fixed views and standards about the meaning of male and female in a society in which those roles were strictly defined and hardly ever challenged. Added to this was her status as an outsider because of her Italian origins, which was repeatedly emphasised by the press.

How should we view Eugenia Falleni's condition today, with the benefit of hindsight, the advances that have been made in the modern medical and social sciences, and our more enlightened views about sexuality and personal identity? Was she a sexual invert, a lesbian, a transgender person, a transsexual, a sufferer of gender dysphoria, or what? Sexual orientation or preference is quite different and separate from sexual identity. The former is an expression of sexual attraction to others, while the latter is an expression of one's own inner sexual identity. The terms 'lesbian' and 'homosexual' refer to sexual orientation or preference. A transsexual is a person whose physical sex at birth conflicts with his or her perceived psychological gender. The medical definition incorporates a number of the following: a marked incongruence between one's experienced/expressed gender and one's primary and/or secondary sex characteristics; a strong desire to be rid of one's primary and/or secondary sex characteristics because of a marked incongruence with one's experienced/expressed gender; and a strong desire to be of the other gender.

Transgenderism is a broader umbrella term which includes people who do not conform to typically accepted gender roles, for example: cross-dressers, drag queens, and people who identify as genderqueer (a catch-all term for gender identities other than male and female). Transgenderism and transsexualism are not interchangeable terms. Transsexualism is a specific category within the realm of transgender. The term 'gender dysphoria' is a medical term referring to feelings of discontent with the biological gender that one was assigned at birth.

The most acceptable term today for Eugenia Falleni's condition is 'gender identity disorder', which is synonymous with transsexualism. It is quite different from homosexuality, in that homosexuals nearly always identify with their apparent sex or gender. It is also completely different from transvestism, where cross-dressing occurs for sexual pleasure but the transvestite does not identify as a member of the other sex. Girls with gender identity disorder prefer, as did Eugenia, to wear boys' clothing, to look like a boy, to have mainly boys as playmates, and to engage in competitive contact sport and rough play of the kind normally engaged in by boys. However, merely because a girl has these preferences does not necessarily mean that the child has a gender identity disorder. As females with the disorder approach puberty, they dread the prospect of developing normal female characteristics and menstruating. Adults with gender identity disorder are often more comfortable living their lives and dressing as members of the opposite sex and have a strong desire to be viewed by others as members of the opposite sex.

Today in Australia, and in most developed western countries, Eugenia would be able to chose, if she wanted, to live openly as a transsexual man, comfortable in the knowledge that there were other people like her in the community. Various laws would protect her from official and institutional discrimination, although she would still face much fear, prejudice and misunderstanding of transsexuals in society. She would have a variety of medical and social services available to her, including hormonal treatment and sexual realignment surgery. She would have a greater chance today than she did in the first two decades of the twentieth century of meeting a female partner who would accept her as a man.

When I tell people about Eugenia's story, I am often asked: 'Do you think she was guilty?' My answer is always the same: 'That is the wrong question. The right question is: Was there sufficient evidence to justify her conviction for murder?' For reasons I have explored in this book, I believe that Eugenia Falleni should not have been convicted of murder. If her trial were held today, I am quite convinced that she would either be acquitted outright or, at most, convicted of manslaughter. Her conviction for murder was based on fallacious scientific evidence, unreliable sighting witnesses, dubious police practices and an avalanche of prejudicial publicity about her gender identity disorder. A number of significant items of evidence would probably not be admitted today. Undoubtedly the body in the park was Annie Birkett's, and unquestionably Eugenia was with her in the park on the day she died, but how she came to die shall always remain a mystery.

EPILOGUE

PEOPLE

Luigi and Isola Falleni

Eugenia's parents, Luigi and Isola Falleni, lived for many years as respected members of their community in Wellington. They celebrated their diamond wedding anniversary in May 1933, an event that prompted the publication of their photograph in the Wellington *Evening Post*. As previously described, they never re-established contact with Eugenia and died within several weeks of her death.

Arthur Raymond Whitby

Josephine Falleni's husband, Arthur, left the Navy and became a telephone linesman. On 5 January 1934, ten years after Josephine's death, he married Alice Maud Nichols, who was a spinster two years older than him. Alice died in 1939. In 1944, Arthur married for the third time, to Dorothy Frances MacCarthy. Dorothy died in 1974. Her death prompted Arthur in about 1974 to send a letter to his daughter, Rita, whom he had not seen since shortly after her mother, Josephine's, death in 1924. Despite her resentment at the father who had abandoned her at such a young age, Rita went with her husband Thomas and their two children to visit Arthur at his home at Oxley Street, Campbelltown. Arthur died of prostate cancer at Bellingen on 16 October 1986 aged eighty-nine. All three wives had predeceased him. Rita was his only child.

Rita Whitby

Rita Whitby, Eugenia's only grandchild, became a very pretty, dark-haired, assertive young woman with distinctive Italian looks. The author has been unable to establish whether, after her release from prison in 1931, Eugenia had any contact with her granddaughter. Rita later married motor driver Thomas Elvy at St Michael's Anglican Church in Sydney on 19 October 1950. He was twenty-seven and she was twenty-nine. At the time, Rita was working as a machinist. One of the companies she worked for was a manufacturer of asbestos industrial filters. Rita and Thomas had two children and lived in Paddington. Rita died of asbestosis on 17 June 1995 aged seventy-four.

Dr Gother Clarke

During the First World War, Dr Clarke enlisted in March 1916 as a medical officer with Headquarters Company, 34th Battalion. He was given the rank of major. At the outbreak of war, the Australian Army Medical Service was a small, part-time, specialised addition to the British Royal Army Medical Corps. By 1918, it had become an independent medical corps that showed great professionalism and dedication. Often short of supplies and sometimes under attack themselves, the members of the AAMC played a significant role in most of the major battles of the latter part of the war. Dr GRC Clarke was killed with members of his staff while tending to wounded soldiers during the Battle of Passchendaele in the Ypres region of Belgium in October 1917. He was buried at Hamburg House on the Zonnebeke Ridge just outside the pill box used as the Regimental Aid Post. The 3rd Division suffered 3,199 casualties in the twenty-four hours of the battle.

Sir William Cullen

Cullen retired as the Chief Justice of New South Wales in 1925. Although he was still at the height of his forensic powers, his physical health had deteriorated. He remained as Chancellor of the University of Sydney for the unprecedentedly long period of twenty years, until 1934. He and his wife spent their retirement years at Leura. Sir William died on 6 April 1935 and was buried in the Wentworth Falls Cemetery.

William Coyle KC

William Coyle KC went on to become a District Court Judge and a Chairman of Quarter Sessions.[1] While he was known as an able and fair judge, he had a reputation for expressing his displeasure at the presence of women in the public gallery during unsavoury trials. This possibly derived from his experience of the public gallery in the trial of Eugenia Falleni. These views resulted in some censure from the appeal courts. He retired from the Bench in 1938.

William Coyle died on 7 September 1951 at his home 'Woodbridge' at 4 Holt Street, Double Bay, just several hundred metres from the home of Mr and Mrs De Angelis, where Josephine Falleni had lived many decades earlier. He was eighty-two years of age. One of his sons became a promising barrister, but unfortunately died very young.

Archibald McDonell

Less than twelve months after conducting the trial of Eugenia Falleni, Archibald McDonell represented the accused in another celebrated and notorious legally aided case: the trial of Arthur Peden. That case was also prosecuted by William Coyle KC, while Drs Palmer and Sheldon again featured as expert witnesses. Arthur Peden was charged with the murder of his wife, Hannah Jane Peden. At the first trial in 1921, the jury could not reach a verdict, as one lone juror would not agree to a conviction. At the second trial, Peden was convicted of the murder. Subsequent appeals to the Court of Criminal Appeal and the High Court of Australia failed. However, a 1922 Royal Commission into his conviction, presided over by Mr Justice Phillip Street, found that there was a doubt about the conviction because of some questionable expert scientific evidence. As a result, Arthur Peden was released and pardoned. The newspapers reported that upon his release from gaol he was met at the gates by Mr Archibald McDonell. A book has been published and a film produced about this highly controversial case.[2]

On 2 June 1926, at his own request, Archibald McDonell had his name removed from the roll of barristers and transferred to the roll of solicitors. According to one of Archibald's modern-day relatives,[3] the Peden trial took so much out of him that when it was all over, he decided to retire from the Bar. However, another account records that his brother Charles, who had been paying the rent on Archibald's professional Chambers, insisted that he leave the Bar and join him in his legal firm, though not as a partner. In 1926, Archibald became an employee in his brother's firm, McDonell & Moffitt. It has been said that even as a solicitor 'success continued to elude him'.[4]

Archibald never married. He continued to live for the rest of his life in the upstairs bedroom of Arundel, his brother Charles McDonell's home. He was well cared for by his brother. His great-nieces and nephews viewed him as a virtual recluse who hardly ever spoke. Archibald died at Lewisham Hospital in Sydney on 10 March 1941 of complications from appendicitis. He was buried at Rookwood Cemetery.

Rod Kidston

The prosecuting officer who conducted Eugenia Falleni's committal proceedings later became a Crown Prosecutor. In 1954, although Kidston was acknowledged as unsurpassed in his knowledge of the criminal law and his experience and dedication as a Crown Prosecutor, he was passed over for the role of Senior Crown Prosecutor when the Government instead appointed William (Bill) James Knight QC directly from the private Bar.

Kidston had to be content with appointment as a QC and the States first Deputy Senior Crown Prosecutor. He was the author of an article published in the Australian Law Journal in 1958 entitled 'The Office of Crown Prosecutor (More Particularly in New South Wales)' which for many decades was the definitive work on the professional and ethical duties of Crown Prosecutors.[5]

Maddocks Cohen
Maddocks Cohen, solicitor, subsequently appeared in some other notable cases, including the third trial of Major James Stewart in 1921, who was finally acquitted after two convictions, death sentences and successful appeals. Maddocks Cohen died in Sydney in June 1942 at the age of seventy-four. He was survived by his wife, Mary Jane, three sons (Frank, Edward George, and Earnest John Maddocks-Cohen), and two daughters (Mary Frances Aston and Dora Josephine Phillips). The firm of Maddocks Cohen & Maguire still survives today.

Dr Arthur Aubrey Palmer
Dr Palmer rose to the rank of Chief Government Medical Officer and Senior Gaol Surgeon. He was also Police Surgeon and a lecturer in medical ethics and medical jurisprudence at the University of Sydney. He retired in 1936 after twenty-seven years of service in the Health Department. He was awarded the OBE in 1941, and died the following year.

Dr Stratford Sheldon
Dr Sheldon went on to become a lecturer in medical jurisprudence and toxicology at the University of Sydney. In all, he performed more than 10,000 autopsies for the City Coroner. He died in 1965 at the age of ninety-one.

Detective Sergeant Stewart Robson
Detective Robson was appointed an inspector in 1928 and superintendent at Broken Hill in 1935. He retired to Maroubra in 1936 after thirty-five years of service, and died in 1946 at the age of sixty-six.

Constable Lillian Armfield
Constable Armfield, the officer who unsuccessfully tried to explain to Lizzie Crawford that her husband was a woman, progressed through the NSW Police service inordinately slowly – much more so than if she had been a man. She was appointed a sergeant in 1923. Most of her police

service was at the CIB in Sydney. For most of her police career, it was known that she was the only policewoman in New South Wales approved to carry a service revolver. She was awarded the King's Police and Fire Service Medal for outstanding service in 1947, and retired in 1949 – still a sergeant and was awarded the Imperial Service Medal. She died in Lewisham District Hospital in 1971 aged eighty-six. Her life story, *Rugged Angel – The Amazing Career of Policewoman Lillian Armfield* by Vince Kelly, was published in 1961. Policewomen were not sworn in as constables like their male counterparts until 1965.

Dr Herbert Moran

Doctor Herbert Moran worked as a doctor in Europe during the Second World War. He was instrumental in establishing the teaching of Italian at the University of Sydney. He wrote three books before he died at sixty years of age in Cambridge, England in 1945.

William McKell MLA

William McKell, who, as Justice Minister, gave permission for Dr Herbert Moran to visit Eugenia Falleni in Long Bay Gaol, was the Premier of New South Wales from 1941 to 1947. He was Governor-General of Australia from 1947 to 1953. He was knighted in 1951 and died at the age of ninety-three in 1985.

Joe Lamaro MLA

Joe Lamaro was Minister for Justice between 1930 and 1931. He then became the Attorney-General of New South Wales from 1931 to 1932. In 1934, he resigned from his State seat to contest one at the Federal election, but was unsuccessful. He then entered private practice as a solicitor and later as a barrister. He was appointed a New South Wales Crown Prosecutor in 1943 and became a District Court Judge in 1947. In 1951, he suffered a cerebral haemorrhage while in court at Hay, and died there. He never married.

Havelock Ellis

The pre-eminent sexologist of his generation, Ellis's own life was hardly one of sexual normalcy. In 1891, at the age of thirty-two and still ostensibly a virgin, Ellis married the English writer and women's rights advocate, Edith Lees. Lees was openly a lesbian. After their honeymoon, Ellis returned to his rooms, where he had previously lived as a bachelor, and Lees resided elsewhere. Ellis later described their relationship as 'a union of affectionate comradeship, in which the specific emotions of sex had the smallest part, yet a union, as I was later to learn by experience, able to attain even on that basis a passionate intensity of love'. In March 1916, Lees suffered a severe nervous breakdown and entered a convent nursing home. She died of diabetes six months later. Ellis's friends were amazed that he came to be considered an expert on sex, as they knew that he was impotent. Ellis died in England in July 1939. Much of the personal information about his life was the subject of Ellis's autobiography *My Life*, which was published posthumously in 1940.

PLACES

Annie Birkett's death scene, Lane Cove River Park

The author has conducted many unsuccessful searches of the bush in the Lane Cove River National Park in an attempt to locate the actual site of Annie Birkett's death. The uniformed officer who was first on the scene after the body was found, Constable John Henry Walsh, described it as being in rough, timbered country about 400 yards from the Cumberland Paper Mills. The first detectives on the scene described the location as: about 140–200 yards from Mowbray Road, about 40 or 50 yards north of the Cumberland Paper Mills and about 400 yards east of the Chicago Flour Mills. In *The Sun* newspaper on 7 July 1920, there was a photograph of 'the spot in the Lane Cove River bush where the remains of Annie Birkett were found'. The photograph shows a level clearing about 5 yards across, a distinctively shaped rock which Constable Walsh described as about nine feet high, a tree growing up the rock in the way typical of angophoras, and some identification tags stuck in the ground to show the location of items of evidence that had been found. While the vegetation may well have changed during the intervening years, the rock is unlikely to have altered significantly, unless it has been buried beneath the six-lane carriageway of nearby Epping Road. The best access to this area of the park is either down a small track that starts at the corner of Epping Road and Sam Johnson Way or via the back of the Shell service station on Epping Road. The author would appreciate being informed if any reader is successful in locating the site.

Lane Cove River Park

In 1938, the park was declared a national park. In recent years, additional areas have been added to it. The park has continued to provide Sydney residents with opportunities for picnics and boating. It has also continued to possess a mystical and sombre side. In more recent times, this was heightened by the mysterious deaths on New Year's Eve 1963 of Dr Gilbert Bogle and Mrs Margaret Chandler, whose bodies were found in bushland near to Fullers Bridge, only several hundred metres from where Annie Birkett's body had been found. Dr Bogle was a CSIRO scientist and, although he and Margaret Chandler were both married to other people, they had left a New Year's Eve party at night to have sex in the park. Their bodies were discovered the next morning by two boys. The cause of their deaths was by poisoning, but the type of poison and the source of it could not be established at the time. However, there has since been a convincing theory advanced that their deaths may have been caused by accidental hydrogen sulphide poisoning, due to the build-up of this poisonous gas in the river bed, largely because of suppurating, polluted mud from the factories formerly operating nearby.

Cumberland Paper Mills

The Cumberland Paper Mills were destroyed by fire in 1928. In 1932, filmmaker Frank Hurley made a dramatised documentary film to highlight the history and heroics of firefighters. The final firefighting scene for the film was staged by re-burning the mills as a re-creation of the actual fire that had taken place there four years earlier. To achieve authenticity, Hurley laced the dilapidated building with highly flammable nitrate film stock and doused it in petrol. Although under fire brigade supervision, the sequence was hazardous to film.

Sydney Morgue, 102–104 George Street, The Rocks

The site was associated with the investigation of unexplained deaths from 1854 until 1971, when the Coroner's Court and morgue moved to their present location in Parramatta Road, Glebe. The court building in The Rocks survives, but the morgue was demolished in 1972 after unsuccessful green bans and protests by local residents.

103 Cathedral Street, Woolloomooloo

Mrs Schieblich's former residence survives as a block of flats.

The Gap

The Gap continues to be enormously popular with tourists and sightseers. It also continues to have an ominous reputation as a place for suicides. The wooden fence has been replaced many times, but is still of a very similar construction to what it was in 1917. There are currently proposals to erect a high metal fence to deter suicides. In 2008, the author prosecuted the trial of Gordon Wood, who was charged with the murder of his model girlfriend, Caroline Byrne, whose body had been found at the base of The Gap. In preparation for the trial, the author was lowered in a harness over the cliff to the rocks below by the police rescue squad. He is therefore one of only few people who can say that they have gone over The Gap and lived to tell the tale! Wood's conviction at trial was overturned by the Court of Criminal Appeal.

Central Police Court, Liverpool Street, Sydney

This court, now the Central Local Court, still functions as a criminal court where magistrates preside over summary hearings and committal proceedings.

Central police station, Central Street, Sydney

The Central police station in Central Street, Sydney, was the headquarters of the New South Wales Police Force until the construction of the Sydney Police Centre in Surry Hills in the early 1980s. The building in Central Street is currently in a derelict condition, except for the cell area, which has recently been renovated and is still used for prisoners attending the Central Local Court next door.

Empire Hotel, Annandale

The Empire Hotel, where police first approached Harry Crawford, still exists by that name on the same site at the corner of Parramatta Road and Johnston Street, Annandale.

INSTITUTIONS

Paulina Rescue Home for women, Wellington, New Zealand

The Salvation Army's Paulina Rescue Home in Cuba Street, Wellington was the place where Eugenia was given refuge at a particularly critical time in her early life prior to her departure from New Zealand. In 1907, the home was transferred to Owen Street and new plans were devised for the Cuba Street property to become the 'The People's Palace', a name used throughout the world for the Salvation Army's affordable and liquor-free hotels. This was equipped to the latest standards, including electricity and hot water throughout. It had 96 bedrooms, slept 134 guests and fed 180. Two more wings were built in 1917, bringing the number of rooms to 288. In 1986, the Salvation Army sold the property and it became the Trekkers Hotel. Today, it is the four-star Wellington Hotel.

Sargent's Tea Rooms

The Sergeant's Tea Rooms flourished all over Sydney and in country towns until about 1960, when eating habits of Australians became more sophisticated. Between 1962 and 1964 all the tea rooms were closed. Ownership of the company left the Sargent family in 1967. In the 1980s, the company began focusing on frozen pies for the retail market. Today the Sargent's pie company is still a private, Australian-owned company providing the major supermarket chains with pies and other baked pastries.

St Margaret's Maternity Home, Darlinghurst

At its peak, St Margaret's was the third-largest maternity hospital in Sydney. From 1961 to 1988, the hospital was a teaching hospital of the University of Sydney in obstetrics and gynaecology. The hospital finally closed in 1998. The art deco building survives.

Riverstone Meatworks

The Riverstone Meatworks served for many decades as one of New South Wales's major abattoirs. A fire onsite in 1970 killed six men. The meatworks closed in the 1980s, but some cottages at the abattoirs built for nightshift workers in the early twentieth century survive.

Perdriau Rubber Company, Drummoyne

The company merged with Dunlop Rubber Company of Australasia Ltd in 1929. In 1977 the factory buildings were purchased by a developer and converted into the Birkenhead Point shopping complex.

State Reformatory for Women, Long Bay Prison Complex, Malabar

The State Reformatory for Women at Long Bay was vacated after Mulawa Correctional Centre opened at Silverwater in 1969.

Senior Crown Prosecutor

Although the first Crown Prosecutor was appointed in 1830, William Coyle KC was appointed as the first Senior Crown Prosecutor in 1920. To date, there have been fourteen Senior Crown Prosecutors. They are: William Thomas Coyle KC (1920–27), LJ McKean KC (1927–40), TS Crawford KC (1940–47), Charles Vincent (Mick) Rooney QC (1947–54), WJ (Bill) Knight QC (1954–69), DF (Don) Kelly QC (1969–73), Leon G Tanner QC (1973–75), Vincent (Vin) R Wallace QC (1975–78), RW (Bill) Job QC (1978–86), JX (Joe) Gibson QC (1986–87), WH (Sandy) Gregory DSC

RFD QC (1987–90), Allan C Saunders QC (1990–91), Ian S Lloyd QC (1991–96), and the author (1997–present).[6]

ANIMALS AND OBJECTS
Zulu
Zulu, the horse that belonged to Archie McDonell's father and unexpectedly won the Melbourne Cup in 1881, and which Archie looked after in its later years, died at Mondrook and was buried on the property. The horse has been memorialised in a road at Mondrook called Zulu Lane.

The 'article'
A year after Eugenia Falleni's trial, Dr A. Palmer and Dr S. Sheldon presented the 'article' for inspection at a medico-legal meeting in Sydney of the NSW Branch of the British Medical Association. The Justice and Police Museum in Sydney has possession of an object which some claim is the 'article' from the trial of Eugenia Falleni. However, the author is firmly of the view that this is not the genuine item, and the curator of the Museum is of the same view. The original article was last seen publicly at the meeting attended by Drs Palmer and Sheldon.[7]

SPIRITUAL
The legend of St Eugenia[8]
Born in 280 AD, Eugenia was the daughter of Philip, the Duke of Alexandria and Governor of Egypt on behalf of Emperor Commodus of Rome. Eugenia was both educated and beautiful. When it came time for her father to screen suitors for Eugenia's marriage, she rejected his choice and fled her home dressed as a man, using the name Eugenius and accompanied by a pair of faithful servants, Protus and Hyacinth, who escorted her to an abbey far removed to assure obscurity. Here she was baptised a Christian by Helenus, the Bishop of Heliopolis. Still pretending to be a man, due to her piety and character she rose to become an abbot. While an abbot, she cured a rich woman of Alexandria named Melanthia of an illness. Melanthia fell in love with the abbot and made sexual advances towards him, which he rebuffed, so Melanthia publicly accused Eugenius of sexual assault. Eugenius was taken to court, where, still disguised as a man, he faced his father as the judge. The father recognised his daughter, whereupon her female identity was revealed, and she was exonerated. Her father was so overcome by the return of his daughter whom he had thought to be dead that he converted to Christianity and became Bishop of Alexandria. The Roman Emperor was not impressed by this and had him executed.

Eugenia and her remaining household then moved to Rome where she converted many to Christianity, especially young women. This led to her martyrdom. Protus and Hyacinth were beheaded on 11 September 258 and Eugenia followed on 25 December 258.

The story of St Eugenia's was included in the *Golden Legend*, a collection of hagiographies by Jacobus de Voragine that became a late-medieval bestseller. It was likely compiled around the year 1260, although the text was added to over the centuries. St Eugenia has been recognised by the modern-day LGBT (lesbian, gay, bisexual and transgender) communities as an example of a transgender saint.

The martyrdom of Eugenia of Rome, from Menologion of Basil II, eleventh-century illuminated Byzantine manuscript with 430 miniatures, now in the Vatican library.

BIBLIOGRAPHY

Rex v Eugene Falleni, transcript of the trial of Eugene Falleni in the Supreme Court of New South Wales, 5–6 October 1920, State Records Office, New South Wales

Handwritten trial notes of Chief Justice Sir William Cullen from the trial of Eugene Falleni, State Records office, NSW

Birth certificates of: Josephine Falleni (1898), Josephine De Angliss (1914), Archibald McDonell (1868)

Marriage Certificates of: Eugenia Falleni and Braseli Innocente (1894), Harry Crawford and Annie Birkett (1913), Harry Crawford and Elizabeth King Allison (1919), Arthur Raymond Whitby and Josephine Falleni (1920), Arthur Raymond Whitby and Alice Maude Nichols (1934), Rita Josephine Whitby and Thomas Elvy (1950)

Death certificates of: Josephine De Angliss (1914), Josephine Rita Whitby (1924), Archibald McDonell (1941)

Commonwealth Electoral Roll for Paddington, NSW, 1949, 1958, 1963, 1980

NSW Census records for the District of Paddington, 1901

The Ryerson Index for Rita Josephine Elvy

Records of the ship *Waikato* in 1877: ancestry.com

NSW Law Almanac, 1920

Register of post mortem examinations, Sydney City Morgue, 1917, 3/2209 p336, State Records Office, NSW

Cadastral Records, Land & Property Information, NSW Department of Finance & Services

NSW Female Penitentiary Records for Eugenie Falleni, State Records Office, NSW

Probate records for Eugene Falleni, State Records Office of NSW

Police Statement of Harry Bell Birkett, 13 June 1920, State Records Office, NSW

Various contemporary New Zealand newspapers: *Wairarapa News*, *Poverty Bay Herald*, *The Star*, *Marlborough Express*, *Evening Post*, *Colonist*, *Wanganui Herald*, *Hawke's Bay Herald*, *Timaru Herald*, *Hawera & Normanby Star*

Various contemporary Australian newspapers: *Evening News, Sydney Morning Herald, Daily Telegraph, The Sun, Melbourne Argus, Adelaide Advertiser, The Melbourne Age, Adelaide Register, Broken Hill Barrier Miner, Brisbane Courier, Hobart Mercury, The Truth, Smith's Weekly, Launceston Examiner, The West Australian*

Sun-Herald article by Harry Cox, 11 June 1961

Evening Post (NZ), 6 May 1933

Daily Mirror, 28 February 1970

Sydney Morning Herald death notices, 21 October 1986

Various obituaries of Archibald McDonell, including a typed manuscript provided by his family, and the St Ignatius College, Riverview Magazine

Obituary of Charles Joseph McDonell, typed manuscript provided by his family

Typed manuscript about the family and descendants of Henry Cohen (1790–1867) by Philip Charles Cohen, provided by his family

Australian Dictionary of Biography, National Centre of Biography, Australian National University

Charles Bean, *History of World War 1*, Vol IV, *The Australian Imperial Forces in France, 1917*, p 927

JM Bennett, *Sir William Portus Cullen - Scholar and Judge*, Canberra Historical Journal, September 1977

Suzanne Falkiner, '*Eugenia – a man*', Pan Books Australia, 1988

Ruth Ford, *The Man-Woman Murderer: Sex Fraud, Sexual Inversion and the Unmentionable 'Article' in 1920s Australia*, in Gender and History, Vol 12 No 1, April 2000

HTE Holt, *A Court Rises: the lives and times of the judges of the District Court of New South Wales (18591959)*, Law Foundation of NSW

Vince Kelly, *Rugged Angel*, Angus & Robertson, 1961, chapter 26

John Laffin, *Guide To Australian Battlefields Of The Western Front 1916–1918*, Kangaroo Press and Australian War Memorial, 1992

Lane Cove Council, *A brief history of Lane Cove*

Herbert M Moran, *Viewless Winds*, Peter Davies, London, 1939

Kate Russell, 'Some of the lost wharves of Hunters Hill', *Hunter's Hill Trust Journal*, May 2009, Vol 47 No 1

Sands Directory, Sydney, 1892, 1897, 1900, 1910, 1912, 1913, 1914

Rachel Simpson, *Tenants' Rights in New South Wales*, Parliament of NSW, Briefing Paper 9/99

St Ignatius College, Riverview, *Jubilee book (1880–1930)*

Wilson's Authentic Directory, Sydney and Suburbs, 1914

The Death of Dr Claude Tozer, by Dick Whitaker, http://passingparade-2009.
blogspot.com.au/2009/06/death-of-dr-claude-tozer.html

Information about Dr GRC Clarke: http://harrowercollection.com/clarke.
html

ENDNOTES

Chapter 1: Discovery on the high seas

1 Consensual homosexual acts between adult males were a criminal offence.

2 Dr Herbert Moran, who met Eugenia four times, describes the event on the ship thus: 'It is said that the Captain, having surprised the secret of her sex, used her violently and then abandoned her in her pregnancy' (*Viewless Winds*, p 243). He refers to it as 'the brutal deflowering by a violent man'. There is not the slightest suggestion that she had any sexual inclinations towards men at any other time, either before she went to sea or after she left the ship. The discovery of Eugene's femaleness inevitably resulted in her being put off the ship at the next convenient port, which was the last thing that she would have wanted. Harry Cox, a journalist who interviewed Eugenia in 1931, wrote in 1961, 'Only one seaman, an Italian named Martello, probed her secret. As they talked together in Italian he caught a word here and there that revealed her sex.' (*Sun-Herald*, 11 June 1961, p 27). Josephine Falleni, in a police statement which was summarised by the newspapers, said that she had been told by her foster mother that her father was the captain of a ship. Eugenia's sister-in-law, Olga Falleni, who was interviewed by Suzanne Falkiner in 1987, said, 'And then she went away. She was about twenty then, I think. With this captain on the boat, so they said. And got married to him. The old lady [Isola Falleni] said this, but this is what she had been told. It might not have been true ... The old lady nearly passed away when it all happened [the charge and trial]. She did not want trouble. She always said, if Eugenia had married this captain, when she went to the court, why couldn't she have used his name, and not bring the family into it?' (Suzanne Falkiner, *Eugenia: A Man*, Pan Books, 1988, p 207).

Chapter 2: Early years

1 The Risorgimento, or Italian reunification, occurred predominantly between the 1840s and 1860s.

2 It is now a suburb of Livorno

3 Provided to author Suzanne Falkiner by Olga Falleni in 1987. Olga was the second wife of Eugenia's younger brother, Louis Falleni. See: Suzanne Falkiner, *Eugenia: A Man*, Pan Books, 1988, p 206. Falkiner used the pseudonym Anna for Olga, who has now passed away; her family have given me permission to name her.

4 To obtain employment or to enter into any contract while pretending to be a person of the opposite sex would have been considered a fraudulent deception. To have sexual contact with another woman while pretending to be a man would have been a sexual offence.

5 The law in this area, in both Australia and New Zealand, derived from English law. The laws against homosexuality had been introduced during the early Victorian age. Apparently, Queen Victoria's advisors found it so hard to explain male homosexuality to their young Monarch, that they gave up explaining the female version to her, and as a result the law did not criminalise the latter.

Chapter 3: Parenthood

1 This name is often recorded as De Anglis, D Anglis or even D Angels, however the correct spelling is De Angelis. See 1901 NSW Census records for Double Bay Ward under the name D Angelis.

2 The Italian name of the Tiber River in Rome

3　Many accounts of this part of Eugenia's life describe her giving birth and then going to the home of Mr and Mrs De Angelis in Double Bay in an attempt to hand over the child. However, Josephine's birth was registered in the adjoining suburb of Woollahra and Mrs De Angelis was one of the witnesses listed on the birth certificate. In Josephine's 1920 police statement she said that Mrs De Angelis had told her that she was born at her house in Double Bay. It is therefore highly likely that Eugenia gave birth in the home of the De Angelis family.

4　Information provided to author Suzanne Falkiner in 1987. See Falkiner, p 207.

5　At that time still part of Paddington

6　The term then used for a Scotsman

7　A copper was a large round container for washing clothes. By this time they were heated by a gas flame, but originally they were heated by a fire underneath.

Chapter 4: Love

1　This term subsequently came to be used for a piece of medical equipment used for internal examinations of bodily cavities, especially of a woman's vagina.

2　Subsequently the Pacific Highway

3　Ethel Turner was the author of *Seven Little Australians* and thirty-three other works of fiction, three of verse, a travel book, and a number of plays. Her husband was a District Court Judge.

4　Colleano's All-Star Circus troupe was made up of all 12 members of the Colleano family, including the ten Colleano children, who performed as acrobats, trapeze artists, wirewalkers, bareback riders and musicians.

Chapter 5: Marriage

1　Designed by Colonial Architect Edmund Thomas Blackett, the same architect who designed the Courthouse in Phillip Street that now houses the Justice and Police Museum.

2　A large rectangular travelling case, generally made of stiff leather, that is hinged at the back so as to open out into two equal compartments

3　Now it would be called oedema due to congestive heart failure.

4　The baby was registered under the name Josephine De Angliss.

5　Evidence of Josephine Falleni in the committal proceedings in the Police Court, 1920

6　Now part of Gipps Street. The modern-day name of the street was identified by Suzanne Falkiner in her book, although she mistakenly thought that all of Gipps Street had previously been known as The Avenue, so that the numbers had remained the same, whereas only the part to the north of Lyons Road was formerly known as the Avenue. She therefore identified the wrong location of these two houses. In the author's view, they correspond with the modern-day 87 and 89 Gipps Street – two wooden workmen's cottages. Number 87 has been totally renovated, but number 89 is still in much of its original condition.

Chapter 6: Exposure

1　The date was estimated three years later by Lily Nugent in her evidence at the trial of Eugenia Falleni.

2　Suzanne Falkiner, p 23

Chapter 7: Picnic

1　16 January 1907 page 5

2　The author recalls swimming in the Blue Hole as a child in the early 1960s, before it became too polluted. It was situated very close to De Burgh's Bridge. The author also recalls from the same period the broken-down remains of the entrance to the Fairyland Pleasure Grounds on Delhi Road near to the Crematorium.

3　An undulating merry-go-round.

Chapter 9: Discovery in the Park

1   Most people at this time expected and indeed accepted the extraction of maloccluded or decaying teeth and their replacement with vulcanite dentures in early or middle life – particularly those people of lower socio-economic status. From 1900, written and pictorial advertisements for painless extractions and inexpensive dentures flourished, as both registered and unregistered practitioners alike competed for business in an increasingly specialised market.

2   In 1917 the ability of forensic scientists to detect low levels of alcohol in the body was nowhere near as sophisticated as it is now. At that time, alcohol was detected by purely chemical methods, which provided nowhere near the sensitivity of present-day methods involving detection by gas chromatography and mass spectrometry.

Chapter 10: Anguish

1   The first Gap suicide was reported in 1863. See Claire McIntyre, *On the edge: deaths at the Gap*, Ginninderra Press, 2001; and the website: http://www.dictionaryofsydney.org/entry/the_gap

2   The Sargent family had a thriving business selling cakes and pies in Sydney, which began in 1891 as a small bakery in Oxford Street, Paddington specialising in meat pies. In 1914 the company opened the first of many Sargent's Tea Rooms in the Sydney Metropolitan area. By 1915 there were thirty-six of them. Their speciality was a meal of a meat pie with peas, potato and gravy, a bread roll, a pot of tea and a slice of apple charlotte for one shilling and sixpence. They quickly became an established part of everyday life in Sydney. In a sense, they were the equivalent of today's McDonald's.

3   The author assumes this was in the vicinity of Cooper Park.

4   The 'Palais de Danse' formed part of the elaborate Crystal Palace entertainment complex on George Street – a lavish amusement venue that combined a deluxe 1000-seat picture theatre with 300 American-style slot machines, a soda fountain and ice-cream bar, a gymnasium, air-conditioning and an opulent wintergarden cafe, with orchestral music to serenade its patrons throughout the day. Opened in 1912, it proved enormously popular with Sydneysiders of all classes. The Crystal Palace primarily catered to and relied upon the patronage of married women through the provision of on-site child care, female attendants, and continuous picture screenings from 11 am to 11 pm. In 1914, with Sydney in the grip of the irrepressible jazz and dance craze then sweeping the globe, the Crystal Arcade Dancing Palace or 'Palais de Danse' was opened adjacent to the Theatre. By 1917, the Palais de Danse was attracting large numbers of young dancing enthusiasts to its popular matinee and evening sessions, offering free refreshments, live music and expert instruction in the waltz, two-step, rag, foxtrot and tango at competitive admission prices. With the introduction of the six o'clock closing time for public bars during World War I, the Palais provided an opportunity for people to mingle with members of the opposite sex in a singularly modern and energetic atmosphere, and to experience the very pulse of modern urban life.

5   From her evidence at the trial at page 69. She was referring to Australian internment camps for enemy aliens during the First World War. Soon after the war started in 1914, the Australian government set up accommodation for the large number of Germans who were resident in Australia. They were interned in so called 'concentration camps' (a term first used by the British Government in the Boer War of 1899–1902). These camps were established in each of the six Australian States. In New South Wales, the Holsworthy Army camp was greatly enlarged to house the internees, and two special camps were established at Berrima (mainly for ships' officers and sailors) and at Trial Bay (for about 500 internees). By the end of May 1915, almost 3,000 people of German origin had been interned. See: Gerhard Fischer, 1989, *Enemy aliens: internment and the homefront experience in Australia, 1914–1920*, University of Queensland Press; and Jürgen Tampke and Colin Doxford, *Australia, Willkommen*, New South Wales University Press, 1990.

6   Mrs Marcellina Bombelli gave evidence in the Falleni trial through an Italian interpreter, Dr Charles Monticone, who also interpreted for the author's grandfather, Guido Tedeschi, during a judicial hearing in Sydney on 2nd August 1941 when an order was made for Guido Tedeschi's release from internment.

Chapter 12: Investigation

1   The old police station building is still there, but substantially moribund and dilapidated.

2. That was exactly how the press reported it at the time of Eugenia's arrest and trial, and how it has since been presented by most commentators.

3   This conversation with the police, as with all such police conversations, is taken verbatim from the evidence given by the police at Eugenia's subsequent committal and trial.

4   In practice it was routine for police officers to take people in for questioning before charging them, until the decision of the High Court in *Williams v R* (1986) 161 CLR 278.

5   The latter building is now the Downing Centre, which houses the District Court and the Local Court.

6   A twilled cloth of worsted or worsted and wool, often used for suits.

Chapter 13: Lizzie's discovery

1   This room was the scene of one of Sydney's most dramatic gaol escapes on 15 December 1949 when well-known escape artist Darcy Dugan and his mate William Mears cut their way through the wire mesh ceiling of this room during a lunch adjournment at the court. They then slid thirty feet down a drainpipe, scaled a twelve foot gate and jumped into Central Street, from where they quickly ran to George Street where they were lost in the dense pre-Chrismas traffic. They remained at large for 62 days until captured at a holiday cottage at Collaroy. The wire mesh was considerably strengthened after their escape. The room is now used as a recreation and gym area for the corrective services staff and police who man the court and station.

2   The photograph on the front cover is one of them. See Peter Doyle and Caleb Williams, *City of shadows: Sydney police photographs 1912–1948*, Historic Houses Trust, 2005, pp 199, 236. See also Peter Doyle, *Public eye, private eye: Sydney Police mugshots, 1912–1930*, Scan Journal (online), Vol 2 No 3, December 2005, Media Department, Macquarie University, Sydney.

3   Menopause. Many people at this time, including clinicians, still believed that menstruation and ovulation were inextricably linked, and only had a nascent appreciation of the possibility that ovulation may continue in the absence of menstruation. Medical practitioners noted the rare cases in which women conceived *after* the cessation of menstruation, producing what would become known as 'change of life' babies. A complete physiological understanding of the perimenopausal phase only emerged later.

Chapter 14: Exhumation and second autopsy

1   X-rays had been discovered by Wilhelm Conrad Röntgen in 1895 at the University of Würzburg, Germany. Röntgen had just retired in 1920.

2   A waxy organic substance produced by the decomposition of tissue in moist burial places.

3   The skull cap, consisting of the frontal, occipital and right and left parietal bones.

4   The join between the occipital and the parietal bones of the skull.

5   A large opening in the occipital bone of the skull. It is one of several oval or circular openings in the base of the skull.

6   A prominent, irregular, wedge-shaped bone at the base of the skull.

7   Jawbone

Chapter 15: The Press

1 Her arrest and trial were extensively publicised in the New Zealand newspapers, so Eugenia's parents must have been aware of the sensation.

2 That is still generally the practice.

3 Today most committal proceedings are conducted on the papers, but they still have the same functions.

4 A reference to a convict ship bound for Botany Bay in New South Wales.

5 A document given to convicts when granting them freedom to work and live within a given district of the colony before their sentence had expired.

6 The author suspects that it was at Sydney Grammar School that Cohen was given the nickname 'Maddocks', which he kept for the rest of his life and transmitted to his descendants, who adopted the surname Maddocks-Cohen.

7 Pomade, after the French term *pommade* (ointment), was a greasy, wax-like substance made of petroleum jelly, beeswax or lard, and used to style hair and to make it look slick and shiny. Pomade did not dry out and often took several washes to remove. A stylish man in 1920 might wear a felt fedora hat, a tweed sports jacket or three-piece suit, a fob watch on a chain, patent leather shoes or boots and an Oxford pince-nez.

8 There were 20 shillings in a pound

9 The Eveleigh payroll robbery took place on 10 June 1914 at the Eveleigh Railway Workshops on Wilson Street, Newtown. What made this crime unique was that it was the first robbery in Australia where a get-away car was used. The amount robbed was a huge £3,300 and the daring crime was remarkable also for being committed in the middle of the day in a busy suburban area.

10 In the later prison records her eyes are described as blue. During evidence they were described as grey.

11 The media today will generally not publish an image of a person accused of a criminal offence, particularly where the identity of the offender is in issue.

12 Jangle: an old-fashioned word for an argument or quarrel, derived from an old French word *jangler*, to whine or complain. See Webster's dictionary.

Chapter 16: Judge, Crown Prosecutor and defence counsel

1 The right to serve on juries was only extended to women in 1947, and then only on their application.

2 In some respects, this crisis foresaw the events of the 1975 federal constitutional crisis.

3 60 kg and 175 cm.

4 A valid engagement was considered to be a type of contract, and a breach of promise to marry created a right (in the woman) to sue for damages.

5 While the first Crown Prosecutor had been appointed in 1830, William Thomas Coyle KC was the first person designated as the Senior Crown Prosecutor, and therefore the first predecessor of the author.

6 While the establishment of the Public Solicitor's Office and the Public Defenders in the 1940s introduced comprehensive salaried services for the poor in both civil and criminal cases, it was not until the establishment of the Australian Legal Aid Office in 1973 and the flourishing of community legal centres in that decade that legal assistance to indigent persons came to be viewed as an inherent right. The High Court of Australia recognised this right in the case of *Dietrich v The Queen* in 1992.

7 Subsequently known as the old Bank of New South Wales building

8 Frederick Wordsworth Ward (aka Captain Thunderbolt) (1835–1870) was an Australian highwayman renowned for his reputation as the 'gentleman bushranger' and as the longest roaming bushranger in Australian history. Over a six-and-a-half year period from 1863, Ward robbed mailmen, travellers, inns, stores and stations across much of northern New South Wales. Ward was finally shot and killed on 25 May 1870 by Constable Alexander Walker at Kentucky Creek near Uralla. A modern-day highway, Thunderbolt's Way, between Gloucester and Inverell via Uralla is named after him.

9   Somerset Richard Lowry-Corry, Fourth Earl of Belmore (1835–1913), Governor of New South Wales from 1868 to 1872

10 See: http://en.wikipedia.org/wiki/List_of_Melbourne_Cup_winners. See also *Daily Mirror*, 28 February 1970, p 13. Some of this information was provided to the author by Frances Kenney, a family historian of the McDonell family.

11 McDonell's time at Riverview overlapped Coyle's for six months in 1886. He later wrote about the young Coyle: 'I was in his company long enough to learn his sterling qualities': See Riverview's Jubilee Book pp 19–39

12 Obituary of Archibald Joseph McDonell published in the *Wingham Chronicle* and *Manning River Observer*, 18 March 1941

13 A metallurgical process in which ores are placed under high temperatures to separate the noble metals, like gold and silver, from base metals, like lead, copper, zinc, arsenic, antimony and bismuth

14 A mixed concept involving both homosexuality and some aspects of gender transference that was thought to derive from an inborn abnormality. See later for a more detailed discussion.

15 Major General Sir Neville Reginald Howse, VC, KCB, KCMG, KStJ, the Surgeon-General of the Australian Army. There is not the slightest suggestion that Sir Neville had any particular knowledge of or expertise in the field of sexual inversion.

16 The preeminent racehorse of his day, and possibly of the twentieth century

17 *Smith's Weekly*, 9 October 1920

18 Today, the legal aid office is administratively independently of any government Department.

Chapter 17: The trial begins

1   A solicitor is entitled today to appear as an advocate in a Supreme Court trial, but in practice it is almost always a barrister that represents an accused.

2   Women were not entitled to serve on a jury until 1947.

3   At that time there were only eight known planets. Pluto was not discovered until 1930.

Chapter 18: Family witnesses

1   Today, the witness would be able to provide this information.

2   Eg: *The Truth*, 11 July 1920, p 9; *The Truth*, 18 July 1920, p 7

3   It seems that Harry Jnr did not notice Harry Snr, who at this time was drowning his sorrows with whisky.

4   *Evening News*, 16 August 1920; *Daily Telegraph*, 17 August 1920; *The Truth*, 22 August 1920

Chapter 19: Sighting witnesses

1   No judge today would allow evidence of such a farcical identification process to be given.

Chapter 20: Expert witnesses

1   The author has not heard of such a procedure occurring during a criminal trial anywhere in Australia in living memory. The prejudicial effect on the jury would be way out of proportion to any probative value that could be gained by the jury personally inspecting the skull of a victim, as opposed to looking at photographs or diagrams.

2   William Dobinson Halliburton (1860–1931) was a British physiologist who was one of the founders of the science of biochemistry. His main work, first published in 1896, became known as 'Halliburton's Physiology' and in its many editions was an indispensable reference work for generations of doctors and medical students.

3   As a young man, from 1875 to 1879 Ellis worked as a schoolteacher in Australia. It was during this period that he read the book *Life in Nature* by James Hinton, which inspired a spiritual transformation and a lifelong search for scientific and artistic truth, that later

led to him to becoming a sexologist. In 1879, Ellis returned to England to qualify as a physician, having decided to take up the study of sex. On his way back to England, he wrote: 'These three years I have spent in Australia seem to me like those three during which Paul was in Arabia.' Ellis believed that sexual freedom could usher in a new era of universal happiness.

4   The term 'transsexual' only began to be used in English in 1949. The seminal book on the topic, published in 1966, was *The Transsexual Phenomenon* by Harry Benjamin (1885–1986). Benjamin was a German-born endocrinologist, sexologist and gerontologist, who spent most of his working life in the United States. In *The Transsexual Phenomenon*, Benjamin described transsexualism in this way: 'True transsexuals feel that they belong to the other sex. They want to be and function as members of the opposite sex, not only to appear as such. For them, their sex organs, the primary as well as the secondary, are disgusting deformities.'

5   This is known as the McNaughton test, and is still the basis of the law of insanity today.

6   Published in 1898

7   He was referring to discredited theories in the field of criminal anthropology – a field of offender profiling. In the late nineteenth century, the Italian School of Criminology, whose most famous member was Cesare Lombroso, performed autopsies on convicted criminals and declared that they had discovered distinctive characteristics in them that had some similarities to early humans, monkeys and apes. These similarities included receding foreheads, head shape and size. Lambroso concluded that criminals were born with inferior and detectable physiological traits. He popularised the notion of the 'born criminal' with a hereditary disposition to crime, and he proposed that such persons could be identified by their physical characteristics before they had an opportunity to embark on a life of crime. In the decade before the trial of Eugenia Falleni, these theories had rightly fallen into disfavour.

Chapter 22: Police witnesses

1   *Crimes Act 1900*, section 352. Police in most jurisdictions now have a defined time to question a suspect before bringing them before a magistrate.

2   This used to be called similar fact evidence. Since the Uniform *Evidence Act* came into operation, it has been called coincidence and tendency evidence, which requires substantial probative value to be admissible.

3   This is not an infrequent occurrence today when prejudicial evidence is inadvertently given by a witness.

4   Many judges today would take it upon themselves to prevent such evidence being led, even without any objection by defence counsel.

Chapter 23: Defence case and case in reply

1   The unsworn statement from the dock was abolished in New South Wales in 1994.

Chapter 24: Closing addresses

1   It is now the Crown that addresses first, followed by the defence.

2   The author has conducted several of these.

Chapter 25: The law speaks

1   A summing-up in a comparable case today would take a day or more.

2   The most famous case in England where this occurred was in *Bushel's Case* in 1670. William Penn and William Mead had been put on trial for illegally preaching a Quaker sermon and disturbing the peace. Four jurors, led by Edward Bushell, refused to find them guilty. Instead of dismissing the jury, the trial judge sent them back for further deliberations, instructing them to return a guilty verdict. The jury returned after a short while and announced that they unanimously found Penn guilty of preaching, but acquitted him on the charge of disturbing the peace, and acquitted Mead of all

charges. The judge refused to accept their verdicts, and had the jury locked up and kept isolated for three days without 'meat, drink, fire and tobacco' in an attempt to force them to bring in a guilty verdict. When they failed to do so, the judge ended the trial and ordered the jurors imprisoned until they paid a fine to the court. Four jurors refused to pay the fine and after several months Edward Bushell sought a judicial hearing by bringing a writ of *habeas corpus*. Chief Justice Vaughan released all four jurors, calling the power to punish a jury 'absurd', and forbidding judges in future from punishing jurors for returning a verdict that the judge disagreed with.

3   It was only in the 1980s that the practice of locking up juries overnight fell into disuse. In exceptional cases today, juries are still housed overnight, but in hotel rooms rather than in dormitories.

4   In NSW, both murder and attempted murder carried a mandatory penalty of death, although judges and juries could make a recommendation for mercy. The death penalty was abolished in NSW in 1955.

Chapter 26: Prisoner

1   The buildings of Darlinghurst Gaol largely still survive as the site of the present-day National Art School.

2   The Morts had been a prominent and prosperous family in Sydney since Thomas Sutcliffe Mort (1816–1878) arrived in Australia in 1838.

3   An alcoholic tincture containing powdered opium. Laudanum was historically used to treat a variety of ailments, but its principal use was as a painkiller, sleeping pill, tranquilliser and cough suppressant. Until the early twentieth century, laudanum was sold without a prescription. Victorian women were prescribed the drug for relief of menstrual cramps and other aches, even though it was highly addictive.

4   At that time there was no speciality as a forensic psychiatrist, so all medical practitioners were considered as experts to some degree in the workings of the mind.

5   The relationship was described by Dr Herbert Moran thus: *There was the ridiculous little sentimental liaison in gaol with another murderess. A bizarre story which is not for here.* (*Viewless Winds*, p 249). There would have been very few murderesses in the Women's Reformatory at that time, other than Eugenia Falleni and Dorothy Mort. Probably for reasons of sensitivity to Mort's family, Moran was reluctant to name her. Later, Dorothy Mort's name was closely associated with the women's crusade to have Eugenia released. *Smith's Weekly* of 8 March 1930 describes the relationship thus: 'During Mrs Mort's incarceration at Long Bay, the two women became close friends. Mrs Mort, once a society woman, and Jean Falleni, 'general useful', during their association of many years, came to know and appreciate one another. In education and general environment they were at opposite ends of the scale, but they had one bond, the bond of suffering. They were two women together expiating their offences.' Falleni is quoted as saying: 'She and I were friends and we still are.'

Chapter 27: Release

1   At that time, a nine-year sentence was considered a particularly lengthy one. Since then, various measures have been introduced that have effectively created a trend for much longer sentences in New South Wales. One such recent measure has been the introduction of standard non-parole periods. A standard non-parole period is the indicative mid-range sentence for an offence of mid-range objective seriousness after a conviction at trial. The current standard non-parole period for murder is twenty years. At that time, life sentences rarely meant that the prisoner would serve the rest of his or her days in custody. Today, due to 'truth in sentencing' legislation, a life sentence means just that. As a result, they are rare.

2   She had, in fact, turned fifty-five the previous January.

3   This may have been literally true, but the clear implication was that Falleni may have done away with her as well.

4 Transcripts of evidence

5 In this sense it was very similar to the modern concept of parole.

6 It is unknown, because it has faded into the mist of time, whether after her release Jean established contact with her granddaughter, Rita Whitby, who had been abandoned by her father after her mother's death, and who had been placed into institutional care in Macksville after being sent north to her father's relatives in Bellingen.

Chapter 28: Jean Ford

1 Two pounds, eleven shillings and eight pence

2 Money paid to a head-tenant to assign a lease to a new tenant. It was prevalent during the period of rent control in New South Wales when a tenant could not be evicted by the landlord without good reason. Rent control in one form or another existed in New South Wales from the Depression until it was progressively abolished in the 1950s and 1960s.

3 The identity of this man has not been ascertained

4 Six stone and seven pounds, which is the equivalent of 41 kilograms

5 Paddington's gentrified reputation was not to arrive until the 1960s

Chapter 29: To the bank

1 It is not known whether Rita had any knowledge of her notorious grandmother, then or later. Her son and daughter-in-law have stated to the author that she never spoke of her early life prior to meeting her husband, Thomas Elvy, except to say that she spent some years at a convent in Macksville.

2 See Suzanne Falkiner, p 207

3 Plot number 3223; see Suzanne Falkiner p 242

Chapter 30: Retrospective

1 This is based on the expert opinion of Dr Rebecca Irvine, Forensic Pathologist at the Department of Forensic Medicine, NSW Department of Health, Glebe Coroner's Court, Sydney

2 Ibid

3 There was one exception to this, which in the author's view is utterly unreliable. In 1961, *Sun-Herald* journalist Harry Cox wrote about his 1931 interview of Eugenia at Long Bay just before her release. He wrote in the edition of 11 June 1961: 'What was her motive? I asked her that when I saw her in 1931, finally a serene, grey-haired woman, enjoying her job in the flower gardens of Long Bay Penitentiary, just before she was released after her term for murder. All I could get from her was that she had to do it – that there was nothing else.' It is highly implausible that Eugenia would have finally confessed just prior to her release. It is even more incredible that Cox would not have published it at the time, and waited thirty years to inform his readers. The answer may be that in this comment Eugenia was referring to her choice to live as a man, but that Cox, relying on his notes made thirty years earlier, mistakenly thought that she had been referring to the murder.

Epilogue

1 The precursor to the District Court in its criminal jurisdiction

2 *Who Killed Hannah Jane?* by Tom Molomby SC, Potoroo Press Australia, 1981; and *Who Killed Hannah Jane?*, directed by Peter Fisk, shown on ABC TV in September 1984. See also: *The Conviction of the Innocent* by Chester Porter QC, Random House Australia, 2007; and *Bloody Relations* by John Kerr, Penguin, 2007

3 Frances Kenney, a descendant of Archibald McDonell's uncle

4 Tom Molomby, p 123

5 RR Kidston QC, *The Office of the Crown Prosecutor (More Particularly in New South Wales)*, (1958) 32 Australian Law Journal, p 148

6   See Mark Tedeschi QC, *History of the New South Wales Crown Prosecutors: 1901–1986*, Forbes Flyer, Journal of the Francis Forbes Society for Australian Legal History, autumn 2006

7   *Medical Journal of Australia*, 3 December 1921, p. 521

8   See: '*The Trial of Saint Eugenia*', by Campbell Bonner, in American Journal of Philology, Vol 41 No 3, 1920

Now that you've read Eugenia's story take a visual tour of the Sydney Eugenia lived in, seen through the eyes of Mark Tedeschi.

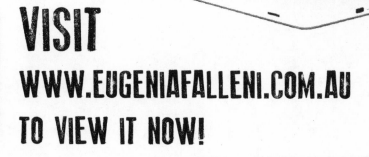

VISIT
WWW.EUGENIAFALLENI.COM.AU
TO VIEW IT NOW!

www.simonandschuster.com.au

Visit www.simonandschuster.com.au for great book recommendations, free chapters, author interviews and competitions.

You can also follow us on Facebook, Twitter and Youtube.

SIMON & SCHUSTER
AUSTRALIA
A CBS COMPANY